# HITLER'S TYRANNY

RALF GEORG REUTH

# Hitler's Tyranny

## A History in Ten Chapters

Translated from German by Peter Lewis

First published in English in 2022 by
Haus Publishing Ltd
4 Cinnamon Row
London SW11 3TW

First published in German as *Hitler. Zentrale Aspekte seiner Gewaltherrschaft*
Copyright © Piper Verlag GmbH, München 2021
Translation copyright © Peter Lewis, 2022

ISBN 978-1-913368-62-3
eISBN 978-1-913368-63-0

Typeset in Garamond by MacGuru Ltd
Printed in the UK by Clays

*www.hauspublishing.com*
*@HausPublishing*

# Contents

# Introduction

This book has as its subject the darkest years of German history and the person whose name is synonymous with that period: Adolf Hitler. The Second World War, which his actions unleashed, visited destruction and millions of deaths upon humankind. Yet the gravest legacy of Hitler and his twelve years of tyranny was the monstrous industrialised extermination of millions of innocent non-combatants, a cataclysmic event encapsulated in the place name Auschwitz. The devastating psychological scars left behind by the genocide of Europe's Jews will seemingly never heal. It shook the very foundations of civilization and, as a consequence, is of universal significance.

To a far greater degree than the Soviet Russian and the Chinese 'universes of destruction', as the German philosopher Peter Sloterdijk has dubbed the three great crimes against humanity in the twentieth century,[1] the German genocide has become the focus of intense scrutiny and interest. Not least, this is the result of the Federal Republic of Germany having confronted its problematic past with a purpose and thoroughness not witnessed elsewhere, but it also has to do with the fact that the Jewish community – in other words, the community which above all has a keen interest in appraising this phase of history – is dispersed across the entire globe. The upshot of both these factors has been a wealth of literature on National Socialism, which in the interim has mushroomed to such proportions that not even those who deal with it in a professional capacity can keep track of it.

Looking back is always subject to change, since history is not a static phenomenon. Instead, it is conditioned by the changing face of contemporary politics. At seats of higher learning in the liberal democracies, especially those in Germany, this has resulted in historical research taking on an increasingly sociological character from the 1970s onwards. In the process, historical turning points are often glossed over and the significance of human planning, decision-making, and agency played down. This school of thought asserts that it is first and foremost societal structures that determine the course of history. This viewpoint has latterly been supplemented by an understanding of history that maintains that any recapitulative interpretations of past epochs are inherently unreliable. According to this view, historians can only recapitulate what individual sources tell us about the past. Alongside, and in response to, the sociologically dominated way of looking at history and deconstructivism on the internet – far removed from the ivory towers of academe – a new, negligible, and vulgar form of historical revisionism has taken root.

The common denominator of all these diverse historical viewpoints is that a substantive appraisal of the historical figure of Hitler has tended to recede further and further into the background. Even though a biographical approach is very hard to reconcile with a sociological viewpoint, this latter tendency has nonetheless still managed to find its way into this realm. Whereas the active personage of Hitler still stood front and centre in Joachim C. Fest's great biography, which first appeared in the early 1970s,[2] later works with more of a sociological bent sought to deny that this architect of genocide played virtually any shaping role in what took place.[3] For example, in the British historian Ian Kershaw's biography of Hitler,[4] which today is widely regarded as groundbreaking, the dictator is presented primarily as a projection screen and focal point of social structures.

This perspective is also broadly true of the recently published work by Volker Ullrich.[5] Wolfram Pyta is among those who have chosen a different approach. In his *Herrschaftsstudie* ('Study of power'), he concludes that Hitler's rise to power and his genocidal regime were founded on the radical application of certain aesthetic principles.[6]

Elsewhere, sociologically dominated historiography does not hold undisputed sway to the same extent as in Germany. In France, for example, there is a far more liberal contemporary historical discourse. Thus, the socialist historian François Furet, author of a definitive study of communism, *The Passing of an Illusion*,[7] wrote that 'the historians of our era, who are obsessed with determinism and a sociological conception of history ... are all too ready ... to [disregard] the role that certain personalities have played in it'.[8] This eminent French commentator, who maintains that 'everything would surely have turned out differently ... had it not been for Hitler's political propensity for evil'[9] is unquestionably correct, given that human beings are not merely the playthings of anonymous political processes but have the capacity to shape historical developments. For the British-Austrian philosopher Karl Popper, this human capacity is a fundamental building block of an open and pluralistic society, the basic principles of which he drew up as a countervailing model to any social construct based on ideology.[10]

Where the shaping of historical developments is concerned, this insight holds good in a negative sense for Hitler to a quite striking degree, since he was indisputably the figure who was most prominent in shaping the history of the twentieth century. He changed the face of the world like no one else. The end of old Europe as the centre of world power; the rise of the two opposing superpowers of the United States and the Soviet Union as heirs to this mantle of power; the dividing of the continent and of Germany; the Cold War, the fall of the Berlin Wall, and the reunification of Germany – none of this would have occurred if Hitler had fallen on some battlefield during the First World War. Future generations are often completely unaware of this possibility.

In history, everything is connected with everything. Accordingly, it is all the more unhistoric for Hitler, and above all his crimes against humanity, to be wrested from their historical context – something that is happening with increasing frequency. What results from this kind of insular thinking is a purely emotional response to the subject, which has already culminated simply in demands to dispense entirely with any historical account of the Nazi genocide on the grounds that such an approach attempts to make comprehensible something that is inherently incomprehensible and is therefore bound to fail. In this context, Joachim Fest, whose work set the tone for numerous subsequent interpretations of Hitler, just as Kershaw's did later, spoke of a 'form of demonological displacement' that encouraged myth-making and legends but in no way contributed to a greater understanding of what had taken place.[11] To achieve such an understanding, the most essential requirement – alongside a sober and objective treatment of the topic – is to firmly embed it within the historical context of German and European history. This is the only way in which the political and moral dimension of Hitler can be properly gauged.

This historicisation, which prominent historians were already calling for even in the 1980s,[12] will be taken full account of in this book. It treats ten central aspects of Hitler's tyranny; taken together, these are intended to give the historically curious reader an overview of the topic 'Hitler and National Socialism' – concisely, clearly, and comprehensibly. It begins with a brief tour d'horizon of the world of European racism and anti-Semitism, culminating in the question of whether a hatred of Jews was more pronounced in Germany than elsewhere in the period before Hitler appeared on the political scene. Following on from this, we examine whether Hitler's rise to the chancellorship in January 1933 was only made possible by the 'unfinished' revolution of November 1918 in Germany and the subsequent split in the German working class – a view still espoused today by intellectuals of the Left. Since the end of the Second World War, the narrative from the opposing political camp has been that the Versailles Peace Treaty was responsible, thus shifting at least part of the blame for Hitler onto the victorious Allied powers in the First World War. But is this view truly tenable?

A major bone of contention among German historians in the 1980s was whether the genocide conducted by the National Socialists was a response to the 'class murder' committed by the communists; this thesis was notably advanced by the historian and philosopher Ernst Nolte,[13] and remains the subject of lively debate today. Moving on from this, we tackle the question of how a politician who advocated a fanatical form of racism and painted scenarios of a 'worldwide Jewish conspiracy' was able to become chancellor of Germany. We also investigate why, in spite of his brutal elimination of all opposition and his racial policies, which displayed utter contempt for human rights, the nation swung behind him. Did the Germans simply take such things as part and parcel of his triumphal rewriting of the terms of the Versailles Treaty – not least because they failed to understand this man with his overweening sense of destiny? Was it this same failure on the part of the German people to grasp reality that fostered a personality cult, allowing Hitler to style himself as some Wagnerian figure from another realm who offered the prospect of salvation?

The Second World War, without which there would surely have been no genocide, occupies a large portion of this book. It began with the campaign against Poland and the act of diplomacy that paved the way for it: the Nazi–Soviet Non-aggression

Pact of August 1939. What really lay behind this unlikely alliance between two arch-enemies that is portrayed nowadays by the Russian president Vladimir Putin – with all the guile of a demagogue – as a necessary self-defence measure enacted by a peace-loving Soviet Union?[14] Why did the Germans still follow their 'Führer' down the road to perdition? This question is lent even greater force when one considers the historical background: in the period between early summer 1944 and the unconditional surrender of German armed forces in May 1945, twice as many Germans died as in the entire four years of war up to that point.

'How could it have happened?' asks the subtitle of the chapter describing the extermination of Europe's Jews. Did Hitler carry out the genocide to compensate for his military defeats, or was it the horrifying enactment of his earlier ideological racial fanaticism? With regard to Hitler's racial fanaticism: an appraisal of his worldview forms a common thread throughout this book. In the process, special attention is given to determining how far this worldview impinged on Hitler's policies and his waging of the war – or even shaped his political and military decisions as a whole. Fifty years ago, the historian Andreas Hillgruber sought to demonstrate that this was indeed the case,[15] a thesis that was hotly contested by a group of early social historians led by the influential left-liberal scholar Hans-Ulrich Wehler.

# 1

# Anti-Semitism in Europe

*Was it especially prevalent in Germany?*


As a general rule, the act of looking back at the history of anti-Semitism and racism in Germany is nowadays defined from its endpoint: namely, the flagrant genocide that was committed against the Jews of Europe. This view naturally implies a moralising and emotional perspective, from a position of outrage so to speak, which can mislead us into seeing connections and consistencies even where none exist. From such a standpoint, every anti-Semitic statement (and there is no shortage of these) is seen against the background of this abhorrent crime against humanity. As a result, almost automatically, a distorted image arises that often has little to do with historical reality. Add to this a propensity to see things in isolation, and our judgement about anti-Semitism before Hitler is a foregone conclusion.

The situation is very different if our consideration of history is soberly and objectively geared to the context of the whole of Europe and to the period in question – in other words, if the values and mindsets of people at that time are taken into account. These differ fundamentally from those of today. Thus, in 1889, when Hitler was born in the Austrian frontier town of Braunau am Inn, the spirit of the age was characterised by a rampant nationalism on both sides of the river, in the Austro-Hungarian Dual Monarchy as well as the German Second Empire. It was no different in the other monarchies of old Europe: one's own nation was considered paramount, and nation states vied with other peoples for supremacy. In this atmosphere, in Prussian military theorist Carl von Clausewitz's (1780–1831) infamous definition, war was seen as the perfectly legitimate continuation of politics by other means.

Attitudes towards certain sections of humankind were markedly different then, too. The peoples of the world were divided up into 'races'. First, there was the white race – in other words Europeans – among whom the Jews, as a 'Semitic race', played a special role. Then there was the 'yellow' race, namely Asiatic people, and the so-called primitive peoples, a group that included 'negroes' – a broad umbrella term embracing both Africans and African Americans. From a European point of view, it was an article of faith that their own white race was the most advanced by far, and that it had an exclusive right to colonise and rule the world. When for example Cecil Rhodes (1835–1902), who had a monopoly of the numerous gold- and diamond-mining concessions in British-governed South Africa in the second half of the nineteenth century, called the British the 'first race in the world'[1] and described the indigenous population of the region as mere 'cheap slave labour' for the extraction of raw materials, his statements were all of a piece with the general spirit of the age.

Over a century before Rhodes – who in Great Britain is still commemorated by statues that have latterly become the subject of much controversy – the 'raw material' was human beings themselves, sold by the British in trans-Atlantic trade to their colonies in North America and the Caribbean. People were a commodity. Much the same was true of the other colonial powers such as Spain, France, Belgium, Portugal, and the Netherlands. They were all involved in the slave trade. However, as we are repeatedly given to understand nowadays, slavery was by no means a European invention that arose with colonialism. Trafficking in humans had its origins in ancient Mesopotamia and was later introduced into Africa by Arab traders. For centuries these merchants held a monopoly over the slave trade in Africa. In his book *Le génocide voilé* ('The veiled genocide') the anthropologist Tidiane N'Diaye concludes that 'the slave trade conducted mercilessly by Arab Muslim robbers ... had a far more devastating effect on black Africa than the trans-Atlantic slave trade'.[2]

This particular poisoned chalice bypassed Germany, as by the time it had become a colonial power in the 1880s the slave trade had been abolished. It was a belated 'place in the sun' that the German Second Empire secured for itself in parts of Africa, the Pacific region, and China. For the world at this juncture had already been largely carved up among the other European powers. Yet in its colonialist behaviour it was no less unabashed than its fellow nations. In Germany, too, everything was conditioned by the spirit of perceived racial and cultural superiority. In the German Empire, the indigenous peoples of the country's eight colonies were regarded as exotics – sometimes quite literally, as when the animal collector Carl Hagenbeck exhibited Somalians in a zoo in Hamburg. The supposed characteristics of 'natives' were described in books. For example, one volume about Germany's overseas possessions claimed that 'in common with many other primitive peoples, the negroes of Togo have a propensity for lying'. This work went on to state that these people knew nothing about the wheel, the plough, wind power, or the principle of levers, and concluded: 'In such matters they are millennia behind the white race and the yellow race.'[3]

Consequently, the colonial powers regarded themselves as being charged with a mission to educate. The British writer Rudyard Kipling (1865–1936), the main theme of whose work was the clash between West and East, and between technology and nature, famously characterised this as the 'white man's burden'.[4] According to prevalent attitudes at the time, it was the task of the white race to introduce the natives to the standards of 'civilized' society. This included converting them to Christianity and getting them to adopt European ways of life. Anyone who rebelled against this agenda was brought to their senses by the application of brute force. This was what happened, for instance, to both the Indians who rose up against the rule of the British East India Company in 1857 and to the Herero and Nama peoples in German South-west Africa who in 1904 staged an insurrection against their colonial masters and were slaughtered in response by German troops.

As already mentioned, in this world of the different 'races', a special role was played by the Jews for they did not live on some far-flung continent but in among the other peoples of Europe – and in no way were they culturally inferior. Indeed, the opposite was often the case, sometimes prompting feelings of inferiority among non-Jewish communities. This factor and their distinct 'otherness' heavily predisposed the Jews to being made into scapegoats, all the more so as this negative characterisation had a long history in the annals of Christian-motivated hatred of the Jews, or anti-Judaism. Some commentators, such as the founder and leader of the Zionist movement, Theodor Herzl (1860–1904), saw this as the real kernel of racial anti-Semitism. In his 1896 pamphlet *Der Judenstaat* ('The Jewish state'), he wrote that the Jewish question was 'a remnant of the Middle Ages, which civilized nations do not even yet seem able to shake off, try as they will'.[5]

Indeed, it is true that the roots of modern racial anti-Semitism lie in the Christian-motivated hatred of the Jews in the Middle Ages. The American Judaic scholar Talya Fishman explains this as deriving from the institution of the Talmud, the great Jewish work of exegesis, which stirred up bitter criticism by the Catholic clergy and was burned on pyres and, she maintains, led directly to the establishment of the Inquisition.[6] The Jews

– several hundred thousand of whom were living in communities in Europe at that time – were now regarded by the Church not as deluded older brothers but as heretics. Hand in hand with structural changes that were taking place in a medieval society hitherto based on estate and feudalism, this period also witnessed a shift from the portrayal of Christ as *Pantokrator*, the ruler of the universe, to his depiction as the man of sorrows on the crucifix. Since in Christian eyes it was the Jews who were to blame for Christ's sufferings, they came to be seen as deicides. In a world that was characterised through and through by Christian metaphysics, such an alleged crime was unforgivable. Accordingly, the Jews found themselves condemned from the pulpits of churches and presently also hunted down by marauding gangs. The Black Death, which swept Europe in the mid-fourteenth century, saw pogroms of Jews in Switzerland, Alsace, the Lower Rhine region, and along the rivers Main and Moselle in the course of which hundreds of villages were razed to the ground and thousands of Jews killed. The bloody expulsion of this community brought many material advantages to the Christian populace and their secular rulers. Yet because the Jews were ultimately indispensable to those in power, they were subsequently allowed to resettle, albeit under worse conditions than before.

The anti-Semitism displayed by Martin Luther (1483–1546) was completely consonant with the tenor of his age. Moreover, the instigator of the Protestant Reformation regarded himself as the mouthpiece of common Christians, 'the true people of God'. Luther had set his face against Rome, and now he saw it as his mission to forcefully repress the 'chosen people' of the Bible, who stubbornly refused to recognise Jesus as the Messiah. In his infamous treatise *Von den Juden und ihren Lügen* ('On the Jews and their lies'),[7] this is precisely what he did, calling on the rulers of German principalities to burn down synagogues and schools in order to destroy Jewish cultural life and drive

Jews out of the country, as had already happened in territories belonging to the Bohemian crown and in Spain. Although, in the event, Luther's demands were not carried out, secular rulers at the time, who were closely allied to the clergy or the forces leading the Reformation, nonetheless segregated Jewish communities, forcing them to live in their own designated quarters of cities, largely without any legal rights, and to earn their living in professions that were considered un-Christian, such as money-lending (usury). As a result, a more or less intense anti-Semitism involving periodic persecutions or pogroms characterised the life of European Jews for many centuries.

Then came the Enlightenment. A Christian worldview that essentially divided humanity up into believers and unbelievers was now supplanted by one that viewed and classified people according to physiological and intellectual criteria. In the wake of this new universalism, while theoretically all people were considered equal, they were also thought to be at different stages of development. This new view of humankind – which was not so very new in actual fact, having originated with Aristotle (384–322 BC) – began to assert itself from the end of the seventeenth century onwards. It was at that time that French physician and traveller François Bernier (1620–88) wrote an essay entitled *Nouvelle division de la terre par les differentes espèces ou race d'hommes qui habitent*, ('The new division of the Earth by the different species or "Races" of man that inhabit it').[8] This form of classification of humanity was shared by almost all the major thinkers of the European Enlightenment. For example, Immanuel Kant (1724–1804) wrote:

> In the hot countries the human being matures in all respects earlier but does not, however, reach the perfection of those in the temperate zones. Humanity is at its greatest perfection in the 'race' of the whites. The yellow Indians do have a meagre

talent. The Negroes are far below them and at the lowest point are a part of the American peoples.[9]

In reviewing the history of racism, commentators commonly overlook the fact that racially based anti-Semitism was also a product of the Enlightenment. During the Enlightenment, theologically derived anti-Judaism gradually metamorphosed into a secular enmity towards Jews. In consequence, the segregated, marginalised, and disenfranchised Jews, who as a result of discrimination had already long since ceased to be regarded as merely a religious community, were now considered as members of a so-called 'Semitic race'. The French philosopher and writer Voltaire (1694–1778) described them in these terms, for instance. For him, Jews were an 'inferior species of mankind' who were 'driven by the urge to procreate and acquire wealth'. He attributed to them 'ignorance, a barbarian language, enmity towards other peoples, cruelty, superstition and a variety of sexual perversions'.[10]

Under these modern auspices, Kant launched a series of polemical attacks on the legitimacy of the Jewish faith with its rigid rules, but in so doing was operating wholly within the tradition of anti-Judaism. However, he did not stop there but also used common clichés in describing the Jews as the 'vampires of society' and castigating their 'propensity for profiteering'. He claimed that their reputation for being swindlers was not unfounded.[11] Voltaire and Kant were just two of a number of Enlightenment thinkers who depicted Jews in a negative light. Yet there were also those who treated Judaism with a degree of tolerance, such as Montesquieu (1689–1755), or even full acceptance, such as the dramatist Gotthold Ephraim Lessing (1729–81). In his play *Nathan der Weise* ('Nathan the wise'), which was only premiered posthumously in 1783, he proclaimed for the first time the idea – thoroughly groundbreaking for the period – of peaceful coexistence between the three great monotheistic faiths, of which no single one is the 'one true' religion.

Although the Enlightenment was the seedbed of modern racism and racially based anti-Semitism, at the same time it also paved the way for means by which it could be overcome. It was Voltaire who was responsible for disseminating this new thinking. Kant, in his *Critique of Pure Reason*, revolutionised philosophy in a way that no one else before him had. Montesquieu devised the concept of the separation of powers that forms the cornerstone of modern democracies. Without these figures, it is impossible to imagine the French Revolution of 1789 ever taking place. This momentous event not only saw the abolition of the feudal, absolutist corporative state but also the implementation of inalienable universal human and civil rights under the motto '*Liberté, Égalité, Fraternité*'.

The French revolutionaries were inspired by the struggle for independence from British rule by the thirteen American colonies, where the 'Virginia Declaration of Rights' was proclaimed in 1776. In the same way as had happened in America, where human rights were to form the basis of the emancipation of white settlers (and slave owners) from the British colonial power, so too in revolutionary France were they of benefit to the Third Estate – principally the urban bourgeoisie but also independent peasant farmers – in breaking the dominance of the aristocracy (the Second Estate) and the clergy (the First Estate). In other words, what demolished the ancien régime and represented a quantum leap towards the modern constitutional state did nothing whatsoever to change the subdivision of humanity into unequal races. Nonetheless, it did at least achieve the swift divestment of the institution of slavery on both sides of the Atlantic of any legitimacy.

The revolution brought emancipation to French Jews, and they were granted full civil rights. Occupation by Napoleonic forces subsequently saw the ideas of 1789 exported to the German-speaking lands, heralding the end of the inferior legal status of Jews living there, too. Jews were granted full equality under the law in the principalities of Anhalt-Bernburg and Anhalt-Köthen in 1810 and 1812, respectively. Emancipation laws were enacted in the kingdom of Bavaria, the Grand Duchy of Baden, and Frankfurt. In addition, the German-speaking states abolished special taxes on Jews. In Prussia, the 'Edict concerning the civil status of the Jews', which was promulgated in March 1812, gave them full citizenship. In formal legal terms, this decree put them on an equal footing with all other subjects of King Friedrich Wilhelm III (1770–1840), although they were still deprived of statutory political enfranchisement.

Even before the French Revolution, an amelioration of the Jews' lot had been discussed in Prussia. In 1781, at the instigation of Enlightenment philosopher Moses Mendelssohn (1729–86), the historian and civil servant Christian Wilhelm von Dohm (1751–1820) wrote a treatise entitled *Über die bürgerliche Verbesserung der Juden* ('On the civil improvement of the Jews').[12] In it, Dohm advocated the step-by-step implementation of full parity with Christians for the Jews, a controversial demand. Then, in the early nineteenth century, the naturalist and geographer Alexander von Humboldt (1769–1859), who was working for the Prussian government at the time, demanded equality for the Jews. In his opinion, the Jews were to be liberated from their 'national character' through a process of 'integration, demolition of their religious nature, and colonisation'.[13] Thus, Humboldt too, who fostered good relations with Prussia's Jews, saw them not merely as a religious community but also as members of their own nation – i.e. race – which needed encouragement to reach the same level of development as the Prussian non-Jewish community.

Yet the Jews too considered themselves a race. They had never really come to terms with the new classification of humanity introduced by the Enlightenment. While their emancipation saw the rise of Jewish criticism of the universalism of the Enlightenment, there was no corresponding critique of the division of humankind into races, let alone of the existence of a Jewish race. The historian Philipp Lenhard (b. 1980) has offered the following analysis:

> The appropriation of the concept of race was an expression of a self-confident attitude towards their own Jewishness. Precisely for those Jews who were not particularly religious or who even espoused secular views, recourse to the idea of 'race' provided an opportunity to continue to define themselves as Jews ... In contrast to ancient and mediaeval Judaism, in the modern period, the unity of a community based on descent and one based on religion began to disintegrate. In this context, the concept of race also assumed a fundamental importance for the development of a Jewish identity.[14]

The concept of a 'Jewish race' had therefore been in circulation long before the late nineteenth and early twentieth centuries, a period when advocates of assimilation and Zionists freely bandied it about in their disputes, as did anthropologists of Jewish origin in the realm of the life sciences.

Not least, Jews' emphasis on their right to autonomy within Christian society hampered their emancipation, a process which started to stall in Prussia after the Allied victory over Napoleon (1769–1821). Unlike the Enlightenment, idealism and the Romantic movement once more stressed the differences between peoples and religions. Johann Gottlieb Fichte (1762–1814), the philosopher of idealism, called the Jews 'a state within a state'[15] – those same Jews of whom so many had just fought for Prussia in the wars of liberation. This climate therefore meant that the provisions of the edict of 1812 were not enacted in any of the territorial gains awarded to Prussia in the Congress of Vienna. Accordingly, Prussia's Jews found themselves under the jurisdiction of no fewer than twenty-two different legal systems. Whereas in the former kingdom of Westphalia (at least theoretically) full equality was guaranteed, in the provinces of Posen and West Prussia, which in around 1830 were home to some 30 per cent of the total Jewish population, the endemic lawlessness from the time when the region was under Russian and Polish control and forcible settlement in ghettos continued unabated. This situation only changed after 1833.

In the years leading up to the March Revolution of 1848, the emancipation of the Jews became a central political issue, often simply referred to as the 'Jewish Question'. In Germany, the so-called *Vormärz* (pre-March) period was a time when liberals, bourgeois democrats, and nationalists made common cause against the restoration of the monarchy and demanded unity, justice, and freedom for all Germans. Jews were also among their number. Yet to many, they still remained alien and were sometimes even regarded as opponents of the new movement. National-liberal anti-Semites such as Ernst Moritz Arndt (1769–1860) took the view that Jews were a 'corrupt and degenerate people'[16] and as such had no place in an aspiring German nation state. Anti-Semitism was also rife in the movement run by *Turnvater* ('father of gymnastics') Jahn (Friedrich Ludwig Jahn, 1778–1852) as well as in the student fraternities that assembled at the Hambacher Festival in May 1832, sporting the German national colours of black, red, and gold. All things considered, however, the ideas of the *Vormärz* were in no way anti-Semitic and exclusive but were inclusive. In this, the German-speaking territories followed anti-restoration movements in Austria, Italy, and Hungary.

At the same time, the growth of socialist ideology in Europe brought with it the rise of a socially motivated form of anti-Semitism that focused attention on supposed Jewish wealth and the controllers of that wealth, the bankers. These financiers were for the most part adherents of Orthodox Judaism, and their detractors accused them of exploiting the people. Those who peddled this kind of anti-Semitism included early socialists in France such as Pierre Leroux (1797–1871) and Charles Fourier (1772–1837), and in *Vormärz* Germany the group known as the Young Hegelians, notably Bruno Bauer (1809–82). Bauer agitated against Jewish emancipation on the grounds that this would only strengthen the state's entrenched structure of privilege. Under the influence of the philosopher and anticlerical thinker Ludwig Feuerbach (1804–72), even Karl Marx (1818–83), who was himself of Jewish extraction, wrote an essay 'Zur Judenfrage' ('On the Jewish question') in 1843,[17] long before his famous analysis of capital. In this treatise, in which he went so far as to deny religious Jews the right to exist, Marx voiced the opinion that while Jewish emancipation was desirable, it could never be real freedom, since such a thing would be impossible in the absence of a complete and unquestioning renunciation of Judaism. Or to put this in simpler terms: the emancipation of capitalist, Orthodox Jews in an equally capitalist society would do nothing to promote the emergence of a classless society.

However, the class hatred of early communists towards prosperous Jews was not devoid of racial anti-Semitic aspects. Thus, Marx lambasted his adversary the labour leader Ferdinand Lassalle (1825–64), who in contrast to the internationalist stance of Marxism was more in favour of a Prussian nation state, as a 'Jewish nigger'. Marx went on:

> It is now crystal clear to me that, as proved by the shape of his head and the way his hair grows, he is descended from the Negroes who joined the Israelites' flight from Egypt under

Moses (unless his mother or grandmother on his father's side cross-bred with a nigger). This combination of Jewishness and Germanness with a negroid base note must of necessity produce a peculiar result. The fellow's pushiness is also very nigger-like.[18]

In addition, Marxism produced some little-known but truly extraordinary mental gymnastics. While individual radical nationalist anti-Semites indulged in rabid fantasies of violence against the Jewish race, leading Marxists took the view that certain peoples or ethnic groups who were not ready to participate in the class struggle had thereby abrogated their right to exist. For example, Friedrich Engels (1820–95) wrote in the *Neue Rheinische Zeitung*, a newspaper founded by Marx in 1848: 'until they are totally eradicated or denationalised, these residual fragments of peoples … will remain the most fanatical standard-bearers of counter-revolution'.[19] Marx believed that these peoples would have to be 'swept away in the global revolutionary hurricane'.[20] In light of this, the Cambridge literary historian George Watson has called Marx the 'ancestor of modern political genocide'.[21]

Thus, while on the one hand the burgeoning ideology of socialism promoted anti-Semitism, on the other hand, in conjunction with liberalism and the bourgeois democracy movement, it laid the groundwork for the revolutions of 1848 that gripped many parts of Europe. The uprising in Germany brought with it full Jewish emancipation. The so-called preliminary parliament convened at St Paul's Church in Frankfurt from May 1848 to May 1849, in which Jewish delegates also participated, resolved that citizens' 'civil and civic rights' should be neither 'conditioned nor limited' by the religious faith they professed. Equality laws were now passed in numerous small German states. In December 1848, the new Prussian constitution granted full emancipation to the Jews. Even though many of these reforms were rescinded

after the failure of the revolution, Germany's incipient indus-
trialisation and economic development nonetheless increasingly
rendered absurd the restrictions placed on the Jews' rights.
Formal resolutions to implement full Jewish emancipation were
passed in both the Prussian state parliament and the North
German imperial diet in July 1869, and the measure was adopted
into imperial law following the formation of the Second German
Empire in April 1871.

At the same time, the rapid and radical changes that society
was undergoing at that time and the nationalism that was beginning to emerge all over Europe fuelled racial anti-Semitism,
which found its most fertile breeding ground in anti-liberal
circles. Among such groups, a hot topic of discussion was a work
by French aristocrat Arthur Comte de Gobineau (1816–82) entitled *Essai sur l'inégalité des races humaines* ('An essay on the
inequality of human races').[22] It had first appeared in the mid-
1850s but only translated into German around the turn of the
century, and was notable for being the first work to broach the
subject of supposed 'racial purity', which was later to become a
key element of National Socialist ideology. Gobineau regarded
racial purity as being of central importance because in his view
the only essential element of history was the law of nature, and
hence race. He categorised the Jewish race as forming a constituent part – a sub-race, as it were – of the white race. He even
accorded the Jews a certain respect for keeping themselves to
themselves and so creating the conditions for a continuation of
their race – conditions that the French aristocracy had also fulfilled, although not the Germans. According to racial theorists,
the Germans were a mixed race of Celts and Slavs. The journalist Joachim Fest, who published his seminal work on Hitler in
1973, wrote of Gobineau that he 'first formulated the fear of
the racial chaos of modern times and linked the decline of all
cultures to the "promiscuity of blood"'.[23]

Gobineau's ideas gained traction through the evolutionary theory of the British naturalist Charles Darwin (1809–82) concerning the 'survival of the fittest'[24] that would presently captivate the whole world – although this term was in fact coined by his fellow countryman, the philosopher and sociologist Herbert Spencer (1820–1903).[25] Henceforth, the theory of evolution was trivialised and traduced as a kind of racial theory. According to the eternal existential law of natural selection, the racial theorists argued, the individual races were fated to engage in a merciless competition for survival. This law then appeared to take on a greater significance in the early twentieth century, when anti-colonial uprisings such as the Boxer Rebellion broke out in China, and alarmist talk of a 'yellow peril' began to circulate in Europe. Yet to dyed-in-the-wool anti-Semites, working from the premise of racial purity, it was obvious which group represented the greatest threat to the Nordic or Aryan race: the race that lived among the Nordic peoples and which was increasingly maligned as parasitic – namely, the Jews.

One individual who drank deeply from the well of contemporary anti-Semitic prejudice was the composer Richard Wagner (1813–83), who met Gobineau on several occasions. An anti-Semitic mythically Germanic worldview combined with an innate genius for musical composition and drama in Wagner, whose name was later to become indelibly associated with Bayreuth, and whose stage works the young Hitler hugely admired, even while he was still resident in Linz. In the opinion of the anti-Semitism researcher Wolfgang Benz, Wagner exerted a 'fateful influence' on Hitler by disseminating his anti-Semitic convictions both in his operatic works and in his 1850 essay 'Judaism in Music', which was 'as influential as it was irrational'.[26] There, Wagner wrote that Jews were 'incapable' of artistic expression, either in words or song. As he later added in his diary: 'Nature is organised in such a way that, wherever there is something to parasitise, the parasite will duly appear.' He went on to explain that: 'an expiring body is immediately located by worms, which set about breaking it down completely and ingesting it. This is precisely what the rise of the Jews means to cultural life in pre-sent-day Europe.'[27]

Wagner's anti-Semitism was also reflected in his operas. Time and again he thematised the conflict between materialism and the human soul. The heroes of his musical dramas are Germanic redeemer figures like Lohengrin, whose aim is to save the world from materialism, or Parsifal, who liberates the wild woman Kundry, whom Wagner characterised as Jewish, by putting her to death. This led the music critic Hartmut Zelinsky to remark that Wagner had thereby 'abetted the exterminatory anti-Semitism of the Holocaust'.[28] Other commentators responded that Wagner, under the influence of Gobineau's racism of blood, had aban-doned his anti-Semitism in favour of a rebirth through the blood of Christ that transcended all divisions, as enunciated in his 'regeneration writings'.[29] Micha Brumlik identifies both tenden-cies in Wagner's work.[30] Hitler considered Wagner the 'greatest prophet figure' the German people had ever had,[31] and almost all the motifs that underpinned the dictator's career can be found in the composer's work, from redemption through destruction to downfall.

At the beginning of the twentieth century, Europe's anti-Semites were then treated to a 'clarification' of the Jewish Question by Wagner's son-in-law, Houston Stewart Chamber-lain (1855–1927), whom Hitler later got to know personally and idolised. In 1899 this independent British scholar, who had a penchant for all things German, published a book that became the standard work of theoretical racial anti-Semitism. In *The Foundations of the Nineteenth Century* (originally published in German as *Die Grundlagen des neunzehnten Jahrhunderts*),[32] Chamberlain gathered together all the anti-Semitic and racist 'findings' popular hitherto into a kind of cultural history. For him, the Aryans were the 'soul of culture', as they carried within them the legacy of classical antiquity – Greek art and philosophy, Roman law, and early Christianity. In his view, as the 'master race', these Aryans were destined to usher in a new era of history for the world. For Chamberlain, too, the essential prerequisite for this view would be upholding the 'purity' of the race, as 'noble breeds of human beings will be forever spiritually impoverished and excluded from the race of humanity striving towards the light by the semitic dogma of materialism, which has kept itself ... free of all Aryan impurities.'[33] Taking Europe's literary salons by storm with his treatise, Chamberlain's admirers included Emperor Wilhelm II (1859–1941), Winston Churchill (1874–1955), and Albert Schweitzer (1875–1965).

Chamberlain's *Foundations*, which were widely read in the German-speaking world, were supplemented by a strong revival of interest in Germanic mythology as dramatised by Wagner. The Austrian occultist Guido von List (1848–1919) linked this with a theosophist cosmology and the call for an unconditional 'racial hygiene' of the kind already promoted by Gobineau. These combined to form an 'Aryan religion' in which old Germanic gods like Wotan had new life breathed into them and magical powers were ascribed to runes. List also influenced another ariosophist, as adherents of this worldview were called: Jörg Lanz von Liebenfels (1874–1954). He too wanted, by means of a new 'Aryan religion', to create the conditions for nurturing a new 'master race' that would be steeled for the existential struggle between the races, and above all for the fight against the Jews.[34]

In the last quarter of the nineteenth century, the pseudo-scientific analysis of human ethnicities in general, and of the 'Jewish Question' in particular, went hand in hand with an ever-increasing political exploitation of anti-Semitism. A prime example was the backward Russian Empire, where fully one-third of the population were serfs until 1861 and the old anti-Judaism had clung on far longer than elsewhere in Europe. Some five million Jews were living in the so-called Pale of Settlement, a kind of giant ghetto covering the western and southern regions of the Tsarist empire: in other words Lithuania, Poland, Ukraine, Volhynia, Bessarabia, parts of Galicia, and the Black Sea. Benz likens their situation prior to the First World War to that of the Jews of Central Europe in the eighteenth century, describing them as a 'marginalised, disenfranchised minority debarred from any social status and hence also from any opportunities to make a proper living and come up in the world'.[35]

Russian Jews were repeatedly made the scapegoats for political ineptitude and failures in the country's notoriously catastrophic food supply. Consequently, after the murder of Tsar Alexander II (1818–81), the 1880s witnessed a series of pogroms. The plight of the Jews grew still worse under the last tsar of Russia, Nicholas II (1868–1918). As a result, many of them joined the newly formed liberal and later socialist parties in the hope that they might thereby realise their desire for emancipation. Yet other motives also played a role. Thus, the researcher and writer on communism Gerd Koenen describes how there was also a general aspiration 'to escape the stifling world of their ancestors and enter into a new form of modernity, not through bourgeois assimilation but through a notional symbiosis with the proletariat'.[36] The response to their political protest was a wave of pogroms and other outrages orchestrated by the authorities in St Petersburg, the worst of which took place in Gomel and Kishinev in 1903 and Odessa in 1905.

It is in this context that surely the most evil of all anti-Semitic fabrications first saw the light of day: *The Protocols of the Elders of Zion*.[37] In the wake of the Bolshevik Revolution of 1917, there was an explosive upsurge of interest in this text, with millions of copies being read worldwide. Many people saw it as a blueprint for the upheavals that were shaking the world. The *Protocols* are an incoherent collage, making it hard for us today to grasp how its conspiracy theories could ever have been taken seriously by people back then – for example, the claim that the chief aim of the 'Elders of Zion' was to establish a 'Jewish world-wide hegemony' to be based on the 'power of gold' but also on repression of the working classes. This hegemony would be established by destroying other peoples. Lies, deceit, and fraud, political ideas like liberalism and democracy, prostitution, and infiltrating the free press, as well as economic crises and naked terror, would be the means through which this total dominance would be achieved.

The *Protocols* purported to be the minutes of the First Zionist Congress, which was held in Basle in Switzerland in 1897 under the presidency of the founder of the worldwide Zionist movement, Theodor Herzl. The main aim of the congress was to create a common homeland founded on the principle of equality for the Jewish diaspora, which was spread throughout the entire globe. Herzl justified the need for a Jewish state in his 1896 pamphlet *The Jewish State* as being about 'our loss of the power of assimilation'. Herzl said of the Jews: 'When we sink, we become a revolutionary proletariat, the subordinate officers of all revolutionary parties; and at the same time, when we rise, there rises also our terrible power of the purse.'[38]

The emergence of the *Protocols* dates from this same period, although these have absolutely nothing to do with the real Zionist conference. Indeed, even Hitler, while still considering their content to be wholly accurate, did not discount their specious provenance.[39] In actual fact, they were the work of the Tsarist secret police. They were first published in 1903 as a nine-part series in a St Petersburg gazette under the heading 'The Jewish Programme for World Domination'.[40] Not long afterwards they appeared in book form with the title *The Great in* the Small, edited by one Sergei Nilus (1862–1929), a Russian Orthodox mystic. The treatise later came to widespread public attention in Russia under yet another title, *The Approaching Antichrist*. This allusion to the apocalypse only served to greatly enhance its deliberately calculated anti-Semitic appeal in the mystical religious world of the Tsarist empire, with the alleged Jewish global conspiracy being equated to the war waged by the forces of evil against the divine order.

This escalating hatred of the Jews in Russia, with its spasms of extreme violence, meant that in the final three decades before the outbreak of the First World War more than two million adherents of the Mosaic faith left the Tsarist empire. They emigrated predominantly to the United States, the Austro-Hungarian Empire, and the German Empire. Very few made it to European countries located farther to the west. This was a contributory factor to the population of Jews in France in the nineteenth century, comprising just 0.2 per cent of the total, or some 80,000 people. Yet even there, anti-Semitism was in evidence; this had a variety of causes and was related to the way in which the Jewish minority was segregated. Whereas the Sephardic Jews of southern France, who had originally come primarily from the Iberian Peninsula, were well integrated, Ashkenazi Jews who arrived from Russia to settle in northern France found themselves – again according to Benz – 'facing all manner of hostility, which had its roots partially in Catholic Christianity – partially in the kind of racism promulgated by Gobineau and by Édouard Drumont in his 1886 book *La France juive* ('Jewish France') – and partially ... in socialist agitation'.[41] One notorious example of how anti-Semitism set its face against a future that was no longer determined by blood ties and traditions was a legal scandal that sowed division in the Third Republic for decades: the so-called Dreyfus affair. This began in 1894 when a young Jewish army captain, Alfred Dreyfus (1859–1935), was put on trial for high treason and unjustly found

guilty. It was only in 1906 – when Republican France finally prevailed against nationalists and clerics who saw Dreyfus, the son
of a manufacturer from Alsace, as epitomising a new, ruinous age
– that the Jewish officer was fully exonerated and rehabilitated.

The Austro-Hungarian Dual Monarchy was also hit by waves
of anti-Semitism in the second half of the nineteenth century.
Here, too, it was fed by a number of diverse sources from Christian, socialist, and populist nationalist standpoints that took
their cue from a variety of greater or lesser racial theorists,
ranging from Gobineau to Chamberlain and Lanz to Liebenfels. The most voluble representative of political anti-Semitism
in Austria was the Pan-Germanist propagandist Georg Ritter
von Schönerer (1842–1921), who was a delegate to the Imperial
Council in Vienna, the so-called multi-ethnic parliament. He
combined hatred of the Jews with a greater-German, anticlerical
nationalism: 'Through purity to unity – Germania's cathedral
will be built without Jews, and without Rome' (*Durch Reinheit
zur Einheit – Ohne Juda, ohne Rom wird gebaut Germaniens
Dom*) ran one of Schönerer's campaigning slogans.[42] He was
an early advocate of the German-speaking parts of the Danube
monarchy being subsumed within the German Empire. Since it
chimed in so well with his anti-liberal and anti-socialist policies, anti-Semitism was also deployed by the eloquent Christian
Socialist politician Karl Lueger (1844–1910). His anti-Semitic
rhetoric was reputed to have played a part in his rise to become
the mayor of Vienna in 1897.

Even though the great metropolis of the Danube monarchy
was widely regarded as the European centre of anti-Semitism, it
was still not the be all and end all of Viennese life. This reputation was only retrospectively assigned to the city, post-Holocaust,
not least because of the presence there of the perpetrator of
this greatest crime against humanity, Hitler, who was resident
in Vienna between 1908 and 1913. In truth, anti-Semitism was

just one of a number of different movements of the age to find expression in Vienna. Thus, for instance, at the municipal elections in Vienna in 1907, at which universal suffrage was extended to all male voters for the first time, the anti-Semitic pan-German and radically German nationalist parties polled just 2.8 per cent – even though the proportion of the city's population consisting of Jews who had emigrated there from the East was not inconsiderable. In 1910, this community numbered some 175,000, or 90 per cent of all the Jews in the Austro-Hungarian Empire. Their foreignness gave the anti-Semites an ideal peg on which to hang their agitation.

In the melting pot that was the multi-ethnic Austro-Hungarian Empire, the vast majority of citizens of the most diverse nationalities and religions co-existed peacefully among or alongside one another. The Jews, whose emancipation was enacted in the Danube monarchy in 1867, belonged for the most part to the petty bourgeoisie. However, a few had become seriously wealthy, either through railway construction or in the textile industry. Their contribution to the cultural life of Vienna, which at that time was a major European metropolis of culture, was immense. Figures who are inextricably associated with this period include Sigmund Freud (1859–1939), Gustav Mahler (1860–1911), Arthur Schnitzler (1862–1931), and Hugo von Hofmannsthal (1874–1929), to name just a few. The Viennese Jewish community, which thanks to Zionist ideas that had been in circulation since the late nineteenth century had – at least in part – resisted assimilation, formed a self-confident segment of the city's social life. In the Union of Austrian Jews they even had their own party, while there was also a Jewish nationalist student movement called 'Kadimah'.

It sounds like a terrible irony of history to note that Hitler, of all people, provided a shining example of this peaceful coexistence. This was the conclusion reached by historian Brigitte Hamann in her book *Hitlers Wien* ('Hitler's Vienna').[43] The findings of her research, for which she undertook a systematic and painstaking study of Hitler's surroundings during his stay in the city, can be broadly summarised as follows: although Hitler, the failed artist from the Waldviertel region, had found himself confronted by the 'Jewish Question' in Vienna and considered the Jews a separate race, he was anything but an anti-Semite at that time. Rather, he was full of admiration for the Jews' cultural achievements, notably the works of the composers Mahler, Mendelssohn-Bartholdy, and Offenbach, and acknowledged the benevolence of Jewish institutions. What's more, after failing at his chosen profession and slipping down the social scale, he maintained extraordinarily good relations with Jewish denizens of men's hostels, craftsmen, and small tradesmen. These individuals had names like Neumann, Robinson, Löffner, Altenberg, Landsberger, and Morgenstern.

In Germany, where Hitler moved in May 1913, he behaved no differently, at least to begin with. As already noted, Germany's Jews, who numbered just over half a million (or 1.2 per cent of the population) had been granted full legal and political equality by the imperial constitution of 1871, although they were still disbarred from holding senior positions in the civil service and the Imperial Army General Staff. As a result, many Jews entered the business and financial sectors, which were then booming, as well as the liberal professions. Here too, they found themselves being integrated into wider society.

Admittedly, this did not alter the fact that whenever a crisis shook the community, the Jews were immediately scapegoated, primarily by the anti-liberal bourgeoisie and petty bourgeoisie but also by the working class. This was the case, for example, when the country threatened to plunge into economic depression in the wake of the so-called Panic of 1873, a global overproduction crisis triggered by the Vienna stockmarket crash in May of that year. Conservative newspapers like the *Kreuzzeitung* exploited Otto von Bismarck's (1815–98) 'Jewish connections' to his private banker Gerson von Bleichröder (1822–93) to campaign against the policies of the German chancellor. The mass-circulation *Gartenlaube*, which had been founded by the anti-Semitic journalist and author Otto Glagau (1834–92) harped on about the Jews' supposedly typical racial characteristics, branding them as 'capitalists' and 'speculators'. Glagau's overstated credo ran: 'The social question is the Jewish Question.'[44]

On the other hand, the Jews who had arrived in Germany from the east – their numbers rose to 46,000 by the turn of the century – were viewed even by their assimilated co-religionists as 'foreign bodies' and as having the potential to cause social unrest. In turbulent times of technological and social upheaval, their presence seemed in particular to trigger anxieties about the future that were very much akin to those voiced nowadays. Such fears were stoked by an article written by the respected historian Heinrich von Treitschke (1834–96) in 1879, in which he spoke out against a feared influx of Eastern European Jewish immigrants into the empire, while at the same time demanding the complete assimilation of Germany's Jews, 'since the last thing we want is for millennia of German civilisation to be followed by an era of German–Jewish mixed culture'.[45]

In addition to Treitschke, who coined the notorious phrase 'The Jews are our misfortune' ('Die Juden sind unser Unglück'),[46] in 1880 a left-leaning journalist by the name of Wilhelm Marr (1819–1904) came to prominence not only by founding the League of Anti-Semites, the first expressly anti-Semitic organisation in the German Empire, but also by publishing the highly inflammatory pamphlet 'The Victory of Judaism over Germanness, Viewed from a Non-Confessional Standpoint'.[47] In it, Marr wrote that Judaism had:

taken over leadership of the international financial conspiracy
… a race of born merchants in our midst, the Jews, has created

an aristocracy, one of money, which crushes everything from above, but also engendered a kind of mercantile mob rule, which eats away and undermines society from below by means of haggling and profiteering.[48]

Marr maintained close contacts with Bayreuth, which had by then become the epicentre of German anti-Semitism around the nucleus of Richard Wagner and his wife Cosima (1837–1930), and spread its influence beyond Germany's borders. It was there, too, that Glagau and the Göttingen biblical scholar Paul de Lagarde (1827–91) also arranged a rendezvous. This academic likened Jews to 'trichinae and bacilli'.[49] Lagarde and his confederates were instrumental in ensuring that anti-Semitism among the Bayreuth circle, where a number of different strands of this prejudice came together, assumed manic proportions. The philosopher Friedrich Nietzsche (1844–1900), who had once been a great admirer of Wagner but later became a fierce critic of his anti-Semitism, described the Bayreuth circle in his work *Ecco Homo* as an 'appalling bunch'.[50]

Another person to foster links with this group was the Berlin court chaplain Adolf Stoecker (1835–1909). Stoecker founded a party that began campaigning not only against the 'Jew-ridden Left' but also 'Jewish-dominated big business'. His 'Berlin Movement', which aimed to break the link between the working class and the Left, was succeeded by other organisations that nailed the colours of a consistently anti-Semitic worldview firmly to their masts. In 1881, the German People's Union drafted a radically anti-Semitic petition, not only calling for Jewish emancipation to be repealed but also demanding that a ban be imposed on Jewish immigration from the East. Seventy-six leading academics, including the historian Theodor Mommsen (1817–1903) and the medic Rudolf Virchow (1821–1902) wrote an open letter of protest against this 'revival of an old delusion'.[51] Yet this delusion remained alive, albeit still within manageable bounds. At the instigation of the Marburg librarian Otto Böckel (1859–1923) and Theodor Fritsch (1852–1933), founder of the notorious Hammer Verlag, a number of smaller groups came together in 1886 to form the German Anti-Semitic Confederation. Three years later, this became the nucleus of the German Social Party. Yet the party only managed to garner 2.9 per cent of the vote in the general election of 1893.

Most prominent of all, however, was the Pan-German League, an organisation founded in Berlin in 1891 as a German counterpart to the Austrian Schönerer's Pan-German Movement. The aim of this organisation, which at the turn of the century boasted around 20,000 members, was to promote German expansion through naval rearmament and to 'revive a German nationalist attitude, especially by reawakening and fostering an awareness of the racial and cultural ties that bind all sections of the German people'.[52] Yet for all the attention currently being focused on anti-Semitism within the Germany of the Kaisers and its dominions as a world power, there is no evidence that this organisation ever exercised much influence on contemporary politics. All the same, it must surely have played a part in encouraging a steady undercurrent of anti-Semitism in the country.

Nor was Emperor Wilhelm II immune to anti-Semitism. However, he cannot be regarded as a real Jew-hater. He once stated: 'The dear Lord knows better than we do that the Jews were responsible for killing Our Saviour, and has punished them accordingly. But neither the anti-semites or others or myself have been tasked and empowered by Him to bully and harass these people for the greater glory of God.'[53] In the late 1890s the emperor even intended to assist Herzl in pushing through his plan for the creation of a Jewish state in Palestine against the opposition of Germany's ally, the Ottoman Empire, and to allow himself to be proclaimed as its patron. For one thing, the emperor believed that this would rid the German empire of any potential socialist unrest. Second, he took the view that 'given the enormous power that is now wielded by international Jewish capitalism, with all its attendant dangers, would it not be a massive achievement on Germany's part if the world of the Hebrew people were to view it with gratitude?'[54] But although Wilhelm II met Herzl during his official visit to Jerusalem in November 1898, he ultimately withdrew his support for the project, evidently after the Ottoman sultan, who controlled Palestine, made known his strong objections. Ottoman support was ultimately more important to the emperor than Herzl and his Jewish state.

In the Bavaria of King Ludwig III (1845–1921), in whose capital Hitler was resident from May 1913 onwards, anti-Semitism was something of a sideshow. Of course, the city also had its share of pan-Germanists. In 1912, the group's president Heinrich Class (1868–1953) wrote an anti-Semitic treatise entitled *If I Was Emperor...*[55] that met with a positive response on the far-right fringes of society. In the literary salons of the city, an intellectual anti-Semitism was also in evidence, based on the racial theories current at the time. Yet thanks to the feeling of separateness prevalent in Bavaria, fuelled by the Prussian claim to hegemony within the German Empire, attempts to link anti-Semitism with populist notions of a 'Greater Germany' gained very little traction there. Instead, any resentment felt by the populace towards the city's longstanding Jewish community, in so far as it existed at all, was based on the customary clichés.

It was quite another matter where new Jewish refugees from the East, with their truly alien appearance, were concerned; they sought refuge in Bavaria too at this time. They tended to elicit a somewhat defensive attitude within the populace. However, this did not apply to Hitler, newly arrived in the city from Vienna. During his brief sojourn in Munich, he thought of himself as an artist and frequented artists' haunts in the Schwabing district – in other words, places where liberal attitudes were the order of the day and there was no place for populist anti-Semitism, not least because Jews were well-represented among the potential clientele. No contemporary eyewitness accounts make any mention of Hitler being a conspicuous anti-Semite during his stay in Munich before the First World War.

When in the summer of 1914, Europe's heads of state led their people like 'sleepwalkers' into the First World War, as the Australian historian Christopher Clark has so appositely put it,[56] no one in Germany, where anti-Semitism had been steadily waning in popularity since the turn of the century, was remotely interested in who was a Jew and who not. Germans of all backgrounds went to war enthusiastically – including Hitler, who volunteered for service in a Bavarian infantry regiment. To many soldiers of the Mosaic faith, it appeared that their emancipation was now reaching full fruition. They read in the papers how the Jewish industrialist Walther Rathenau (1867–1922) had risen to become the head of the department supplying raw materials for the war effort, while the shipowner Albert Ballin (1857–1918) had been made head of the imperial procurement agency. And they saw how more and more Jews were becoming commissioned officers. Many believed that, in performing military service, they were passing a kind of final test for full social recognition. Men of Jewish extraction fought and died alongside their non-Jewish comrades on the battlefields of East Prussia, Flanders, Champagne, the Somme, the Marne, or outside the fortress city of Verdun.

It was only when the far-reaching hopes of the nation had been dashed by the grim reality of bloody trench warfare, and after hundreds of thousands of men had lost their lives and a crisis gripped the empire, that anti-Semitic resentment started to gain momentum once more. The Jews were now blamed by ultra-nationalist circles for the mood of defeatism that swept the country. They were also accused of being shirkers, prompting the Prussian war minister Adolf Wild von Hohenborn (1860–1925) to investigate the matter in the autumn of 1916. The survey he commissioned, which became known as the 'Jewish census' (*Judenzählung*),[57] was designed to ascertain exactly how many soldiers of the Jewish faith were actually engaged at the front. The results showed that their number – pro rata to population – was no lower than that of their non-Jewish counterparts.

The results of the 'Jewish census' were initially hushed up by the war ministry, as it swiftly became clear to the imperial government, which was intent on assimilation and integration, how divisive this whole affair could become. Instead, there was a concerted effort to sweep everything under the carpet, which the anti-Semites construed as confirmation of the alleged Jewish draft-dodging. Only in January 1917 did new minister of war Hermann von Stein (1854–1927) concede to the Association of German Jews that 'the conduct of Jewish soldiers and their fellow citizens gave no cause for the review ordered by my predecessor and therefore does not in any way relate to it'.[58]

In the light of what happened at Auschwitz, the tendency nowadays is to exaggerate the significance of the 'Jewish census' as a clear indicator of the radicalisation of anti-Semitism in Germany. We do not know whether Hitler had any knowledge of this measure and – if so – what he thought about it. Certainly, there is no record of anti-Semitism in his military unit or of any dismissive comments about Jews made by him during this period. In the First World War, Hitler was no Jew-hater, as the German–Scottish historian Thomas Weber has recently demonstrated in his book *Hitler's First War*.[59] After the war, when Hitler entered politics and became a fanatical anti-Semite, the regimental aide-de-camp Fritz Wiedemann (1891–1970), who like Hitler had been a messenger and spent every day in his company, spoke for many others when he said that he had 'puzzled long and hard' as to the root causes of Hitler's loathing of the Jews but was adamant that 'his experiences with Jewish officers during the Great War could not have played any significant part in it'.[60] One key aspect was that Hitler owed his Iron Cross, First Class – a decoration he was awarded in the autumn of 1917 and which he wore with pride throughout his life – to a Jewish territorial army lieutenant, Hugo Gutmann (1880–1962). Hitler was said to have had a very cordial relationship with Gutmann, who hailed from Nuremberg, even supposedly running some off-duty errands for him.

It sounds very odd: when anti-Semitism was on the rise as discontent grew in Germany, Hitler himself was still no anti-Semite. At a time when the only news coming from the front was bad and when hardship and misery were rife back home, people started clamouring for scapegoats. For some, it was the emperor and the aristocratic officer corps; for others it was the capitalists who were profiting from the war; while for still others it was the Left, which was maligned for allegedly undermining the heroic struggle of the entire nation. And for those who had always been anti-Semites, the archetypal war-profiteer capitalist and seditious socialist alike were naturally Jews.

In actual fact, there were indeed many Jews to be found in the ranks of German socialists. They often fronted the strikes that from 1916 on had been steadily eroding the tacit truce called between capital and labour when war broke out. Jews were also well-represented among those radical Social Democrats who split from their party in April 1917 to form the Independent German Social Democratic Party (USPD), which called for a swift end to the war. They were also leading lights in the insurrectionary Marxist Spartacus League, which called for global revolution by the international proletariat and made common cause with the USPD. Plus, many Jews were at the forefront of the Bolshevik

November Revolution of 1917 in Russia that gave huge encouragement to rebellious radical leftist groups worldwide. All of these provided grist to the mill of those peddling anti-Semitic conspiracy theories. This ugly face of anti-Semitism remained implacably unmoved by the knowledge that some 12,000 Jews had given their lives for their German fatherland in various theatres of the First World War.

That sacrifice in turn did little to alter the overall picture of German anti-Semitism. It was not the case that it had been steadily on the rise over several centuries. Instead, there were alternating phases where it flared up and abated, such as after the 1848 revolution or the period from the turn of the century until far into the First World War. Periods of unrest and crisis also caused a spike in anti-Semitism. Even then, those who espoused this view remained a small minority who failed to find any resonance for their ideology in mainstream politics. They only became a mass movement as a result of the attitude towards contemporary history that set in following the total collapse of Germany after the war, which put them centre stage.

Anti-Semitism in Germany was no more pronounced than in other European countries, not to mention its virulent expression in Tsarist Russia. It was not, therefore, a specifically German characteristic but rather a European one, which had its roots in the long history of the West and not in the late emergence of the German nation state. In that polity, the Jews found themselves emancipated unlike anywhere else. This acceptance chimes in with the early history of the man who would later give the order to implement the 'Final Solution', the genocide of Europe's Jews. At this stage, as recent research has shown, Hitler, who was wounded during a gas attack in Flanders and was sent to a military hospital in Pasewalk in Farther Pomerania in October 1918 to recuperate, was anything but an anti-Semite. It would be more accurate to call him a 'rudderless political nobody'.[61]

# 2

# The Civil War after the Great War

*Did Friedrich Ebert and others bear some responsibility for Hitler?*

The majority of scholarly opinion holds that the resurgence of reactionary politics in Germany – in other words, of those forces that had set the agenda prior to 1914 – was triggered by the country's defeat in the First World War. In this interpretation, the driving force behind this revival was a nationalistic, anti-Jewish spirit of revanchism that had its roots in the period of empire, along with a desire to turn Germany finally into a truly global power. Standing in opposition to this agenda, according to the customary narrative, was the November Revolution of 1918, which – had it succeeded – would have offered the beaten country the chance to forge a genuinely democratic future. Instead, Germany drifted into Hitlerian fascism and the catastrophe of the Second World War and the Holocaust. Commentators place some measure of blame for this outcome at the door of mainstream social democracy, claiming that it was complicit in joining forces with the old imperial army to thwart the revolution and in so doing paved the way for Hitler and National Socialism.

The key to an understanding of the events that took place in revolutionary Germany in 1918–19 resides in the Russian factor: namely, the way in which contemporaries responded to the powerful ripple effect of the Bolshevik Revolution. In the

vast empire to the East, which many people even before the First
World War assumed would be the up-and-coming power of the
twentieth century, given its huge stocks of raw materials, a brutal
civil war had been raging from late 1917 that had cost the lives
of millions of Russians. However, the leader of the Bolshevik
faction, Vladimir Lenin, and his followers were intent not only
on bringing this conflict to a victorious conclusion. They also
saw themselves as the vanguard of a worldwide class struggle
and Russia as the 'beacon of global revolution'. Their sworn
enemy was the capitalist entente – that is, Great Britain, France,
and the United States. These Western powers dispatched troops
to Russia to aid the 'White' (imperialist) forces in their struggle
against the 'Reds'. The 'victorious group of imperialist powers',
to use a phrase of Lenin's, saw its primary task as 'strangling
global Bolshevism to death'.[1]

To try and force the Western powers onto the defensive by
facing them with the prospect of civil war in their own countries,
Lenin planned to export the proletarian revolution to Central
Europe. It was only natural that Lenin's main focus here was
on Germany. The country was on the brink of losing the Great
War. Two million Germans had been killed on the battlefield,
and almost as many had starved to death on the home front.
Faced with hardship and misery of every conceivable kind, the
populace of the German Empire was weary of the war and of
those who seemed incapable of bringing it to an end. From Moscow's perspective, Germany was ripe for revolution. A push was
all that would be needed for it to fall into the hands of Bolshevism like a ripe fruit, whereupon it could be added to the united
front opposing the 'imperialist powers'.

The coup was to be directed and coordinated by Soviet Russia's
embassy in Berlin, specifically its ambassador Adolf A. Joffe,
a political confederate of the Bolshevik leader and founder of
the Red Army, Leon Trotsky. Joffe became the conduit through

which large quantities of propaganda material and weapons were channelled to the radical Left, who were determined to bring the German monarchy to a violent end. The Russian envoy also forwarded large sums of money to his German legal counsel Oskar Cohn, a USPD delegate in the Reichstag, to fund the planned revolution. It is one of the great ironies of history that the German imperial government's machinations in fanning the flames of Bolshevik revolution during the First World War, and thereby plunging its military adversary Tsarist Russia into chaos, backfired on Germany with astonishing speed. At a party conference, Lenin once declared: 'I am *often accused* of having used German money to achieve our revolution. I have never sought to deny this fact – nor will I do so now. I would, however, like to add that we will stage a similar revolution in Germany with Russian money.'[2]

As early as mid-October 1918, a secret meeting took place in the ROSTA, the branch of the Russian telegraph agency in Berlin, at which Joffe and other Bolshevik leaders got together with radical leftist ringleaders, USPD officials, and representatives of the Spartacus League. The Spartacists' main spokespeople, Rosa Luxemburg and Karl Liebknecht, were not present because they were in custody at the time, as they had been so often in the preceding war years. After much discussion about the situation in Germany, those who were at the conspiratorial gathering agreed to issue a call for revolution, including demands for expropriation, nationalisation, socialisation, a minimum wage, and so forth. The wording of this declaration had been drafted by Joffe and agreed with Lenin.

As the collaboration with their German comrades began to take concrete shape, the Russian Bolsheviks looked towards the future with growing optimism. Sven Felix Kellerhoff and Lars-Broder Keil, whose outstanding book *Lob der Revolution. Die Geburt der deutschen Demokratie* ('In praise of the revolution.

The birth of German democracy')[3] is one of very few works to investigate this cooperation, report an announcement by Lenin's adviser Karl Radek to the effect that Bolshevism would henceforth be a phenomenon in Germany. According to Radek, it was 'a force which, in terms of ideology, overtrumps anything our enemies can muster'.[4] The radical Left and the Spartacists matched the Bolshevik Radek's words with deeds, and with Russian help tried their utmost to stir up the German populace. The situation, however, remained relatively calm, although Karl Liebknecht, who by this time had been released from prison, believed the moment was now ripe to 'strike the decisive blow'.[5]

As it turned out, it was the actions of the 'class enemy' – namely, the emperor, the army, and the government of Prince Maximilian of Baden – that really lit the fuse. Yet this politician, a liberal aristocrat who had been elected imperial chancellor on a ticket of peace through reconciliation, was actually very much in favour of social reforms. He was supported by a cabinet that included, for the very first time in German history, ministers from the mainstream Social Democratic Party, Philip Scheidemann and Gustav Bauer. Under Maximilian's leadership, a request for a ceasefire was duly dispatched to the American president. The German imperial government fully expected a just peace settlement from Woodrow Wilson, given that he had, in his 'Fourteen Points' of January 1918, called among other things for the creation of a Europe based on democratic ideals, in which state frontiers would essentially be identical with the borders between different nationalities.

In the diplomatic notes that were presently exchanged between Washington and Berlin, the American side demanded the following preconditions for a peace settlement: the cessation of unrestricted submarine warfare, the withdrawal of German troops from occupied territories, and the democratisation of the empire, necessarily meaning the abdication of the emperor.

This final provision was met with outrage in the emperor's third Supreme Army Command under Paul von Hindenburg and Erich Ludendorff. The German military, which in September 1918 had virtually issued an ultimatum demanding that the war be brought to an end and placed the empire's fate in the hands of the politicians once more, now performed a volte-face and insisted, in view of what it deemed to be wholly disproportionate peace demands made by Wilson, that the war should go on. Ludendorff, who was responsible for this intervention, was duly relieved of his post, with Wilhelm Groener succeeding him as quartermaster general.

The high command of the navy strongly disapproved of Ludendorff's dismissal. For the admirals had welcomed the last-ditch offensive ordered by the quartermaster general in 1918 – the so-called fight to the death. Ever since the inconclusive Battle of Jutland in May/June 1916, the Imperial High Seas Fleet had lain idle, quietly rusting away in its home ports. On 22 October 1918, the Chief of the Naval Staff Reinhard Scheer informed the Supreme Commander of the High Seas Fleet Franz von Hipper that he intended to engage in a decisive battle with the British Grand Fleet in the North Sea, on roughly the same latitude as the West Frisian island of Terschelling. An operational plan was swiftly drawn up, to be put into action by the end of October. Why the naval high command now wanted to risk everything on a single roll of the dice is unclear. Did they perhaps hope to turn the tide and thereby improve the conditions for peace negotiations? Despite the Royal Navy's clear superiority, many maritime historians still believe that Scheer's plan had a realistic chance of success.[6] Others think that the naval high command wanted to send out a clear signal by sacrificing itself for the Fatherland in a heroic battle. What the admirals actually achieved, however, was absolutely not what they intended: their plans stirred up a revolt among ordinary sailors that acted as a spark for a wider revolution.

Unguarded comments by officers meant that news of the plan to engage the British in one final apocalyptic battle leaked to the crews of the warships. Now that the end of the war seemed imminent, naval ratings had little desire to be used as 'cannon fodder'. The sailors mutinied, dousing the fires heating the steam boilers and opening ships' seacocks to prevent them from putting to sea. They ran up revolutionary red flags on vessels anchored in the roads off the naval bases of Kiel and Wilhelmshaven and pledged solidarity with the workers at rallies and mass demonstrations. Sailors' soviets were formed. In no time, military and civil power at the bases was in the hands of the rebels, who demanded an immediate end to the war and the emperor's abdication. With their power rapidly ebbing away, the naval top brass and the state authorities tried in vain to restore order and discipline. The uprising that had begun in the north German naval ports on the eve of November 1918 quickly escalated into the event that has gone down in German history as the November Revolution.

Unlike in Russia, however, the revolt in Germany was primarily about securing peace. However, the radical Left and its Soviet Russian backers, who had tried to foment revolution in Berlin, did not recognise this. Blinded by superficial similarities – after all, as in the naval mutiny in Germany, it was shots fired by the armoured cruiser *Aurora* that had given the signal for the Bolshevik Revolution to commence with the storming of the Tsar's Winter Palace in St Petersburg – they were convinced that their hour had come. Karl Liebknecht earmarked 4 November as the ideal day for the coup. In the event, everything had to be postponed, as preparations could not be finalised by then. A far more serious blow for the revolutionaries was the embarrassing slip-up that unmasked the Bolshevik string-pullers. Crates of materials destined for the Russian Embassy accidentally broke open at a railway station in Berlin. They were found to contain propaganda material in German for the Spartacus League. The

German government responded accordingly, breaking off diplomatic relations with Soviet Russia and ordering Ambassador
Joffe and his staff to leave the country. The Russian telegraphic
agency ROSTA was also shut down. Thereafter, logistical
support for the German insurrectionists, who saw themselves as
part of the global Bolshevik revolution, had to come through
other, clandestine channels.

Not least in the light of what they now knew, the imperial government of Prince Maximilian of Baden, and above all the SPD
leaders Friedrich Ebert and Philip Scheidemann, now feared that
the radical Left in Berlin would use the support it had already
gained from Moscow to seize the initiative. This had already happened in Braunschweig, Leipzig, and elsewhere. Consequently,
the majority Social Democrats went on the offensive themselves
and issued the chancellor with an ultimatum that the emperor,
who was resident at the time at the German Army General
Headquarters at Spa in Belgium, should abdicate. When the
chancellor refused, the SPD ministers resigned from the cabinet.
To try and save the monarchy, on 9 November Max von Baden
decided to tackle the issue head-on. Since he too was well aware
that Wilhelm II had used up the majority of his credit with most
Germans and that they held him responsible for everything that
had happened, he summarily announced the emperor's abdication. This time the emperor acceded and went into exile in the
Netherlands and Prince Maximilian stepped down as chancellor,
naming Friedrich Ebert as his successor.

As a result, the majority Social Democrats now had at their
disposal all the institutional tools required to restructure the
country as a democracy, although Ebert still toyed with the
idea of making Germany a constitutional monarchy. To prevent
Ebert's reforms from stealing his thunder, Liebknecht resolved
to act by proclaiming a Soviet Republic. When Scheidemann
learnt of this, he decided to pre-empt the Spartacists. Early on

that same afternoon of 9 November 1918, he appeared on a balcony of the Reichstag building and announced to the invited crowd assembled below that 'the old, moribund world of the monarchy has collapsed. Long live the new world; long live the German Republic!'[7] Shortly afterwards, Liebknecht addressed his supporters from the flatbed of a lorry parked in the Berlin pleasure gardens and later from a balcony of the city palace. He proclaimed the 'Free Socialist Republic of Germany' demanded that diplomatic ties be restored with 'our Russian brothers', and called for Germans to embrace the global socialist revolution.[8] However, as Scheidemann had acted promptly and because the mainstream SPD had, despite all its differences with the secessionist USPD, offered to put in place until the upcoming elections a provisional government, a 'Council of the People's Deputies', it had effectively claimed leadership of the revolutionary movement and so drawn the sting of the radical Left.

Of necessity, the top priority of the majority Social Democrats was ending the war, as the revolution had meanwhile taken hold throughout Germany. An armistice was thus concluded between the German Empire and France, Belgium, Great Britain, Italy, and the United States. Initially, it was not really seen as a capitulation by the German populace, despite this being what the ceasefire, signed on 11 November 1918 in a railway carriage in the Compiègne Forest just 60 kilometres from Paris, amounted to. The terms of this agreement provided for the immediate withdrawal of German forces, not only from all occupied territories but also from what were then still the German sovereign regions of Alsace-Lorraine and the left bank of the Rhine. Huge quantities of war materiel were to be handed over to the Allies, while the High Seas Fleet's modern warships were interned. The Catholic Centre Party politician Matthias Erzberger, who was sent to Compiègne by the imperial government to negotiate the armistice terms, sought concessions in view of the revolutionary unrest sweeping Germany but was rebuffed. The French Supreme Commander Marshal Ferdinand Foch tersely informed him that this was the defeated nation's own problem.[9] Triumphalism and sheer hatred of the vanquished enemy had blinded the French administration to the very real possibility that the revolution in Germany might drive the country into the arms of Bolshevik Russia. Only the British prime minister David Lloyd George was persistent in warning of the danger of such a development and its potential consequences for Europe.

It was, however, precisely towards such an outcome that the Spartacists and their allies were working. Their propaganda methods included protest marches, rallies, and not least their newly founded campaigning party newspaper, the *Rote Fahne* ('Red flag'). In this paper they accused Ebert of wanting to restore the old order. In its place, they proposed establishing a unified socialist republic, in which all the key industries would be nationalised. The Reichstag and all the regional parliaments in Germany were to be dissolved forthwith. Workers' and soldiers' councils would take control of all civil and military authorities and command centres. To enhance the organisation's efficiency, Liebknecht made the Spartacus League, rechristened the Communist Party of Germany (KPD) in December 1918, into a nationwide fighting organisation.

For the time being the irreconcilable contradictions of the German revolution were still swept under the carpet. This was the case, for instance, on 20 November 1918, when the funeral of those who had been killed in the uprising took place, with Ebert, Scheidemann, Liebknecht, Emil Barth, and others all attending a mass rally on the Tempelhofer Feld parade ground. One of those who witnessed the huge funeral procession that followed as it wound its way past the Berlin City Palace was Adolf Hitler, who had just been discharged from hospital in Pasewalk and was passing through the capital on his way back to Munich, where he was due to report for duty with his regiment's replacement battalion.[10]

It was not long before violent clashes broke out between a motley band of revolutionary militiamen, egged on by the Spartacist leaders, and more moderate socialists. At the beginning of December, fourteen people died in these disturbances after the Berlin city commander – a member of the majority SPD who would subsequently, in March 1933, bravely make his voice heard in opposition to Hitler's notorious 'Enabling Act' – called in the regular army to quell the violence. From the very outset, Ebert had calculated on having to deploy troops on the streets. He knew that millions of soldiers returning from the front would pose a huge threat of unrest. As a result, he considered it of crucial importance to carry these men along with him in building the new state. It was even more important for Ebert, in the event that civil war broke out, that he should have some way of countering leftist revolutionaries supported by Moscow. No sooner had Liebknecht proclaimed the Socialist republic than Ebert secured the support of Wilhelm Groener and the officer corps. Thus when Ebert, who had lost two of his sons in the war, greeted the troops returning to Berlin at the Brandenburg Gate in mid-December, this was also intended to send a signal to the Army High Command. In his address, he paid homage to the army's heroism in defending the Fatherland and acknowledged that they had been undefeated on the battlefield before exhorting them to 'get involved in the great task of building a new future for Germany'.[11]

For the Spartacists and other radicals of the Left, Ebert's performance at this assembly was final proof that the majority Social Democrats were nothing but revanchists in disguise and stooges of the old elites. Their battle cry hereafter was: 'Get rid of ... those who try to seduce the unenlightened masses of soldiers: Wels, Ebert, Scheidemann, and their associates!' They

denounced the Social Democrats as 'class traitors' and called
for them to be beaten down 'with an iron fist'.[12] The radicals
now made a clean break with the still-controversial Independent
Social Democratic Party (USPD).

In a manifesto published in the *Rote Fahne* under the title
'What Are the Aims of the Spartacus League?',[13] Rosa Luxemburg, who had meanwhile been released from jail in Breslau,
called for all policemen, army officers, non-proletarian soldiers, and members of the ruling class to be disarmed and the
whole proletariat to be issued with weapons to form a militia
that would secure the victory of the Spartacus League and the
triumph of the working class. These were the words of a dedicated advocate of class warfare who, driven by her hatred of the
ruling classes, was intent on establishing a Bolshevik dictatorship in the context of a global revolution – even though, not long
before, she had been keen to point out the differences between
the German and Russian revolutions. For Luxemburg, the latter,
while undeniably being 'the greatest consequence of the World
War', also represented unfinished business, since 'in Russia, the
problem could only be identified. It could not be solved there; it
can only be solved internationally. And in this sense, the future
everywhere belongs to "Bolshevism".'[14]

On Christmas Eve 1918, after members of the People's Marine
Division, which saw itself as the spearhead of the revolution,
occupied the Imperial Chancellery and the City Palace with the
support of Spartacists, and troops loyal to the government were
only able to retake the buildings at the cost of almost seventy
dead, the USPD summarily suspended all cooperation with the
majority SPD and walked out of the Council of the People's
Deputies. At the turn of 1918–19, in the presence of two envoys
sent by Lenin – Karl Radek and 'Friesland' (the pseudonym of
Ernst Reuter) – the German Communist Party (KPD), formed
from the Spartacus League, elements of the USPD, and other

radical leftist groups, was founded in the ceremonial hall of the Prussian Parliament. By a two-thirds majority, it immediately voted to boycott the forthcoming elections to the national assembly, and in so doing set itself on a course of revolutionary extra-parliamentary opposition. This was the same path taken by Lenin in Russia in 1917, once he had realised that the Bolsheviks could never gain power through democratic means.

One remarkable thing in this context was the change of heart shown by Liebknecht and Luxemburg. Counter to the hardline stance they had taken hitherto in boycotting elections to the national assembly, at the inaugural meeting of the KPD they urged the party to take part. This decision, which left-wing historians cite as proof that the radicals of the Left were prepared to cooperate with the moderates, Kellerhoff and Keil see as nothing more than a tactically motivated manoeuvre. They point out that the very next day, Luxemburg and Liebknecht, who went along with the majority vote of the party conference, advocated a return to the theory of the violent overthrow of democracy in their comprehensive policy paper 'Our agenda and the Current Situation'.[15]

Indeed, that is exactly what the Spartacus League attempted on 5 January 1919. The handy excuse for the uprising was a row concerning Berlin Chief of Police Emil Eichhorn of the USPD. His dismissal was taken as yet another attack on the working class, which called for a response. Some 500–600 Spartacists, KPD members, and USPD activists who had not yet joined the KPD occupied key locations in the city, including the newspaper quarter. They also invaded the editorial offices of the majority-SPD newspaper *Vorwärts*, the bourgeois publishing houses of Mosse, Ullstein, and Scherl, as well as the premises of the Wolff telegraphic bureau. At the same time, mass demonstrations were held, while Luxemburg, Liebknecht, and their confederates published articles in the *Rote Fahne* inciting people to rise up against the 'Ebert–Scheidemann reactionaries'.

Convinced that the radical leftist revolutionaries had popular momentum behind them, the leaders of the majority SPD were slow to respond to the threat. Besides, they were all too aware that Berlin was awash with weapons. Eventually, the party leadership turned to Gustav Noske, the people's deputy for the armed forces, who had already gained control of the situation at the coast to some extent. They were mindful of his famous assertion that 'someone has to be the bloodhound'.[16] As he made preparations to restore order, the situation in the capital escalated after the KPD and the USPD called for a general strike. Hundreds of thousands of people came out to demonstrate on the streets of Berlin; these gatherings often ended in gunfights. All this was played out to a constant backdrop of agitation by the *Rote Fahne*, which called for a 'final reckoning' and a struggle that would 'crush the bloodstained Ebert and Scheidemann once and for all'.[17]

On the night of 11 January 1919, government forces – mainly comprising sailors loyal to Noske and volunteer units of mainstream Social Democrats – advanced on the newspaper quarter using mortars and flamethrowers. Violent clashes occurred, both there and outside the police headquarters, in which 160 people lost their lives. Before long, calm was restored in Berlin, as the revolutionary militias were no match for the battle-hardened, well-equipped government troops. The rebels were scattered and their ringleaders Liebknecht and Luxemburg went to ground. In the proclamation he issued to the German people, Ebert called them 'misguided fanatics' who had made common cause with 'shady elements of the city ... to try and seize control with the aid of a foreign power'. The author of this speech left his audience in no doubt that this 'foreign power' was Soviet Russia when the proclamation, which was published in *Vorwärts*, continued: 'Bolshevism means the death of peace, the death of freedom, and the death of socialism, the only force that can bring about the emancipation of working people from the bonds of economic exploitation.'[18]

On 15 January 1919, Rosa Luxemburg and Karl Liebknecht were captured by the Rifle Division of the Cavalry Guards of the *Freikorps* (the government-backed militia). Luxemburg was tortured and then executed with a shot to the head fired at close range. The official communiqué on her death claimed that she had been 'killed by an angry mob', and went on to state that the 'mob' had carried off her body.[19] In actual fact, the *Freikorps* had thrown her corpse into the Landwehrkanal, from where it was only recovered several months later. Liebknecht was also shot dead by the *Freikorps* in Berlin's Tiergarten. The report of their murders in *Vorwärts* maintained that they were 'victims of a bloody terror that they themselves, impelled by a crazy delusion, had visited upon the country'.[20]

However, obituaries like this and Scheidemann's, which expressed regret at their deaths and condemned their murder, could do nothing to prevent Luxemburg and Liebknecht from becoming martyrs. The bloody deed provoked a wave of outrage that was felt even among the middle classes. Hundreds of thousands of mourners turned out on 25 January 1919 to accompany the cortège carrying Liebknecht's coffin to the Friedrichsfeld Cemetery in Berlin, where he was buried alongside thirty other victims of the Spartacist uprising. As a sign of the incipient canonisation of the dead communist leaders, an impressive mass demonstration organised by the KPD and the USPD included an empty coffin carried symbolically alongside Liebknecht's funeral procession. It was meant to be for the missing corpse of Rosa Luxemburg.

The death of the two KPD leaders irrevocably severed any last ties between the various factions of the Left. Henceforth, the relationship of the radicals with the majority Social Democrats was hallmarked by sheer hatred. Anti-fascists of later generations in both the East and the West accused the SPD of having paved the way for Hitler's National Socialism by throwing in its lot with the German military. In the 1960s and 1970s the journalist Sebastian Haffner, much vaunted at the time in the culture sections of German broadsheet newspapers, was largely responsible for spreading this viewpoint, which still has widespread currency among historians nowadays. In his bestselling 1978 work *Anmerkungen zu Hitler* ('The meaning of Hitler'),[21] Haffner wrote that the leadership of the majority SPD bore greater responsibility for the demise of the Weimar Republic than leftist revolutionaries. In putting down the revolution, Ebert, Scheidemann, and Noske, he claimed, only succeeded in creating a lasting, embittered opposition on the Left and an even more dangerous one on the Right, both of which ultimately crushed the tender flower of Weimar democracy and prepared the ground for the ensuing catastrophe. Several years beforehand, in his book *1918/1919: Eine deutsche Revolution* ('A German revolution: 1918–1919'). Haffner had even accused social democracy of 'betraying its own revolution'. Following the findings of Marxist historian Arthur Rosenberg,[22] Haffner declared that it was a myth that the revolution was ultimately Bolshevik-inspired and that 'the SPD saved Germany from "Bolshevik chaos"'.[23]

Such a distorted, ideologically led reading of events – which in the West Germany of the time was fully in accord with the spirit of the 1968 student revolutionary movement and its rapprochement with communism, and which misrepresented the leaders of the majority SPD as quasi-fascist members of the petty bourgeoisie – disregards not only the fact that it was the radical Left that terminated the democratic consensus but also that Bolshevism, and its Russian instigators, were seen as an ever-present, existential threat in Germany after the First World War. The Russian journalist Elias Hurwicz, who was living in Berlin during that period, identified a prevailing sense among contemporary Germans that Bolshevism was a 'raging torrent or at least an intellectual wave of overwhelming virulence, or perhaps ultimately an inescapable socialist reaction to the First World War heralding a new age of mankind, which would, sooner or later, inevitably swamp the whole of the civilized world'.[24] Famous German contemporaries of Hurwicz, such as Thomas Mann, Count Harry Kessler, and Ernst Troeltsch, took the same view. Bolshevism appeared to be inexorably clutching at the heart of European civilisation. These facts continue to be left out of the reckoning even in more recent Hitler biographies like that of Volker Ullrich.[25] The idea that Lenin's capacity to influence events was really not so great and that the threat in 1919 might have been overestimated may be the hindsight view of later historians, but it was not shared by those living at the time.

In the light of the 'great threat ... looming over Germany in 1918', to quote the words of Harvard political scientist David Zieblatt,[26] the majority SPD leaders had little choice but to stand in lockstep with the army, for the fight against Bolshevism was not just any old conflict. For them, it was a struggle for the future of civilisation. The fear that large sectors of the populace had of Bolshevism thus meant that these much-maligned upstanding figures were able to steer the ailing country onto the path of democracy all the more quickly. On 19 January 1919 a national assembly was elected which, because of the unstable situation that still prevailed in Berlin, met initially in the National Theatre in Weimar, behind the famous memorial to Goethe and Schiller. As the first free and secret ballot in which women were also allowed to participate, the poll was a great moment for democracy in Germany. The so-called Weimar Coalition of the majority SPD, the Catholic Centre Party, and the newly founded German Democratic Party (DDP) that was to form the country's government won 76.1 per cent of the votes cast. The majority

SPD secured 37.9 per cent, while the USPD won 7.6 per cent. The forces of reaction were trounced, with the German National People's Party (DNVP) gaining 10.3 per cent and the German People's Party (DVP) a paltry 4.4 per cent.

The thesis of those who are intent on seeing Hitler and his genocide against the Jews as an inevitable continuation of an imperialism and anti-Semitism that began during the German Second Empire is therefore unmasked as a historical fabrication. Casting an eye over the works of those historians who have cornered the market in interpreting the history of National Socialism, it is striking how few make any reference at all to the first free and fair election ever held in Germany and its impressive outcome. For example, it appears nowhere in the 2,000 pages of Ian Kershaw's socio-historical biography of Hitler, since the total absence of anything in January 1919 to suggest that Hitler might one day be chancellor or his genocide against the Jews does not fit with Kershaw's thesis.

Rather it was the case that the results of the January 1919 election were a resounding vote in favour of a democratic-republican and hence peaceful future for the country. Majority social democracy – or rather the Weimar Coalition under the leadership of Scheidemann, the 'Imperial First Minister' as the chancellor was originally entitled – supported by Imperial President Ebert, was thus endorsed by the overwhelming majority of German people in pursuing the political course it had set for itself and in fighting against those who wanted to see Bolshevism come to power in Germany.

The crushing of the Spartacist uprising by no means signalled the end of this struggle. For in the Moscow-funded KPD, the murder of Liebknecht and Luxemburg acted as a clarion call to widen the planned civil war. Together with elements of the USPD, the party was able to establish a number of power bases throughout the country. A wave of strikes, fanned by workers' and soldiers' soviets, swept the industrial Ruhr region and many other parts of Germany. Soviet republics on the Bolshevik model were established in Bremen, Mannheim, and Braunschweig. Armed clashes broke out in many places. During the first half of March, the fighting and killing erupted in Berlin once more.

In Munich, the situation was initially as confused as in the capital. The Wittelsbach monarch Ludwig III had abdicated, leaving moderates and radicals to vie for power. The journalist and manufacturer's son Kurt Eisner, from the city district of Schwabing, eventually emerged ahead of the pack. On 8 November 1918, in circumstances resembling a coup, he was appointed prime minister of Bavaria. The aim of this USPD politician was to govern the 'Free State of Bavaria', as the kingdom was now known, as a 'living democracy deriving from the authority of the workers' councils'. Whatever Eisner may have understood by this, he flatly rejected any 'dictatorship of a Bolshevik kind'.[27] Eisner thus sat between all stools, facing just as vehement opposition from the majority Social Democrats as he did from the radical Left both within and outside his own party. The situation in Bavaria was further complicated by the region's separatist leanings.

In the elections for the constitutional Bavarian regional assembly in January 1919, Eisner got his comeuppance for his unrealistic political ideas. He was roundly defeated, with just 2.5 per cent of votes cast. The majority SPD made a strong showing (33 per cent), while the Bavarian People's Party (BVP), as the sister organisation in the Free State to the national Centre Party was called, emerged as the strongest party, with 35 per cent. The German People's Party (DVP) gained 14 per cent and the Bavarian Farmer's League (BB) 9.1 per cent, followed by the National Liberals and Eisner's USPD. On 21 February 1919, while en route to the constituent assembly of the regional parliament, the defeated prime minister was shot dead by a nationalist zealot, Count Arco auf Valley. The assassination was greeted with delight by extra-parliamentary revanchists and populist anti-Semites, such as the ultra-nationalist Thule Society. A few days later, when Eisner, who was of Jewish extraction, was buried amid much pomp and ceremony, Hitler also paid him his last respects. Preserved film footage shows him among the group of men who made up the official mourning party from the 2nd Bavarian Infantry Regiment; one still photograph captures him standing outside the chapel at the Eastern Cemetery in Munich.[28]

In late November 1918, Hitler had returned to Munich from Pasewalk, and served in his demobilisation battalion in the Bavarian capital (in addition to a few weeks in Traunstein). The fact that he was present at all at the Eastern Cemetery that day was due not least to the company he was keeping at the time. The troops at the Karl Liebknecht barracks, where Hitler was stationed, had decidedly left-wing sympathies. The men of the Munich garrison stood four-square behind the revolution and its socialist agenda. This was not only because the soldiers blamed the old regime for their defeat in the Great War; it also had to do with their experience at the front. Active service in the field had broken down all class divisions. The term 'trench socialism' was later coined to describe this phenomenon. For in the secluded world of the trenches, it was no longer of any consequence where an individual came from. Survival was only possible if men stuck together.

In the foreword to his 1919 book *Preußentum und Sozialismus* ('Prussian values and socialism'), the historian and philosopher Oswald Spengler gave the excessively pathos-laden view assessment that 'true socialism was ... only [to be found] in life-or-death struggles at the front or ... in the mass graves that covered half of Europe'.[29] Also dating from 1919, a document written for the use of the Bavarian Defence Force – the unit in which Hitler served is described as being 'susceptible to radical ideas' – goes on to state that mistrust of the old order and of tradition had become widespread within the army.[30] Eisner had ushered in the demise of tradition in Bavaria and, despite his electoral defeat in January and his death, had become something of a patriarch of the revolution who was accorded great respect, even among the common soldiery.

At this stage Hitler, who retrospectively tried to airbrush his participation in Eisner's state funeral from history by post-dating his return to Munich from Traunstein by a few weeks, was no longer just a fellow traveller either. As early as February 1919 – as revealed by a battalion directive – he was elected as the shop steward for the demobilisation battalion of the 2nd Infantry Regiment. If Hitler had had nationalist leanings, he would hardly have attained this position, nor would he have addressed his comrades on the burning question of 'Parliament or Workers' Councils?'[31] There is no shortage of evidence to suggest that Hitler actually sympathised with the majority SPD at this time. In the spring of 1923, when Hitler was already leader of the NSDAP, the *Münchner Post* reported that he had even worked for the MSPD.[32] 'The same Hitler who now bandies about the term "November criminals" [the representatives of the Weimar Republic who advocated acceptance of the Versailles Peace Accord] with gay abandon,' the newspaper wrote, quoting the words of the Social Democrat vice-president of the Bavarian regional parliament Erhard Auer, 'was well known among his colleagues in the propaganda division as a staunch majority Social Democrat and masqueraded as such, though like many others he never had a firm political or trade union affiliation.'[33]

Other sources also reported that Hitler had been a Social Democrat at this time. One was the left-wing intellectual Ernst Toller, who was later involved in establishing the first Bavarian Soviet Republic. Another was the Social Democrat Konrad Heiden, who as a journalist observed the political scene in Munich in the years immediately after the First World War and who, after Hitler came to power, was to author the first critical book about the German dictator. Heiden wrote that Hitler argued the case for the majority SPD government against his comrades.[34] There was nothing unusual in this, since the party amply represented the interests of the army and cooperated fully with its commanders. The troops knew the speeches given by President Ebert, including the one he delivered at the homecoming of the Berlin units and many others elsewhere. It was also well known that at the beginning of March the imperial government had laid on a triumphant reception in Berlin for the returning 'Lion of Africa' General Paul von Lettow-Vorbeck and his troops and that Noske lost no time in appointing the general to new roles. All this could only have played well with the former frontline soldiers, especially deracinated individuals like Hitler, for whom the army had become home and who did everything in their power to ensure that this situation would continue to be the case, at least for the time being.

Reflecting on this period, Sepp Dietrich, who later commanded the SS Adolf Hitler Bodyguard Division, once asserted that all National Socialists had at one time been Social Democrats.[35] Dietrich himself had formerly been the elected spokesman of a soldiers' council, and Herman Esser, one of Hitler's earliest acolytes, had previously worked as a journalist for a Social Democrat newspaper. When, after becoming a national socialist, Esser was attacked for his political past, Hitler is reputed to have spoken up for him by stating: 'Everyone was a Social Democrat at one time.'[36] In private round-table discussions with his innermost circle of confidants, the 'Führer and Imperial Chancellor' was said to have spoken warmly about social democracy on many occasions. For instance, he praised it for having 'got rid of' the Hohenzollern monarchy, 'that bunch of vermin', and he claimed that the only thing wrong with social democracy was 'that it lacked a Supreme Leader'.[37]

Anyone who was on the side of social democracy in February–March 1919, like the government soldier Adolf Hitler, must have been gratified by the turn of events in Bavaria in the wake of Kurt Eisner's murder. His martyr's death, which effectively elevated this political failure to the status of a saint, appeared to temporarily transcend all political differences and to place the vision of a strong Left acting in concert in the realms of the possible. The MSPD (which was engaged in talks with the BVP on forming a government), the USPD, and even the KPD – which had shunned the election in Bavaria just as it had in the rest of the country – now began to work together in a central council of the Bavarian Republic under the chairmanship of the USPD politician Ernst Niekisch. However, it soon transpired that everything once again ultimately came down to the fundamental question: should Bavaria become a soviet republic or a parliamentary democracy? No consensus could be reached. In mid-March 1919 the majority Social Democrat Johannes Hoffmann was duly elected prime minister of Bavaria.

The manner in which Private (First Class) Adolf Hitler – who by now was almost thirty years old – reacted when the newly elected Bavarian government was ousted by left-wing radicals shows once again the gulf that still separated him from nationalist anti-Semites. This action had been preceded by the news from Hungary on 21 March 1919 that Lenin's Bolshevik envoy to the country, Béla Kun (Kohn) and Mátyás Rákosi (Rosenfeld) had proclaimed a 'dictatorship of the proletariat' there. Under the leadership of the Communist International (Comintern), which had just been formed in Moscow, worldwide revolution now appeared to be advancing inexorably westwards from its source in Russia. The floodgates opened in Munich and a motley group of fanatically idealistic, anarchist revolutionaries led by the writers Ernst Toller, Erich Mühsam, and Gustav Landauer, all of whom were of Jewish heritage, seized power. Along with others – though not the KPD, which lurked in the wings, waiting for its chance – they formed a twelve-man 'council of people's deputies'. Under the motto 'Germany will be next', the 'Bavarian Soviet Republic' was proclaimed on the night of 7 April 1919.

What now took place was a bizarre drama. A root-and-branch social revolution was enacted in a flurry of decrees, plans were drawn up for a programme of forcible expropriation and nationalisation, 'juristic thinking' was abolished, and Munich University was repurposed as an adult education centre. Newspapers were ordered to print poems by Hölderlin and Schiller on their front pages alongside the latest verdicts handed down by people's tribunals, which had been convened along the same lines as in the French Revolution. It was the council member Franz Lipp, however, who had been put in charge of foreign policy, who really took the biscuit; his first action on taking office was to sever all diplomatic ties with Prussia. Nor did matters end there: the revolutionary Lipp summarily declared war on Switzerland and Württemberg after they refused to place locomotives at the disposal of the new red Free State. Eventually, Lipp was relieved of his post by Toller and his declarations of war were rescinded.

All this had been made possible because the Bavarian revolutionaries, with their idealistic gaze firmly fixed on Bolshevik Russia as their model, had somehow managed to win the soldiers' soviets in the Munich garrison over to their cause. Commanding virtually no support among the general populace, the revolutionaries needed the power of the bayonet. The soldiers who took up arms were now hailed as the nucleus of a 'Red Army' that would defend the Bavarian Soviet Republic. The shop-steward Hitler was clearly supportive of the revolutionary literati, most of whom were of Jewish origin, and he remained on the side of the revolution, or at least took a neutral stance, when armed clashes broke out between the 'Reds' and army units loyal to Hoffmann's mainstream administration, which had in the

meantime decamped to the city off Bamberg in Upper Franconia. These battles ended in a debacle for the government forces.

The hour of hard-bitten communists who unquestioningly
toed the Moscow party line had now come. The Jewish literary
scholar Victor Klemperer summed up the situation: 'Hamstrung
by their dreamy, Bohemian mindset and forever at loggerheads
with one another, this handful of outsider adventurers found
themselves from one hour to the next having to give more and
more ground to hard-nosed figures of a criminal bent.'[38] The provisional 'council of people's deputies' now became the 'Bavarian
Soviet'. It was led by a four-man executive council comprising
the political functionaries Max Levien, Tobias Akselrod, Eugen
Leviné, and Arnold Wadler, all of them bar one (Levien) of
Jewish extraction, and all of whom without exception had cut
their teeth in either the Moscow Comintern or the KPD. These
men now proclaimed the 'Dictatorship of the Proletariat', which
would herald the dawning of an age of global revolution. The
journalist David Eliasberg, a contemporary eyewitness to these
events, said of the Second Bavarian Soviet Republic:

> It seems gratuitous to stress the Russian character of the
> Munich Soviet leadership. The inhabitants of the city of
> Munich played out the Russian drama according to familiar
> patterns under Russian direction. The manipulated puppets
> all played their allotted parts with panache: The proletariat
> was 'inflamed with revolutionary zeal'. The aristocracy and
> the bourgeoisie were 'counterrevolutionary', and majority
> Social Democracy had been 'deluded'.[39]

Just how right Eliasberg was in his assessment is revealed by the
telegrams exchanged between the Kremlin and the communist
revolutionaries in Munich. Grigory Zinoviev, the head of the
Comintern, observed with satisfaction that there were now three

Soviet Republics: Russia, Hungary, and Bavaria. No doubt in the full knowledge that soviet republics had also been proclaimed in the cities of Augsburg, Würzburg, Rosenheim, and elsewhere, Zinoviev added: 'The whole of Europe will be communist within a year.'[40] The great Lenin sent a message of greeting to Munich in which he requested his comrades 'to tell me as specifically as you can what steps you have taken to combat the bourgeois hangmen Scheidemann and Co'.[41]

As the 'Bavarian Soviet' expected the German government to organise a military intervention, the Munich garrison needed to swear allegiance once more to a new set of political masters – this time the puppets of Moscow. On 15 April 1919, under the supervision of commander-in-chief of the 'Red Army' Rudolf Egelhofer – a naval deserter who had been condemned to death but pardoned – barracks' delegates were renominated in order to weed out any anti-revolutionary elements. In the process, and doubtless without any special effort on his part, Hitler's eloquence and his Iron Cross, First Class, which must have earned his comrades' respect, saw him elected as the replacement battalion delegate of the second company of the demobilisation battalion of the 2nd Bavarian Infantry Regiment, which was integrated into the 'Red Army'. Although this might seem incredible, it is confirmed in the records in black and white:[42] the man who not long afterwards would claim that it was a 'cast-iron certainty' that Bolshevism was an 'infernal instrument of international Jewry' had once been, at least nominally, a cog in the machinery of communist world revolution! How can that be squared with the image that much of the research on Hitler keeps trotting out – namely of someone imbued with a hatred of the Jews from an early age?[43]

The Second Bavarian Soviet Republic, which brought Bolshevik terror to Munich, did not last beyond a fortnight. At the end of April, government troops reinforced by detachments of the

*Freikorps* – a total force of 30,000 including heavy artillery and supported by a squadron of aircraft and two columns of tanks – advanced on the capital of the Free State. After ten hostages were shot dead in the grounds of the Luitpold Grammar School in Munich on 30 April, the MSPD leadership finally resolved to put an end to the spectre of Bolshevism. Gustav Noske called the events in Munich a 'carnival of insanity'[44] and, ultimately, even where they chose to offer resistance, the city's defenders could do little against the forces he dispatched. By 2 May, it was all over. Retaking the city left 600 people dead, most of them civilians, as the *Freikorps* men showed extreme brutality in dealing with the 'Russians'. As a Great War veteran schooled in the art of survival, Hitler lay low in the Karl Liebknecht barracks until the storm had passed.

From Berlin's perspective, the country's most dangerous revolutionary conflagration had been snuffed out by sending government forces to Munich, who received a rapturous welcome from the city's inhabitants. In the process, the revolution in Germany, supported by Moscow, had been put on the back foot. Democracy was in the ascendant. The Weimar constitution was being drawn up. As for the Versailles Peace Conference, which had been in session since January without the participation of the defeated nations, in spite of some alarming reports from that quarter, Germany remained cautiously optimistic about the outcome. The Scheidemann administration saw the Compiègne armistice, with its harsh demands, as a trust-building down payment on a lasting entente. Another factor was the civil war raging in Germany, which it was assumed would temper the victorious nations' strictures, as no one wanted to see a Bolshevik Germany. For these reasons, the majority Social Democrats hoped to be treated more or less fairly by the Allied Powers. Accordingly, the imperial government called upon the Allies to negotiate a European peace on the basis of an equitable settlement of interests and Woodrow Wilson's Fourteen Points. German hopes rested heavily on the American president.

If the Social Democrats proceeded with a degree of self-confidence, then it was born of the awareness that they had driven out those who had been responsible for the war and that they stood for the new Germany, a democratic republican state, which they had so consistently defended from the challenge of the extreme Left. As the representatives of a democratic Germany, they were also motivated by the sincere desire to ensure that a tragedy like the First World War should never happen again. In the course of an official government statement, Scheidemann had stated:

> The peace that this administration is tasked with concluding should not be the kind of peace that is all too familiar from history – a short breather in a state of otherwise permanent war between nations that is filled with preparations to resume hostilities; instead, it should establish a state of harmonious coexistence between all peoples on the basis of a global constitution which accords equal rights to all.[45]

From the perspective of the period, this may have sounded somewhat naive, and tactical considerations may also have played a role, yet Scheidemann's sentiments were far ahead of their time. If these far-reaching hopes, indeed illusions, had ever become a reality, then the Weimar coalition of the MSPD, the Centre Party, and the DDP would surely have continued to represent a firm middle ground in politics. The revolution staged by the radicals would have been put down far more swiftly, and in all likelihood a National Socialist German Workers' Party of the kind that Hitler formed from the original German Workers' Party would not have come about either. For the First World War private would surely have continued to support social democracy and never made a name for himself.

The Social Democrat leaders were no intellectuals. They were first and foremost pragmatists, although they also had visions of a peaceful future for the peoples of Europe. Plus they were honest brokers who led Germany down a good path. Nonetheless, in the memorial culture of modern social democracy, Scheidemann, Ebert, and Noske are condemned to a shadowy existence. Some party members blame them for splitting the Left and for the 'unfinished revolution', and hence for missing a great opportunity – although it must be said that such an opportunity never existed. At a key historical juncture that now lies over a century in the past, contemporaries were faced with a simple either/or decision: a parliamentary democracy or a soviet republic controlled by the communist regime in Moscow. Hugo Preuss, who at Ebert's behest drafted the Weimar Constitution, expressed this in the pithy formula: 'Lenin or Wilson'.[46] It is even more ahistorical that Karl Liebknecht and Rosa Luxemburg should be venerated in modern social democracy – those radical left leaders who in 1918–19 advocated a totalitarian system, sowed terror, and encouraged their supporters to open fire on majority Social Democrats. In the light of this, there is every reason to be proud, rather, of Ebert, Scheidemann, and Co.

# 3

# The Dictated Peace of Versailles

*Did the treaty pave the way for Hitler?*

The Versailles Peace Treaty of 1919 is of enormous significance, for with it the victorious powers of the First World War effectively reshaped Europe and the Near East.[1] In the process empires were broken up, borders shifted, and new states created. This was all done quite haphazardly. The consequences were sometimes devastating and continued to have repercussions throughout the twentieth century, but was the Third Reich also a product of Versailles? Views on this question are often diametrically opposed. For Ian Kershaw, for example, Versailles is evidently irrelevant in this context, as he excludes it entirely from the 2,000 pages of his Hitler biography. By contrast, the renowned American historian George F. Kennan, who called the First World War 'the great seminal catastrophe of the twentieth century',[2] judges that it was 'the vindictiveness of the British and French peace terms' that prepared the ground for National Socialism and another war.[3]

At first sight, this thesis seems entirely plausible, when one considers how, more than a century ago, at the beginning of May 1919 in the Parisian suburbs, the victorious powers of the Great War presented the defeated nations with the most draconian of peace terms: to the Germans at Versailles, the Austrians at St Germain, and the Hungarians at Trianon. In addition, the futures of Bulgaria and Ottoman Turkey were decided upon at Neuilly-sur-Seine and Sèvres, respectively. Universally, the dictated peace was imposed upon countries that had been shattered and laid low by the conflict. Civil war and dire economic conditions were rife not only in Germany. This situation had been brought about chiefly by the Allied naval blockade, which continued after the war's end. The popular mood was correspondingly volatile in the defeated nations, as people were pulled this way and that, between hope that their living conditions might soon improve and fear that the world they had known was about to come crashing down.

Gloomy scenes appeared to signal a cold, impersonal future of the kind described by the historian Oswald Spengler in the first volume of a seminal work that compared and contrasted various historical eras, and which was published in 1919. The Golden Age of European 'culture' was, Spengler claimed, inexorably giving way to a form of 'civilisation' dominated by pure materialism. A human race that had degenerated into an amorphous mass and was vegetating in 'barracks cities' would do the bidding of any leader so long as he promised them bread and circuses, Spengler prophesied in his pessimistic swansong to a better world, which he wrote before and during the First World War. Given the reality of life on the ground in Germany, the book's title *Der Untergang des Abendlandes* ('The decline of the West') carried an even greater poignancy when it finally appeared.[4]

In Russia, where the civil war had been raging since 1917, the West had already declined. News from there coalesced into a picture of sheer horror in the spring of 1919. This made it unmistakably clear to the European middle classes – especially in the nations that had lost the war – that 'the old principles of humanity devised by the bourgeoisie' no longer existed 'nor could they continue to exist', as a Bolshevik credo of the time proclaimed.[5] Wiping out entire strata of society, which the leaders of the revolution authorised with the stroke of a pen, became an essential requirement underpinned by an ethic of murder, whereby hundreds of thousands, indeed millions of people were slaughtered by the Red Amy and the Cheka, the Bolshevik secret service. These victims included the aristocratic and bourgeois elites of the Tsarist Empire, the clergy, and before long also the different nationalities of Russia who strove to break free of Moscow's centralised grip on power. All this was done in order to supposedly create the 'new man' and to 'liberate mankind'. The Great War, in which mass extermination was facilitated by modern technology, which brutalised and disinhibited people in the act of killing, undoubtedly played a major role in sweeping away the last taboos in Russia and ushering in developments that had no parallels in history.

In the light of the ongoing civil unrest, many Germans feared that Bolshevism, with its aspiration to spark worldwide revolution, would spill over to engulf their country too. The title pages of news magazines in Germany portrayed this threat as a gigantic octopus, with its tentacles encircling bourgeois Europe.[6] The inside pages contained dramatic appeals to halt Bolshevism, such as that by the Russian writer Leonid Andreyev. In a May 1919 edition of the SPD newspaper *Vorwärts*, Andreyev addressed an urgent wake-up call to the 'people of Europe'. Everything that had taken place thus far in Germany, he claimed, would continue, 'and escalate from there – everything that you have seen is not a revolution, it's a chaos and a darkness that the war has summoned up from deep, dark recesses. And that chaos and darkness has declared war on the world, with the aim of destroying it.'[7]

In these difficult circumstances, Versailles came like one final great upheaval delivering the coup de grâce to bourgeois Germany. For the outcome that Foreign Minister Ulrich von Brockdorff-Rantzau cabled from Versailles to Berlin on 7 May 1919 was, many people believed, destined to keep Germany downtrodden for years to come and make it even more vulnerable to the threat from the East. The predominant tone of the diktat issued by the victorious Allies was one of unbounded hatred and a spirit of settling scores. The economist John Maynard Keynes, a member of the British delegation at Versailles, wrote: 'Their [i.e. the Allies'] preoccupations ... related to ... revenge, and to the shifting by the victors of their unbearable financial burdens on to the shoulders of the defeated.'[8] The scale of the destruction wrought by the first industrialised war in history was too immense, and the cost in human lives and the devastation suffered by Belgium and above all France too great for members of the Entente to have the strength to put aside all thoughts of vengeance and establish a sustainable peace settlement.

This same mentality of settling scores had already conditioned the existing framework and operation of the Paris Conference, since the defeated nations were excluded from the negotiations. They were only summoned to be told the peace terms and were obliged to enter the Palace of Versailles by a side gate. A Polish observer described the entry of the German delegation under von Brockdorff-Rantzau into the Hall of Mirrors at Versailles. 'They were led in like defendants appearing before a tribunal,' he recalled, and added that the German foreign minister was trembling and barely able to stand upright.[9] It was the height of indignity to make the Germans receive the peace terms in this setting, where almost half a century before the formation of the German Second Empire had been proclaimed, as a humiliating coda to France's defeat in the Franco-Prussian War of 1870–1.

The conditions that were put before the delegation from Berlin bore no resemblance to Woodrow Wilson's proposed Fourteen Points. And they only accorded to a very limited extent with the ideas of British prime minister David Lloyd George, who, in line with London's doctrine of equilibrium, wanted to see Germany's position preserved, at least in part, as an economic and political factor in the balance of power between the continental European nations. Ultimately, both Wilson and Lloyd George had deferred to the wishes of French prime minister, Georges Clemenceau, who saw another conflict with the Germans as inevitable. The French leader was therefore concerned that the peace terms should weaken France's 'arch enemy' for as long as possible.

One particularly striking result of the Versailles Peace Conference, or rather of the Versailles diktat, was that the right to self-determination and the principle of national sovereignty, which Woodrow Wilson had set great store by, were no longer to apply to the defeated nations. Thus, a union between the German Empire and German Austria was vetoed, despite having been /approved by a majority of the freely elected Social Democrat-led administrations in Berlin and Vienna. Furthermore, Germany and Austria were forced to relinquish control over a whole series of almost exclusively German-speaking territories – a move that Lloyd George had expressly warned against: 'I cannot conceive,' he wrote, 'of any greater cause of future war than that the German people ... should be surrounded by a number of small States ... each of them containing large numbers of Germans clamouring for reunion with their native land.'[10] Thus, South Tyrol became part of Italy, the Sudetenland and the Hlučin region were ceded to the newly created state of Czechoslovakia, the Klaipėda region fell to Lithuania, and Danzig (Gdańsk) became a Free City under the jurisdiction of the League of Nations. Areas of the German Empire that were not settled exclusively by Germans, such as Posen, West Prussia, and later some parts of Upper Silesia as well, were ceded to a resurgent Poland, while Eupen-Malmedy went to Belgium and Northern Schleswig to Denmark. In addition, there were also certain regions like the Saarland whose nationality was to be decided upon in plebiscites. Eventually, a seventh of the German Empire's former territory was lost. These areas were home to six and a half million people and also housed key industries.

Nor was that the end of it. The peace terms envisaged reducing Germany, which also had to give up all of its colonies, to a negligible military power. The army, once the pride of the nation, was to be cut to a force of just 100,000 men, while the navy was to number just 15,000. The High Seas Fleet, which had been the apple of the Kaiser's eye, would in large part be surrendered to the enemy. At the Scapa Flow anchorage in Orkney, where the German warships were escorted after the armistice, Admiral Ludwig von Reuter organised a mass scuttling of the fleet in June 1919. In the course of this spectacular action, fifty-two ships were sunk. In response, the Entente demanded that almost the entire German merchant fleet be handed over. In addition to all these clauses, the Versailles Treaty also made provisions for regions on the left bank of the Rhine plus a 50-kilometre-wide strip of land on the right bank to be demilitarised. This measure was to include the demolition of all fortresses there and the disbanding of all garrisons.

Over and above this, the massive treaty – with its 440 separate articles, which even regulated the size of police forces within Germany – also contained a firm provision for Germany to supply fully 60 per cent of its coal output to the Entente powers for a period of ten years. In addition, almost all the country's modern locomotives, hundreds of thousands of railway wagons, every other inland vessel, over half its dairy cows, and a quarter of its chemical and pharmaceutical products were to be ceded in reparation. In the case of the pharmaceuticals, German companies were forced to relinquish the licences. Although the cession of territories alone that was required already meant losing half the country's iron ore capacity, 25 per cent of its deep-mined coal, 17 per cent of its potato crop, and 13 per cent of its wheat, the victorious powers were determined not to let it go at that.

Above all, Germany was also expected to make financial reparations. As yet, the victorious powers had not agreed on the scale of these payments. That was beside the point, however, since the defeated nations were obliged to agree in advance to whatever level of compensation was decided upon. For, contrary to all historical reality, Article 231 of the Versailles Treaty (the so-called 'War Guilt Clause') stipulated that 'Germany accepts the responsibility of Germany and her allies for causing all the loss and damage to which the Allied and Associated Governments and their nationals have been subjected as a consequence of the war imposed upon them by the aggression of Germany and her allies.'[11] It was a new historical departure for a country to be held solely to blame for instigating a conflict and hence for it to be ostracised the world over as a 'nation of barbarians'. This was also true of the demand that the emperor, as the supreme military commander, and almost 900 of his subordinates should be extra-dited so that an Allied tribunal could pass sentence on them. The German government simply sat on its hands on the extradition question. As for the emperor, by that stage he was living in exile at Doorn in the Netherlands, and the Dutch – who had remained neutral in the First World War – steadfastly refused to accede to the Entente's insistent requests that he be handed over.

Within the Entente, many voices were raised in opposition to the harsh conditions imposed by the Versailles Treaty. Keynes saw in it a 'policy of reducing Germany to servitude for a gen-eration, of degrading the lives of millions of human beings, and of depriving a whole nation of happiness'.[12] The more farsighted conference delegates warned of a new conflict, such as the prime minister of the Union of South Africa, Jan C. Smuts, who was part of the British Empire delegation. He wrote to Wilson: 'This peace could ... spell even greater calamity for the world than the war.'[13] And, looking back just two years later, Italian prime minister Francesco Nitti, who was a co-signatory in Versailles as a representative of the victorious powers, saw the treaty as 'a means of prolonging the war'.[14]

Versailles came as a profound shock to the Germans. All the hopes for light at the end of the tunnel – in other words, for a better, more peaceful future and an end to the naval blockade and to hunger – culminated in sheer despair. Even worse was the humiliation of a nation that had been forged in wars and which saw the military as part of its core identity. Germany believed that it had fought a just war, but the War Guilt clause disputed this, making Germany into a malevolent aggressor. This was particularly unacceptable to frontline soldiers and called for revision.

The humiliated, run-down nation was of one mind: namely, that this treaty could and would never be accepted. Preserved in the archives of the Reichstag is the famous address Scheidemann delivered on 12 May 1919 at the University of Berlin, where parliament was sitting at the time. The prime minister declared: 'I ask you, who as an honest, compliant person can possibly accept such terms? By rights, shouldn't the hand that thereby condemned itself and our nation to such bondage wither away? In the view of the Imperial Government, this treaty is wholly unacceptable.' The parliamentary record goes on to note: 'Tumultuous applause for minutes on end in the house and the galleries. The assembly gives a standing ovation.'[15] In the event, 12 May 1919 proved to be the last great expression of parliamentary consensus in Weimar Germany.

A month later, that consensus had evaporated. On 16 June 1919, the victorious powers presented the German government with an ultimatum. Unless Germany accepted the peace terms within five days, they would resume hostilities. Berlin was now caught between Scylla and Charybdis. If it submitted to the ultimatum, this would be seen as a betrayal of the Fatherland not just by those who had fought at the front, and the country's internal unity would be severely shaken or even utterly destroyed. If, however, the deadline were to lapse without acceptance, then war-weary Germany, which thanks to the armistice

agreed at Compiègne would scarcely stand a chance of successfully defending its sovereign territory, might well descend into
total chaos. Considering the separatist movements that were
active both in the Rhineland – with strong French backing – and
Bavaria, this might well mean the break-up of the entire country.
Defence minister Noske spelt out the dire situation: 'We have to
recognise that a resumption of fighting in the West would result
in an independent southwest Germany, an independent Rhineland, and possibly even an independent Hanover.'[16]

Another consequence might well have been the success of the
revolution, whose sponsors in Moscow now sensed a new opportunity. Lenin declared that 'this brutal and infamous peace[17] ...
is the best recruiting sergeant for Bolshevism'.[18] Lenin invested
all his hopes in a resumption of the war, which would favour a
violent coup within Germany. For this reason, the Comintern
should, he maintained, no longer be an organisation headed by
the Bolsheviks fighting to free the global proletariat from capitalism and imperialism but also a liberation movement for the
forces that were being oppressed by the Versailles Treaty.

If prime minister Scheidemann and the members of his cabinet
had been able to look into the future, they would have seen the
extermination camps of the Holocaust and would doubtless
have reached a different decision, and instead of tearing the
nation apart would have shouldered all the attendant risks and
uncertainties and taken up arms once more against the Entente.
From the perspective of June 1919, however, it was the lesser of
two evils to accept the ultimatum rather than resume hostilities,
which had already cost the lives of two million German soldiers
and crippled hundreds of thousands of others. Under protest
and in the certain knowledge that every course of action he took
would be the wrong one, a resigned Scheidemann, followed by
his cabinet, stepped down after he, his party, and some members
of the Catholic Centre Party and the USPD had voted in favour

of accepting the Allied diktat. A minority of delegates, comprising the rest of the Centre, the DDP, the DNVP and the DVP, voted against.

The truly disastrous thing about the vote in favour of acceptance that the victorious powers gained by coercion was that it henceforth split the parties that had formerly been united in their rejection of the Versailles Treaty into two irreconcilable camps. In the light of the economic burden placed on the Republic by the provisions of the treaty, the ever more acrimonious antagonism that developed within German politics drove a wedge between the groups. Whereas the governing parties, first and foremost the majority Social Democrats, were constantly having to justify their decision in the face of the economic misery of millions upon millions of people, the focus of the right-wing parties was on pillorying the acceptance of the treaties as weakness and failure.

The forces of reaction, which were growing ever more radical, now increasingly began to decry the agreements reached at Versailles as a 'betrayal of the Fatherland'. This supposed betrayal was now placed within a wider context. For the attitude of the ruling parties appeared to have vindicated those who had seen Erzberger's signature at Compiègne as a 'betrayal by the home front'. It was no longer of much interest to anyone that Berlin had intended the withdrawal from the occupied territories and the left bank of the Rhine – which the Entente had demanded as a precondition of the armistice – to be taken as a trust-building measure and a declaration of intent that it was willing to cooperate in good faith in securing a 'just' peace settlement for all the peoples of Europe. In the eyes of the conspiracy theorists, Compiègne was the first step towards the permanent military containment and economic despoliation of Germany. A decisive second step had now been taken with acceptance of the Versailles Treaty conditions.

The myth of Germany's politicians on the home front aiming a 'dagger blow' at the frontline forces began to be fabricated precisely by those who were responsible for the disaster of the First World War and who traditionally saw the German National People's Party (DNVP), which was now gaining support, as their political home. Together with the German nationalist politician Karl Helfferich, Ludendorff drafted a declaration which the well-respected Hindenburg read out on 18 November 1919 in front of a commission of inquiry set up by the National Constitutional Assembly. In it, the generals levelled an accusation that was as inaccurate as it was monstrous:

> The political parties undermined the home front's spirit of resistance ... in addition to this, there was a systematic degradation of the navy and the army and a revolutionary demoralization of frontline forces. As a result, our operations were doomed to failure, and a collapse was inevitable. One English general quite rightly observed: 'The German Army was stabbed in the back.'[19]

This declaration, which exonerated the third German Supreme Command for its failure in 1918, went down in history as the 'stab-in-the-back myth'. It came about as a direct result of the ultimatum issued by the victorious powers and the ensuing loss of consensus within German society, and was not, as is often claimed, a simple reflex response to having lost the war. It was only post-Versailles that millions of Germans began to see the 'great betrayal' as the reason for the country's defeat in the Great War, and for the anti-Semites among them, it was self-evident that the Jews were to blame.

In particular, Versailles caused many of the men who had fought for Germany at the various fronts in the First World War to turn their backs on majority social democracy. One of them was the as-yet-unknown Private First Class Adolf Hitler, who experienced at first hand the period of great uncertainty, martial law, and escalating anti-Semitism that ensued in Munich after the collapse of the short-lived Soviet Republic and the imposition of the Versailles diktat. It was during these months that he developed his ideology, a process that we will examine in greater detail presently. Hitler had managed to keep a low profile as delegate for the replacement battalion in the Munich Soviet Republic, but now – by a lucky twist of fate[20] – avoided fading into total insignificance by becoming a propagandist for the Bavarian Reich Defence Force. Under the influence of the environment he now inhabited, the Adolf Hitler with socialist ambitions became Hitler the anti-Bolshevik and fanatical Jew-hater. August and September 1919 thus provide the first indications of anti-Semitic tirades by a man who quickly came to see Versailles and Bolshevism as the corrosive instruments of international Jewry.

In October of that year, Hitler – who in his capacity as an army propaganda officer now found himself moving in populist anti-Semitic and ultra-reactionary circles – first encountered the 'German Workers' Party' (DAP), an insignificant fringe grouping that swam in the same political waters as Alfred Brunner's 'German Socialist Party' and the Sudetenland-based 'German National Socialist Workers' Party'. The DAP had set out to try and reconcile socialism and nationalism. The little group around the sports journalist Karl Harrer and the proletarian activist Anton Drexler, who were soon joined by an engineer by the name of Gottfried Feder, believed that it was the antagonism between these two tendencies that had brought about Germany's defeat in the Great War.

Thanks to Hitler's talent for public speaking, which the populist anti-Semites recognised in him and did their best to encourage, the DAP was soon able to emerge from its shadowy backroom existence. As early as October 1919 it was holding its first large gatherings in the beer halls of Munich, drawing an audience of a couple of hundred people with Hitler as the main speaker. His constant theme was the 'murderous shameful diktat' and increasingly the Jewish conspiracy that was presumed to be behind it. From late 1919 to early 1920, Hitler and the DAP leadership devoted themselves to fleshing out this ideology, work which culminated in the publication of a nationalist, socialist, and anti-Semitic manifesto for the DAP, comprising twenty-five guiding principles.[21]

Its central demand was of course a revision of the Versailles Treaty, a policy that all parties of the Weimar Republic had nailed to their masts. The very first principle espoused by the DAP thus called for the creation of a 'Greater Germany' on the basis of people's right to self-determination. This state was to include all regions settled by German speakers, including German Austria and the Sudetenland. Within the planned 'Greater Germany', Jews would be stripped of their citizenship and an economic system created that would dispense with 'Jewish stock-market capitalism'. This programme was introduced at the party's first truly mass rally in February 1920. Just a few days before, the DAP had been renamed the National Socialist German Workers' Party (NSDAP), which before long would adopt as its emblem a black swastika inside a white roundel on a red background. Hitler identified the swastika flag as 'a symbol of labour, with the white as a token of our national ethos and the red as a symbol of our truly socialist attitude. The cross itself provides a further symbol, namely the spirit of the idealism of an Aryan outlook and not the spirit of the Jews.'[22]

Subsequent developments in the civil-war-torn country provided further impetus to this Bavarian splinter party, whose sphere of influence at the outset barely extended beyond Bavaria. In the capital Berlin, communists and other radical left-wing groups called for a mass demonstration to be held in mid-January 1920.

The Shop Stewards' Bill that was about to pass into law in parliament, and which actually promised fundamental improvements to the lives of most workers but was seen by the USPD and the KPD as a tool to oppress the proletariat, was merely a pretext for this rally. In actual fact, the organisers were hell-bent on a confrontation with the state authorities, having deliberately relocated the demonstration to within the protest exclusion zone around the Reichstag. Fearing the start of a coup, the police cracked down so violently that they left forty-two protestors dead and more than a hundred injured. This sparked a wave of communist-led unrest throughout Germany, leading to the declaration of a state of emergency in several regions, while defence minister Noske assumed executive powers throughout Berlin and Brandenburg.

These events prompted the right wing to accuse the majority SPD of lacking firmness in dealing with the unrest, or even of being a spineless instrument in the hands of enemy powers. Resentment against the Social Democrat-led administration in general, and in particular widespread doubt over whether a 100,000-strong army, as required by the terms of the Versailles Treaty, would even be sufficient to contain the situation within the country, led the director of agricultural policy for East Prussia, the civil servant Wolfgang Kapp, to stage a coup with the assistance of General Walther Freiherr von Lüttwitz. The latter, who had the support of the notorious *Freikorps* naval brigade, commanded by the frigate captain Hermann Ehrhardt, which had already been involved in crushing the Munich Soviet Republic, presented the national government with an ultimatum demanding new elections and the immediate cessation of the troop reductions required by Versailles. However, the government decamped, first to Dresden and then to Stuttgart, and disregarded the ultimatum, whereupon Ehrhardt ordered his irregular forces, many of whom sported the swastika on their uniforms, to occupy the government quarter in Berlin. On

13 March 1920 Kapp announced the dissolution of parliament and the dismissal of the president, the national government, the Prussian government, and named himself Reich chancellor and Prussian prime minister.

The official German army, the Reichswehr, watched these events unfold and did nothing. Torn between its duty of loyalty to the government of Gustav Bauer on the one hand and its complete sympathy with the view of the putschists that the troop reductions dictated by the Entente would cut the very lifeblood of the country on the other, the commanders of the 100,000-strong army retreated to a neutral position. With the slogan 'Troops don't fire on other troops'[23] the operational chief of the Reichswehr, General Hans von Seeckt, tried to wash his hands of all responsibility to intervene, while at the same time acknowledged that many of his soldiers supported the cause of their putschist comrades, alongside whom they had fought in the Great War.

The national government responded to the Kapp Putsch – which Hitler enthusiastically welcomed – by calling for a general strike. In the Ruhr industrial cities of Bochum and Elberfeld, in an uneasy show of unity the majority SPD, USPD, and KPD formed an alliance against the forces of reaction and seized political power in the name of the 'dictatorship of the proletariat'. Steering committees sprang up everywhere, many of them containing representatives of the anarcho-syndicalist Free Workers' Union of Germany (FAUD). The Kapp Putsch had already run aground thanks to the dilettantism of its leaders by the time a 'Red Ruhr Army' took control of the region. After one ultimatum had elapsed, the government sent in regular troops to the Ruhr but also a unit of *Freikorps* irregulars, who cleared the cities one by one of rebel forces. Once again, this latter group displayed particular brutality in confronting the 'Reds', with drumhead courts-martial and summary executions. By the beginning of April it was all over in the Ruhr, at a cost of over 1,600 lives.

That the official government, in combatting the 50,000 armed men of the 'Red Army', once again found itself having to rely on units whose members wanted no part of this democratic republic, was just one of two problems for the government that had their roots in the Versailles Treaty. The other was that French troops now promptly proceeded to occupy Frankfurt and other cities in the Rhein-Main region because, according to the letter of the Versailles Treaty, the military action ordered by Berlin had also taken place in what was officially designated a demilitarised zone. Yet it was rebellion within its own ranks that plunged the German government into crisis. In view of what had happened in the Kapp Putsch, the trades unions complained that the administration was too close to the right wing to recognise the threat it represented. Noske was forced to resign – much to the annoyance of President Ebert. Another casualty was majority Social Democrat Chancellor Gustav Bauer. Hermann Müller now took occupancy of the chancellor's palace in Berlin.

Müller, another MSPD member, then bowed to pressure from the right-wing parties to bring forward the national elections originally scheduled to take place in the autumn of 1920. As expected, the poll on 6 June 1920 resulted in heavy losses for the governing parties. Support for the so-called Weimar Coalition slumped from 76.2 to 43.6 per cent. The SPD alone lost 16.3 percentage points, emerging from the ballot with just 21.6 per cent. The winners were those opposition parties that had voted against accepting the terms of the Versailles Treaty – the DNVP (14.3 per cent) and the German People's Party (DVP; 13.8 per cent). The election victors also included above all the USPD (18.4 per cent), whereas the KPD garnered a mere 2.1 per cent of the votes.

It was an irony of history that that very same election day, 6 June 1920, which saw the implementation of the Weimar Constitution throughout the entire country, also marked the moment when conditions of parliamentary stability definitively came to an end – conditions that had enabled the young republic to gain a foothold in these perilous, turbulent times in the first place. A minority government under the leadership of the centrist politician Konstantin Fehrenbach, comprising the Centre, the German Democratic Party (DDP), and for the first time also the DVP – but without the strongest party, the majority SPD – now guided the country's destiny. This was the fourth of ten cabinets to govern Germany between 1919 and the elections of 1924.

In the Bavarian Free State, the era of SPD rule also came to an end for the time being. Arnold von Möhl, the commander of the Bavarian army units, had cleverly exploited demonstrations by the workers of Munich against the Kapp Putsch to force the Hoffmann government to sign over executive powers to him. Möhl thus became state commissar for the city and province of Munich, and when Gustav von Kahr was named government commissar for the region, the disempowerment of the majority Social Democrats in Bavaria was complete. Hoffmann stepped down. On 16 March 1920 Kahr, a dyed-in-the-wool monarchist who had never made any secret of his hostility towards 'Red Berlin' and Jews, was elected Bavarian prime minister. Munich thus became fertile ground for the local agitator and rabble-rouser Hitler, who by this stage was well on the way to adopting a self-contained worldview based on racial ideology that would govern his thinking for the rest of his life.

The polarisation of society continued as the victorious powers increased the pressure on Germany. In January 1921, the Allied Reparations Conference in Paris once again demanded that Germany pay a reparations bill of 269 gold marks over a period of forty-two years. In addition, within the same timeframe, 12 per cent of its exports were to be sent to the Entente – demands which, if met, would mean that it would be only a matter of time before the already moribund German economy collapsed entirely. The reparations payment demands were greeted with mass protests throughout the country.

Meanwhile, the radical Left was once more plotting an uprising. In October 1920, the USPD had split over the question of whether to join the Moscow Comintern or not. Most of the delegates at the party's annual congress, held in Halle, voted in favour and subsequently joined the Communist Workers' Party of Germany (KAPD), the left-wing KPD splinter group that had come into being in the autumn of 1919. The resulting United Communist Party of Germany (VKPD), which as a full member of the Comintern received its instructions directly from Moscow, thus became a significant parliamentary force, although its principal activity henceforth consisted of extra-parliamentary opposition to the republic. The *Rote Fahne* reported that the proletariat 'must again impress upon its memory the words of Rosa Luxemburg, which the delegate Zinoviev recalled when he came to Halle – namely, that the struggle for socialism is the greatest civil war in history'.[24]

In March 1921 the revolution – the so-called March Action – duly began in the central German industrial zone around Halle, Leuna, and Merseburg as well as in the Mansfeld Land region. At the start of that year, twenty-four Soviet civil war experts, tried and tested in armed combat and strategy, had left Moscow for Germany. Lenin tasked Béla Kun with leadership of the operation; Kun's own Hungarian Soviet Republic had been forced to capitulate after 133 days of fighting a Romanian army supported by the Entente and a Hungarian national army under the former Austro-Hungarian imperial admiral Miklós Horthy. In the *Rote Fahne*, Kun called for workers to 'disarm the bourgeoisie',[25] in order that the proletariat – in other words the KPD, as the unified party soon came to style itself again – might finally come to power. However, the central German uprising failed in the face of a determined response by the police and the army but above all from an unwillingness by German workers to follow the revolutionaries. The sad result of the 'March Action' was 145 dead and several hundreds wounded.

No sooner had this insurrection been put down and the 'state of military emergency' lifted than the victorious powers put forward a new set of unreasonable demands. This time they concerned Germany's second-most important industrial region after the Ruhr, Upper Silesia. In Versailles it had been decided that the nationality of the region, which was split between Germans and Poles, should be decided by a plebiscite. After violent altercations and bloody battles between *Freikorps* units and the Polish army, the plebiscite resulted in a clear majority for German nationality, but in April 1921, the League of Nations appointed a commission that divided up the region with a marked bias in favour of Poland. The government in Berlin was thrown into turmoil, culminating in the resignation of the first cabinet of the centrist politician Joseph Wirth.

While Hitler in Munich railed against the 'stranglehold' of 'international capitalism', in London reparations payments were revised down to 132 billion gold marks, which still corresponded to an unimaginable 47,000 tones of bullion. One billion of this was to be raised within twenty-five days, otherwise – the Entente decreed – the Ruhr would be occupied. Berlin's decision to comply with the demand did not, however, resolve the reparations question, for in the medium term the enormous sums simply could not be raised. Nonetheless, at the end of 1921, foreign minister Walther Rathenau, derided by the National Socialists as a 'Jewish pig', succeeded in striking a deal with the French, with Paris agreeing to accept more payments in kind rather than hard cash. The following year, the Germans managed to negotiate a reparations moratorium, since the British were concerned to protect German purchasing power and industrial production to ensure that the defeated nation could continue to be tapped for payments. The hopes that this postponement raised in the German government that the Entente might finally realise that the level of reparations payments they demanded were out of the question were dashed at the Genoa Conference.

The radical right responded to this development by launching a campaign of targeted terror against those they held responsible for Germany's misery, branding them 'appeasers' who had colluded in 'rendering Germany defenceless'. The murder by the right-wing group Organisation Consul in August 1920 of the centrist politician Matthias Erzberger, who had signed the armistice agreement in Compiègne, was followed in June 1921 by the assassination of the Bavarian USPD politician Karl Gareis. In June 1922 – Scheidemann survived an attempted poisoning by hydrogen cyanide that same month – Walther Rathenau, loathed by the extreme Right as a representative of the 'Jewish Republic', was gunned down in the street. Once again, the perpetrators were members of the Consul terrorist group.

Two months before, in April 1922, Rathenau, who was foreign minister in the centre politician Joseph Wirth's second cabinet, had signed the Treaty of Rapallo with the Russian delegates, the People's Commissar for Foreign Affairs Georgi Chicherin and Adolph Joffe. This was actually something of an outrage, given Moscow's ongoing revolutionary agitation within Germany, but some measure of rapprochement with Soviet Russia was the only possibility open to German foreign policy at the time. Having defeated the 'Whites' in the Crimea in November 1920 and following the withdrawal of Entente troops, the Bolsheviks had finally triumphed in the civil war. Like Germany, Russia was left isolated and ever since Versailles had been geostrategically cut off from Central Europe by a 'cordon sanitaire' of medium-sized and smaller states that had mostly once been part of the Tsarist Empire – from Finland through the Baltic states and Poland down to Romania. Unlike the politicians of the SPD, who refused to recognise the treaty because of their bitter hostility toward the Bolsheviks, foreign minister Rathenau, who was wholly focused on trade, hoped that by taking such a step he might persuade Moscow to desist from its promotion of revolutionary terror in Germany.

The agreement at Rapallo, which Hitler saw as a prime example of the German 'system politicians' he so hated and regarded as being Jewish-dominated collaborating with 'Jewish-Russian' Bolsheviks, only served to confirm the NSDAP leader in his worldview. The treaty came as a bolt out of the blue for the rest of Europe. That Germany, defeated in the war and destitute, was on the point of breaking out of its political and economic isolation and strengthening its position vis-à-vis the Western powers, prompted a concerted move to resume diplomatic and economic relations. The latter were especially important to Germany, since its goods had been boycotted by Western European states since the end of the war. The most explosive part of the treaty with Russia was the establishment of secret military cooperation between these two very different countries, something which had already begun. Soldiers of the Reichswehr were trained in Russia in tank and aerial warfare, in other words in the use of modern weapons systems which, according to the terms of the Versailles Treaty, Germany was banned from possessing. There was something deeply schizophrenic about German generals cooperating with the very people who were fanning the flames of revolution within Germany, but their absolute determination not to become totally disengaged from the latest developments in military technology – born of their hostility toward the Western powers – enabled them to turn a blind eye to this.

The foreign policy of the Soviet leadership in Moscow, meanwhile, was still firmly focused on promoting global revolution. Thus, with the Treaty of Rapallo, the Kremlin hoped to be able to advance the class struggle of their followers in the KPD, which had up to that point been characterised by setbacks. The Russians calculated that the treaty would escalate the conflict between Germany and the victorious powers, which in turn would have a major knock-on effect on the country's internal stability. Revolution needed a crisis in order to succeed, and it was certainly the case that Rapallo galvanised the Western powers into action. Paris in particular feared a shift in the European balance of power and the post-war order created by Versailles. French prime minister Raymond Poincaré publicly aired the possibility of a military intervention.

At the beginning of 1923, Moscow's calculation paid off, as French and Belgian troops marched into the Ruhr, the heart of German heavy industry. Nor did they stop there: the occupying forces advanced into western Westphalia and expanded the French bridgeheads on the right bank of the Rhine – Mainz, Koblenz, and Cologne – by merging them into one large area. They also occupied key strategic positions further south in Baden. France's intention in setting all these 'productive forfeits' – to quote the words of the Germanophobe Poincaré – was, he claimed, to give its reparations demands teeth. Actually, Paris was trying, bit by bit, to realise the war objectives that it had not fully achieved at Versailles. The occupiers, who justified the invasion (which they are thought to have weighed up even before Rapallo) by claiming that Germany had not met its reparations obligations in time, imposed a state of emergency in the area they controlled and put in place a harsh occupation regime. The government of Wilhelm Cuno (DVP) – the seventh since the January elections in 1919 – responded with a campaign of 'passive resistance'. Yet the loss of production completely wrecked the German economy, with unemployment topping the four million mark. Severe hardship in the populace increased accordingly. Battered by hyperinflation – in November 1923 one US dollar was worth 4,200,000,000,000 Marks – Germany threatened to finally slide into total chaos.

Everything was on a knife edge after Cuno's administration stepped down and the new chancellor, Gustav Stresemann of the DVP, was forced to announce to the German public the end of 'passive resistance' and the resumption of the interrupted reparations payments at the end of September. These events were still being played out against an increasingly clamorous backdrop of revolutionary propaganda from the KPD and its allies. As early as July, Stresemann conceded: 'We are dancing on the rim of a volcano, and we'll be faced with a revolution if we can't reconcile competing interests with policies that are as decisive as they are smart.'[26] On becoming chancellor, he wrote to the industrialist Hugo Stinnes: 'It's an existential struggle that we are waging now to save the German nation, and everything else must be subordinated to this.'[27]

Stresemann was not wrong in his assessment of the situation. For the Kremlin and its German supporters really were attempting to take advantage of the moment to trigger the 'second wave of global revolution' in Germany, beginning in Thuringia and Saxony, where popular front regimes had already come to power. 'Revolutionary Hundreds' were created on the model of the St Petersburg 'Red Guards'. Under the leadership of Radek and the experienced civil war commander Yuri Piatakov, who had been dispatched by Moscow, these fighting units were intended to stir up revolution from the heart of the German Reich and have it spread like wildfire, creating the 'German October' after the 'Russian October'. In concert with this, an uprising was to be staged in Hamburg too. There was a plan in place, drafted in Moscow by the military commission of the Central Committee of the Russian Communist Party in consultation with the KPD leadership, that made provisions for up to 2.3 million Red Army troops to march through Poland 'to hasten to the military aid ... of the German proletariat'.[28] With victory in Germany, the 'centre of the world revolution would shift from Moscow to

Berlin', wrote Josef Stalin, who since 1922 had been the general
secretary of the Central Committee of the Russian Communist
Party, in the *Rote Fahne*.[29] Stalin was convinced that only revolution in Germany would provide the all-important impetus for a
global revolution.

Even before the 'German October' so loudly trumpeted by
communist propaganda had failed – once again thanks to an
inability to mobilise a critical mass of workers and because the
German Army was able to contain the incipient uprising – in
Bavaria, the self-proclaimed saviour of the world Adolf Hitler,
who believed he had the support of a number of armed groups,
resolved to take decisive action himself. His ambitions were
fanatical and irrational in equal measure. To try and prevent
Germany from falling prey to 'Jewish Bolshevism' and 'Jewish
big business' and its accomplices in parliament, he intended to
usurp power in Bavaria and then march on Berlin. Although the
authorities in the Free State, notably State Commissar Kahr and
his chief of police, initially wavered when Hitler urged them to
join him, they ultimately refused to heed his call.

The Beer Hall Putsch of 8–9 November 1923, which collapsed
under a volley of gunfire from the Bavarian state police outside
the Feldherrnhalle in Munich, eventually descended into farce,
albeit a bloody one. The upshot was sixteen dead National
Socialists, who were later canonised as 'martyrs of the movement'; a coup leader on the run, whose first reaction was to take
his own life (although he then found he was incapable of doing
so); and an ensuing trial that ended with an extremely lenient
sentence for Hitler of five years' imprisonment. As it turned out,
he was released after serving just a year: the prevailing view was
that the First World War private with the Iron Cross, First Class,
had acted out of a sense of patriotism, as had his co-defendants,
including Erich Ludendorff, former quartermaster-general of
the German Army, who was likewise freed.

The Republic had withstood assaults from both extremes of the political spectrum. In time, hard-pressed Germany found its way out of the crisis. Stalin was forced to resile from his aim for a swift implementation of global revolution in Germany. By all reasonable estimates, Hitler and his NSDAP, the leadership of which he had secured in the summer of 1920, had ultimately also run into the sand on 9 November 1923. Everything seemed to suggest that this clearly repressed individual with the awkward bearing of an obsessive anti-Semitic zealot would now fade into obscurity and remain just a footnote in Bavarian history. His overwrought, racially motivated agitation had failed to capture the attention of the masses. In the general election of May 1924, his party, in alliance with the German Popular Freedom Party, could only garner 6.6 per cent of the vote. By the subsequent ballot in December 1924, this figure had fallen further to just 3 per cent – the trend was clearly downwards. The programmatic exposition of his worldview, which he wrote while imprisoned in a comfortable cell in the fortress at Landsberg, and which was later to appear under the title *Mein Kampf*, did nothing to alter his situation. In this work, he expounded his ideas about a 'Jewish world conspiracy' and his struggle to combat it.

This decline in the appeal of extremist parties was directly linked to a steady improvement in Germany's economic circumstances. The tide of rampant inflation had been stemmed. The introduction of the 'Rentenmark' (mortgage mark) saw the creation of an intermediate currency to replace the former, unstable paper mark; it, in turn, would presently be supplanted by the 'Reichsmark'. In the West, France was prevented from wresting the Rhineland away from Germany. Moreover, it was threats such as this, coupled with Berlin's seemingly boundless tenacity, that began to win the defeated country some sympathy once more in the outside world and led to a reassessment of the reparations question at the instigation of Great Britain

and the United States. Under the Dawes Plan, which was rati-
fied by the German parliament in August 1924, payments of
5.4 billion gold marks up to 1928 were linked to the country's
economic performance. The average yearly rate would be set
at around 2 billion Reichsmarks – just a fraction of the annual
repayments originally demanded in gold marks. Constraints on
German sovereignty, such as foreign control of the national bank
and railway network, were also lifted. These were the first steps
towards a thoroughgoing revision of Versailles. In sum, the dictated Peace of Versailles did not smooth Hitler's path to taking
power on 30 January 1933, as was repeatedly claimed after the
end of the Second World War. It did, however, lead the Weimar
Republic to the edge of the abyss and created in this period a
climate that would provide fertile soil for Hitler's insane racially
based ideology to take root in.

# 4

# Hitler's National Socialism

## *Was it a response to Lenin's Bolshevism?*

The 'historians' dispute' (*Historikerstreit*) of the 1980s over how to treat the phenomenon of Nazi Germany is now itself history, although it has lost none of its topicality. At the time, the historian and philosopher Ernst Nolte wrote that Bolshevism stood in a causal relationship to National Socialism, having originated at an earlier date. Put more succinctly: Nolte's claim was that National Socialism was a response to Bolshevism. This assertion caused horror and outrage among more left-leaning West German historians, who saw in it an interpretation of National Socialism as a purely defensive ideology, and accused Nolte of being an evil revisionist. The chief spokesperson for this group was the philosopher and sociologist Jürgen Habermas. In the ensuing period, Nolte was actively ostracised by the German academic community. This goaded him into escalating the dispute in what were often unacceptable ways, and he died in 2016 as an isolated figure. In other Western countries, Nolte was and still is regarded as a respected academic whose controversial hypothesis, which was shared by many of his peers, has been a catalyst for lively debate. For all his differences with his German counterpart, the eminent French historian François Furet has stated that Nolte's works are some of the most important studies of the period encompassing the two world wars in Europe.[1]

Even the most superficial study of the two ideologies that had such a devastating impact on twentieth-century history shows that communism came earlier. Seen from this perspective, it could well be the case that National Socialism was a response to the former. Current historiography takes a different view. It holds that anti-Bolshevism was an adjunct to the original anti-Semitic worldview of the National Socialists. Consequently, it argues, Bolshevism cannot stand in a causal relationship to National Socialism and its crimes against humanity. According to this viewpoint, Hitler would have been visited upon Germany and the world even without Lenin. However, if we look at Hitler the returning frontline soldier, we see that in April 1919 – in other words in the Munich of the Soviet Republic – he was neither an anti-Bolshevik nor an anti-Semite. When and how did he become both of these things in the period following the Munich Soviet Republic? And which came first, his anti-Bolshevism or his anti-Semitism?

A factor that is of central importance in answering this question is a myth that is almost never mentioned in more recent historical accounts: namely, the canard of 'Jewish Bolshevism'. Following the revolutionary period of 1918, the notion that Bolshevism was a Jewish phenomenon spread rapidly and soon became prevalent. It began to appear everywhere – from serious newspapers to inflammatory anti-Semitic pamphlets. Sometimes, the idea of an association between Bolshevism and Judaism was even promoted by Jews themselves, as for example when the *Jewish Chronicle* in London wrote in April 1919 that the message of Bolshevism accorded in all its key aspects with the tenets of Judaism.[2] Evidently, the world Zionist movement, which was socialist at heart, was uppermost in the writer's thoughts here. In his book *Der Judenstaat* ('The Jewish State') the founder of Zionism, Theodor Herzl, made a connection between Judaism and revolution when he wrote that 'Educated Jews without means are now rapidly becoming Socialists.'[3]

Indeed, that Bolshevism was intrinsically Jewish seemed self-evident above all from the large number of revolutionary leaders who were of Jewish extraction. For instance, of the seven-strong First Politburo of the Russian Communist Party, no fewer than four had Jewish backgrounds: Trotsky, Zinoviev, Kamenev, and Sokolnikov. The proportion of men and women of Jewish origin was similarly high among prominent revolutionary figures in Hungary and Germany too. They included, among others, Béla Kun, Rosa Luxemburg, and Paul Levi, along with most of the leading members of the Bavarian Soviet Republic. Little wonder, then, that US president Woodrow Wilson was also convinced that Bolshevism was a Jewish-led movement. Likewise, Winston Churchill, who at the time was British secretary of state for war and air, wrote in 1920 that Bolshevik Jews were a 'band of extraordinary personalities' that had risen to become the undisputed masters of the vast Soviet empire. Churchill believed that 'a prominent, if not indeed the principal, part in the system of terrorism ... has been taken by Jews'.[4] He was clearly not so far wide of the mark, for, according to the minutes of a politburo meeting of April 1919, Trotsky complained that 'among Cheka employees at the front, executive committee members at and behind the front lines, and in the central Soviet bureaucracy ... the proportion of Latvians and Jews is very high'.[5] The American Russia expert Richard Pipes quite rightly sees the identification of Jews with communism as one of the most 'disastrous consequences' of the Russian Revolution, for this linkage was the main driver of the anti-Semitism that spread throughout the countries that had lost the Great War.[6]

The canard of 'Jewish Bolshevism', which was the subject of a wide-ranging dissertation by Johannes Rogalla von Bieberstein in 1976,[7] naturally gained widespread traction in Bavaria too, as it was in the midst of revolutionary upheaval. Thus, in early December 1918, the unofficial organ of the Bavarian People's

Party (BVP) ran a leader stating that while party members had 'high regard and respect for all honest Jews ... what must be resisted at all costs are the many atheistic elements of an unscrupulous international Jewry with a predominantly Russian flavour'.[8] This view was a reference to the Bolshevik revolutionaries controlled by Russia. This group was also seen by long-established religious Jews as a major threat to the bourgeois world of which they were part. A large number of demobilised soldiers of Jewish origin even opted to join *Freikorps* units fighting against the Bolsheviks.

As early as March 1919, far-sighted Jews had warned that popular hatred might be directed against the entire Jewish community. On the eve of the Bavarian Soviet Republic, the spokesperson for Orthodox Judaism in Bavaria, the industrialist Sigmund Fraenkel, had signalled the 'enormous danger facing not so much individual members of our faith community as Judaism itself should the great mass of Munich's working population come to associate the sublime doctrines and dogmas of the Jewish religion with the false doctrines of Bolshevism and Communism'.[9] The Jewish speaker of the Social Democrat-led Prussian government, Hans Goslar, wrote in 1919 that the Jewish revolutionaries had caused 'the sparks of anti-Semitism to be fanned into the bright flames of a roaring conflagration'.[10]

At the same time, other representatives of German Jewry also saw fit to warn of the incipient danger that threatened when Bolshevism was identified with Judaism, based not least on an awareness of the persecutions that their Eastern European co-religionists in the Baltic region, Byelorussia, and the Ukraine were suffering as a result of the Russian Civil War. According to newspaper reports, in the Ukraine, for example, more than 100,000 Jewish men, women, and children had been butchered by 'White' troops and Ukrainian nationalists in the course of the counter-revolution between December 1918 and August 1919.[11]

Pogroms against the Ukrainian Jews had occurred time and time again in the Tsarist Empire, but what happened in 1919 represented a new dimension in the persecution of the Jews in Eastern Europe. These were massacres in which the last vestiges of any civilised norms seem to have been completely abandoned. In this context, the London *Jewish Chronicle* used a term for the first time in May 1919 that originally denoted a 'burnt offering' in ritual sacrifices, when it reported that a 'Holocaust' was taking place in the Ukraine.[12] The paper identified one of the principal reasons for the scale of the atrocity as being that the Jews, who had always been the victims of discrimination, were now also being seen as sponsors and supporters of Bolshevism.

Developments followed the same pattern in Bavaria, although matters did not come to such an extreme pass there. Once the brief rule of the workers' and soldiers' soviets – which the general population saw as alien and Russian – had come to an end, bloodily crushed by regular army units and *Freikorps* detachments, anti-Semitism only increased further, as it appeared obvious that the Jews were behind the rise of Bolshevism. The situation was further inflamed by the dictated Versailles Peace of May 1919, which coincided with the end of the *Räterepublik* and which had as shattering an effect on the citizens of Munich as it did on the rest of the country. The city was gripped by an hysterical fear of a resurgence of the revolution. With Hoffmann's regular civilian government still exiled in Bamberg, Möhl, commanding officer of Bavarian detachments of the Reichswehr who had sole control over Munich, overreacted accordingly, declaring a state of siege and calling up local defence units.

Möhl's regime was driven by the desire to be rid of the 'Reds' once and for all. A wave of purges swept across the city. Leading members of the revolutionary regime were detained and subjected to brutal treatment. Those who weren't immediately butchered like animals were sentenced to death by a swiftly convened courts-martial and executed. They included the Jews Landauer and Leviné, whose last words to the firing squad were 'Long Live the Revolution!'[13] Egelhofer, the commander-in-chief of the 'Red Army', was shot dead 'while attempting to flee'. Others, like the writers Erich Mühsam and Ernst Toller, who were also of Jewish extraction, were handed long prison sentences. Thomas Mann noted at the time: 'A world that still has the instinct for self-preservation must proceed against these sorts of people with all the energy it can muster and with short, sharp justice.' By 'these sorts of people' the future Nobel laureate, who turned his back on Germany when Hitler came to power, meant 'the type that is the Russian Jew, that explosive mix of Jewish intellectualism and radicalism on the one hand and Slavic Christian fanaticism on the other'.[14]

The Jews who had emigrated from the East quickly got to feel this spreading anti-Semitism, being collectively associated with the rule of the Soviet Republic. A proposal was put forward that anyone from this cohort of people who had come to Germany after 1914 should be expelled. The idea was also mooted that even Jews of Bavarian nationality should suffer the same fate. The Munich chief of police Ernst Pöhner was one of many who thought that Eastern European Jews were and remained 'a harmful foreign body within the German nation'. In his view, they did not serve the general interest but instead only pursued their own 'private and racial ends', in the process stopping at nothing, 'even going so far as to subvert the state itself when it suits their purposes, as the events surrounding the Soviet Republic this year have shown, where it was primarily Eastern European Jewish elements who were the promoters of Bolshevik ideas'.[15]

As already noted, these Bolshevik ideas circulated primarily in the Munich army garrison, which as part of the 'Red Army' provided vital support for the Bavarian Soviet Republic. Consequently, as early as May, Möhl had ordered the formation of 'commissions of inquiry and dismissal', which were designed to track down Bolshevik agitators within the unit and hand them over to the courts martial. Private First Class Hitler now also turned up on one of these commissions, having managed to save his skin and switch sides to join the counter-revolutionaries, where he directed all his efforts at airbrushing out of history his flirtation with the revolution. Furthermore, he also hoped that his adroit move might help him avoid being cashiered from the army.

And so it was that Hitler was also present when, at the end of May, an intelligence (for which read 'propaganda') division was formed under the command of Captain Karl Mayr. Its task was to school members of the Bavarian transitional army in civic awareness. Before the men of the propaganda unit could get to work, they themselves had to be tutored. An introductory course took place between 5 and 12 June. Five more classes were to follow. The 'educational goal' was to devise 'pure anti-Bolshevik propaganda … on the exclusive basis of the Russian, Hungarian and German examples'. The content of the course was further delineated: 'In this context, we will touch upon Lenin, Marx, Bolshevism, Communism, and the Communist Manifesto.'[16] Before long, the propaganda students also had at their disposal a course book, a slim volume by a naval officer called Ernst Lindemann with the title *Was man über den Bolschewismus wissen muss* ('Everything you need to know about Bolshevism').[17] One of the propagandists later wrote to Mayr: 'The examples based on genuine sources prove that it is predominantly Jews who are going about their dirty work as the principal ringleaders of Bolshevism.'[18]

Such a statement would surely have met with no contradiction from the course tutors. One of them, for instance, was Count Karl Ludwig von Bothmer, who had accused Kurt Eisner of being called Kosmanowki, hailing from Galicia, and wanting to 'use the means of national desperation to drive the people into the arms of Bolshevism'.[19] Then there was the more left-orientated Gottfried Feder, whose focus was on 'Jewish capitalism' but who nonetheless also saw Bolshevism as a 'Jewish sham'. The propagandists also included the historian and Bavarian particularist Alexander von Müller who first recognised Hitler's gift for public oratory, the economist Walter L. Hausmann, and the president of a farmers' association, Michael Horlacher. Although the lecturers articulated a diversity of positions, it was they who were responsible for triggering Hitler's politicisation and radicalisation. From being someone with leftist sympathies, Hitler now emerged as an anti-Bolshevik and anti-Semite.

This process was hastened and intensified in mid-June 1919, when the Versailles ultimatum issued by the victorious powers dealt another body blow to German and Bavarian society. The historian Thomas Weber talks in this context of Hitler's 'Road to Damascus experience'.[20] Weber believes that the signing of the treaty signalled the moment when his 'metamorphosis and radicalization' set in. Everything points to the fact that the whole process, from when the treaty conditions were made public in early May to the signing of the treaty in early July, steadily drove Hitler to an extreme position. The continuation of the war, this time against a twofold enemy, began at this point for him; he soon became a protégé of the fanatical anti-Bolshevik and Jew-hater Mayr.

The sheer drama of these weeks is also reflected in the Munich press. On the one hand, Versailles – the humiliation, the 'betrayal', and the resistance to the treaty – was the great emotive topic of the moment. On the other hand, a wide-ranging reappraisal of the Bavarian Soviet Republic now ensued. This period was seen as a 'Bolshevik reign of terror' and its protagonists as 'beasts in human form'.[21] Time and time again, commentators invoked the incident when the 'Reds' murdered a group of hostages in the grounds of the Luitpold Grammar School. The talk was of caved-in skulls, bits of brains spattered around, and severed male genitalia – in short, of an 'incredible atrocity, in which all humanity and human dignity went by the board'.[22] The revolutionaries responsible were demonised as 'brutal', 'bestial', and 'the spawn of the devil'. When the perpetrators were finally brought to justice, the presiding judge referred to a 'Russian strategy' that was presumed to lie behind the atrocity.[23]

The events in Munich were repeatedly related to the 'bloodbath', and the 'Asiatic starvation and terror regime' in Russia. Over and over again, the newspapers reported on the Red Terror unfolding on the Volga, in Siberia, and Ukraine, on the torture chambers run by the Cheka, on the butchering of the bourgeois intellectual elite, and on the bodies of officers and aristocrats being disinterred and desecrated. Other stories recounted the fate of the Tsar's family, who had been murdered on Lenin's order. Bavaria, the papers claimed, had been saved once more from this apocalypse, of which the hostage murders at the Luitpold school was just a foretaste. Yet the barbaric threat was still lurking below the surface as it always had been – that was the message of a significant section of the press that did not omit to hint at the Jewish provenance of Bolshevism.

By the autumn of 1919, these reports of the atrocities committed by the Munich Bolsheviks, whether real or fabricated, and about Eastern European Jews allegedly earning a living from extortion and profiteering had generated in Munich an anti-Semitic atmosphere hitherto unknown. In October, a daily report by the police intelligence division identified 'the distinct possibility that pogroms of the Jews might occur in time'. Another report from the intelligence division in the same month refers to such pogroms being imminent in Munich 'just like in Vienna and Russia'.[24] How greatly hatred of the Jews had flourished in Munich is also evident from a diary entry written by a journalist named Josef Hofmiller who in his own mind had a ready-made final solution to the problem: 'The Galicians ... should all be shot.'[25]

Hitler's first recorded attacks on the Jews also date from this period. During a sojourn at the Lechfeld hostel for demobilised soldiers in Augsburg in the second half of August 1919, while delivering an impromptu lecture to 'troops infected by the disease of communism and Spartacism' and presenting 'the Jewish in a very clear way, paying special attention to the German aspect', he worked himself up into such a frenzy that the head of the guard detail there found himself obliged to 'order the speaker to tread very carefully indeed when treating this question and where possible to avoid making any direct references to this race that is alien to the German people'.[26] The officer who raised this objection was clearly one of those who still took seriously the guidelines issued by the Reichswehr.

The subject of Hitler's address to the soldiers at Lechfeld was capitalism. His radical rejection of it became the second main route by which he arrived at his fanatical anti-Semitism. For at around the same time as the bogeyman of 'Jewish Bolshevism' became a fixed trope in his worldview, so too the idea crystallised in his mind of a 'rapacious Jewish capitalism' that he believed was having no less a corrosive effect on post-war German society. This belief derived not least from an anti-capitalist chip on his shoulder as one of the 'have-nots', and had already found expression in his flirtation with social democracy and his tacit acceptance of the Bavarian Soviet Republic. Now, however, his resentment took on a pronounced anti-Semitic flavour.

In the course of his ideological training, in addition to gleaning information about Bolshevism, Hitler, who was wholly unversed in economic matters, was also taught about 'Jewish capitalism'. Bothmer, who lectured on 'Socialism in Theory and Practice', took the view that 'international socialism' (and hence also the majority Social Democrat-led German government) was merely an instrument of 'international capitalism'. Therefore, in his opinion, 'workers' leaders were not contributing to combatting the plans hatched by plutocrats and Mammonists for world domination but to their ultimate triumph'.[27] For Bothmer, this also explained his supposed discovery that modern Bolshevism 'has the support, sometimes overt and sometimes covert, of all those groups that are consciously or unconsciously in thrall to the free-market system of mobile capital'.[28]

Bothmer's conspiracy-theory views on the subversive collaboration between capitalism and Bolshevism resembled those of Gottfried Feder, who in May 1919 published *Manifest zur Brechung der Zinsknechtschaft* ('A manifesto on breaking the shackles of interest').[29] Feder, a civil engineer by training who developed an interest in financial and economic affairs and who, like Rudolf Jung in his later work *Der nationale Sozialismus* ('National socialism'),[30] took as his yardstick the model of a medieval economy, and contrasted 'good' capital, i.e. creative capital, with 'bad' capital – namely acquisitive capital – which he associated with Jews. Feder's criticism of all the democratic parties without exception was that their revolution had not even come close to addressing the real crux of the problem. In his eyes, a 'truly socialist state' would need to take 'acquisitive big business' properly to task for having been the root cause of the world war. Instead, he claimed, the revolutionaries of the Left had aided and abetted the 'Mammonistic enslavement and corruption of the German people' by the Jews. According to Feder's ideas, which came to form part of the NSDAP's political programme as articulated in the twenty-five principles of February 1920,[31] it went without saying that international Jewry was pulling the strings behind the scenes in Versailles too.

The crudely conspiratorial world of Bothmer and Feder, who saw their economic blueprint as the alternative German model to Western democracy à la Weimar, is also evident in a

positional paper that Hitler produced on 16 September 1919 at
Mayr's behest on the topic 'Government Social Democracy and
the Jews'.[32] By this stage, Hitler, who had turned away from the
Social Democrats after they yielded to the victorious powers'
ultimatum, had already adopted a scathing attitude towards
Ebert's party. Thus, in his 'position statement' he rather clumsily
lamented the fact that there were no 'nationalistically minded
leaders with an inner sense of responsibility', and that contemporary political leaders were compelled 'to seek support from
those who have done nothing but profit from the reconstitution
of Germany, and still continue to do so, and who for this reason
were also the driving force behind the revolution – the Jews'.
These politicians were obliged, Hitler went on, to accept the
support readily offered by Jews for their own benefit, and hence
also to provide some quid pro quo. 'And this service in return
consists not only in promoting Jewish interests at every opportunity but also in frustrating the deceived populace's fight against
their deceivers and in suppressing the anti-Semitic movement.'

However, in his diatribe Hitler did not stop at accusing the
majority SPD of being a passive accomplice of international
Jewry. He also called for 'emotional knee-jerk anti-Semitism' to
be countered by an 'anti-Semitism based on reason'. For it was
a 'fact', he wrote, that Jews were a racial rather than a religious
community, and to back this up trotted out some anti-Semitic
clichés that were commonly heard in Munich:

As a result of a thousand years of innbreeding [sic], often
within a very limited circle of people, the Jew has for the most
part done a better job of preserving his race and its characteristics than the peoples among whom he lives. And this is the
reason why there is a non-German, alien race now living in
our midst.

For this race, he claimed 'everything is simply a means to satisfy its lust for money and power'. Inasmuch as their activities infected their fellow citizens with a kind of 'racial tuberculosis', Hitler called for a 'systematic legal challenge to and curtailment of the privileges enjoyed by the Jews'. In this paper of 16 September 1919, he was already anticipating a measure that he would put into practice twenty-two years later – most chillingly when he concluded: 'without a doubt, our ultimate goal must be to get rid of the Jews altogether'.[33]

When Hitler advocated an 'anti-Semitism based on reason' in his position statement, he was of course taking a pseudo-academic approach to the subject. He was introduced to this milieu by a fiction writer manqué called Dietrich Eckart, whom he most likely got to know through Mayr in the summer of 1919 and who would presently become his mentor. Eckart belonged to a circle of nationalist anti-Semitic fanatics who formed the 'Thule Society' in Munich, which identified the 'parasitic Jew' as the destroyer of all forms of national community. The group had spawned a paramilitary 'combat league' that waged a guerrilla war against the Munich Soviet Republic. It also had its 'martyrs', such as Countess Hella von Westarp – a friend of Hitler's later deputy, Rudolf Hess – who was among the hostages shot by the 'Reds' in the grounds of the Luitpold Grammar School.

Since December 1918, Eckart had been publishing a periodical, most of which he wrote himself, entitled *Auf gut deutsch* ('In plain language'). The January 1919 edition, entitled 'Jews Within and Without' was the first to broach the theme of the corrosive effect of the Jews on the German nation.[34] Other contributors to this small pamphlet, which appeared in a print run of a few hundred, included Bothmer, Feder, and the Baltic German Alfred Rosenberg who had studied in Moscow and experienced the Russian Revolution at first hand before emigrating to Germany. In the February 1919 issue of *Auf gut deutsch*, he wrote an article headlined 'The Russian-Jewish Revolution',[35] in which he accused the Jews of having plotted to destabilise the Russian state. 'The heart and soul of this entire tendency were the well-known Braunstein [*sic*], alias Trotsky, a Jew from the Yekaterinoslav Governorate, and his close confederate Apfelbaum, who styled himself Zinoviev', Rosenberg wrote. Throughout, he referred to the Bolshevik leadership as a 'Jewish regimen' or 'Soviet Judea'.

The semi-educated Hitler proved to be an eager pupil of Eckart. In his quest to find a racially-based ideology to underpin his worldview, Hitler may well have been pointed in the direction of the pseudo-academic, rambling disquisitions of various racial theorists by Eckhart. It was most likely at this point that Hitler first encountered the works of Gobineau or Chamberlain, the latter of whom he met in Bayreuth in 1923. For Hitler, Wagner was now no longer just the great composer who had introduced him to the mythical world of the Teutons but instead was the prophet of racial conflict. Only now did he begin to comprehend the connections that were presumed to exist between the various allegedly subversive activities of the Jewish race. Only now was he able to grasp the supposed importance of 'racial purity'. And he internalised all of this. He came to see himself in the role of a chosen one, as a member of an elite band who had been initiated into the mysteries of how the world worked and what really lay behind the events in Germany. It was no accident that he later called Eckart his 'Pole Star'[36] – in other words the heavenly body that lights the way for someone struggling to get their bearings in the darkest of nights.

For his part, Eckart was quick to spot the 'future leader' in the gifted orator. Before he met Hitler, the cynical Eckart listed the requirements that such a person should fulfil:

We need a bloke at the top who can stand the sound of a machine gun. The rabble must start to shit themselves in fear.

I've got no time for officers, people have no respect for them anymore. What would be ideal would be a working man with a gift of the gab and his heart in the right place ... He doesn't have to be super-smart; politics is the most idiotic business going.[37]

Henceforth, Eckart made Hitler his protégé and put him in touch with the 'right sort of people'. For the most part, these were nationalist, anti-Semitic businessmen who were staunch members of the Thule Society, but they also included anti-Bolshevik Russian émigrés who had gathered around the aforementioned Baltic German Alfred Rosenberg and his compatriot Erwin Scheubner-Richter who would subsequently be killed during the Beer Hall Putsch of 1923. Without these contacts, who steadily helped Hitler become more socially acceptable, his rise from a rank-and-file army propaganda speaker to Munich's foremost nationalist, socialist, and anti-Semitic agitator would have been unthinkable.

It was also Eckart who inducted Hitler into the German Workers' Party (DAP) and did his utmost to support his work there. This work consisted of permanent political agitation, either at party meetings or speaking engagements before larger audiences in the beer halls of Munich. The constant thrust of Hitler's speeches was 'Jewish capitalism' and 'Jewish Bolshevism' in the guise of Versailles or revolution. That campaigning against the treaty and leftist insurrection was one of his main priorities right from the outset is evident from an anecdote told by Hitler's former trenchmate Max Amann, who ran into Hitler again in early 1920 on the Odeonsplatz in Munich and asked him whether he was still in the army. Hitler replied that he was now an 'education officer' who gave 'lectures against Bolshevism'.[38] Against the background of the Polish–Soviet War, a later Nazi Party member by the name of Riedl attended one of these lectures in early February 1920 and took the following notes: 'Bolshevism on the march. Liberation of the proletariat. Global r[evolution]. Russians and Poles face off.'[39] At the end of March, as Riedl also recorded, Hitler, who had then just left the army, spoke on the topic of 'Bolshevism in the Ruhr'.[40] In July, according to a report in a Rosenheim newspaper, Hitler himself is said to have declared that the Jew was master in Russia and wanted to 'permanently enslave' Germany.[41]

Those who contest the viewpoint that Hitler found his way to anti-Semitism through anti-Bolshevism cite the fact that there is no mention whatsoever of Bolshevism in the twenty-five-point manifesto of the NSDAP from February 1920. They extrapolate from this that anti-Bolshevism was of no consequence to Hitler at that point and that he only began to espouse it from mid-1920 onwards as a corollary to his anti-Semitism. Yet how this could possibly have been the case, given that Hitler was heavily under the influence of Mayr, Bothmer, Feder, and Eckart, and also taking into account the general climate in Munich in the period after the Soviet Republic, is a mystery known only to historians who espouse this view. They completely overlook that the first and only party manifesto of the NSDAP was intended to appeal primarily to the working class: namely, to those who, like Hitler, had once thrown their lot in with, or were still wedded to, the Left. When the last but one of the twenty-five points tersely announces that the party will declare war on 'the Jewish materialist spirit within and without',[42] this pronouncement was also directed at those who had once stood on the side of the revolution. Hitler himself later wrote that one had had to show some consideration for 'psychological factors'.[43]

It was only natural that Hitler's anti-Semitism should have had a universal dimension from the very beginning; after all, he was convinced that 'the Jew' was behind both Bolshevism, with its global revolutionary ambitions, and capitalism, in the

form of the 'world tribunal' of Versailles. In a way, it was perfectly consistent with this insane perspective for him to work
from the premiss of a 'Jewish world conspiracy'. An old line of
argument dating from the late nineteenth century thus experienced an enduring renaissance. The 'Jewish global conspiracy'
was a pervasive theme in nationalistic and anti-Semitic publica-
tions. For example, a leader in the *Deutsche Zeitung* of June
1919 noted that 'the preponderance of recent events' – in other
words, Versailles and the revolution, which Jews were presumed
to have masterminded – had shown beyond a shadow of a doubt
'that the Jews really do have such a master plan ... which they
will carry out using every means at their disposal, unless we
Germans finally wake up to the colossal danger threatening us'.[44]

Anyone who was minded to believe this myth duly did so. All
too often, critical voices went unheard. The Social Democrat
Hans Goslar wrote resignedly in 1919:

> The desperate and dysfunctional mood at this time, the impo-
> tent rage at the shame we were feeling and not least also the
> participation of a large number of men of Jewish ancestry in
> the radical socialist and Bolshevik movements brought about
> a situation where the essentially meaningless and demagogic
> phrase 'Jewish world domination' got stuck in the heads of
> many German men and women who would normally have
> been perfectly capable of exercising sound judgment. Now-
> adays, though, they are no longer able to do so, because
> whichever way they turn there are always the same poisonous
> words being dripped into their ears.[45]

Those same ears – to stay with Goslar's image for the present
– were assailed by a positive clamour in 1920, when a German
translation of *The Protocols of the Elders of Zion* appeared. By
1933, hundreds of thousands of copies of this work, in forty-five

editions, had been bought. The treatise about a 'Jewish global conspiracy' caused a huge stir throughout the world. Its authenticity was the subject of discussion in both *The Times* and *The New York Times*. In Washington DC, a US Senate subcommittee even looked into the *Protocols*. The furore surrounding the work also prompted a famous American to address the issues it raised, in the form of a series of pamphlets. This was none other than the industrialist Henry Ford, whose anti-Semitic diatribes appeared under the title *The International Jew: The World's Foremost Problem*.[46] In these writings, Ford too argued that there was a 'Jewish conspiracy' that was being directed above all at Germany. For, he maintained, there was no greater contrast in the world than that between the pure Aryan race and the purely Semitic race. 'Therefore the Jew hated the German people; therefore the countries of the world which were most dominated by the Jews showed the greatest hatred of Germany during the recent regrettable war.'[47] According to Ford, who referred to Versailles as a 'kosher conference',[48] this hatred had been continued in Paris.

However, Ford's global bestseller, which was also distributed by Nazi Party headquarters in Munich, became essential reading not only for National Socialists. While Hitler did not share Ford's conviction that the *Protocols* were genuine, he did subscribe to the general truth of their content. They provided material for his speeches; there are a number of parallels between Ford's book and *Mein Kampf*. As a result of gaining the propagandistic support of the cosmopolitan figure Ford, the petty-bourgeois Hitler was more than ever convinced that that his take on world affairs was the only correct one. When the 'German October' began to unfold, he told a reporter from a New York magazine what conclusions should be drawn from it: 'The Versailles Peace Treaty and Bolshevism are two heads of the same monster. We should cut both off.'[49]

This 'Jewish monster' thus played a central part in Hitler's autobiographical manifesto *Mein Kampf*, the first volume of which he wrote in 1924 after the failed putsch and during his subsequent incarceration in the fortress at Landsberg. In the book, he linked its 'pernicious influence' to his own life story. As an anti-Semite from an early age, as he now claimed to have been, he maintained that he had encountered it at every twist and turn, but the tale that Hitler clumsily and stiltedly concocted in *Mein Kampf* has absolutely nothing to do with the outlook of his younger self, the picture-postcard artist in Vienna and flâneur with a less than perfect command of correct spelling. Even so, he insists that he learned a 'truly malign object lesson' in the Austrian capital, which led him to recognise 'the Jew' as a 'vector of disease', a 'maggot in a rotting corpse', and a 'spiritual plague'.[50] For, Hitler went on to assert, Jews were behind prostitution in the city every bit as much as they were at the root of socialism and Marxism. 'I have noted the names of almost all the [socialist] leaders there; the vast majority of them are likewise members of the "Chosen Race".'[51]

The anti-Semitic tirades become more concise when he goes on to describe his time in Munich in 1913–14. He says that he put the perceived relationship between Marxism and Judaism to a thorough test there. Accordingly, during the Great War, he claims to have identified Jewish soldiers as 'cowards' and 'defeatists' to a man. Everywhere, he continues, he could see the undermining influence of the Jews, be it at the front, in the field hospital in Beelitz where he was sent after being wounded (1916), during his convalescence in Munich in 1917, and of course in Berlin as well the same year. Hitler essentially omits to mention the period of revolution between the end of the war and the demise of the Bavarian Soviet Republic. It is covered in a scant few words and the observation that the *Räterepublik* was a 'Jewish regime'. And what of Dieter Eckart? In all this, there is no place for the mentor who, from the autumn of 1919 onwards, first enabled

Hitler to embark on this retrospective rewriting of history. In the first volume, which Hitler 'dedicated' to the National Socialist martyrs – those who had been shot dead in the Beer Hall Putsch of November 1923 – there is not a single mention of Eckart, who died that same year. At the end of the final chapter of the second volume, Hitler finally acknowledges his 'Pole Star' as someone 'who as one of the best dedicated his whole life to awakening his people – our people – in his writings and his thoughts and ultimately in his actions too'.[52]

In view of his claim to be the leader of the National Socialist movement, however small it may have been in 1924, Hitler could not afford to reveal his true political trajectory. Thus, he couldn't write about his Jewish friend in the early days in Vienna, the Iron Cross that he owed to the intervention of a Jew, the part he played in the state burial of the Jew Kurt Eisner, of his early allegiance to Social Democracy, or finally his election as shop steward in the replacement battalion of the 'Red Army' of a Soviet Republic that was seen as a 'Jewish' enterprise. Instead, what he committed to paper was surely the most enduring of all his propaganda lies. After all, those lies still predominantly shape the image of the dictator to the present day – both in the public eye and within historical research.

By contrast, Hitler's political and ideological aperçus, which blend together in his book to form a mixture of alleged first-hand experiences and supposed ultimate realisations, strike the reader as wholly authentic. For all of his lack of talent as a writer, what emerges loud and clear is Hitler's cohesive racial ideological worldview. Yet this is also a programmatic manifesto for future National Socialist policy, whose constituent elements he would later put into practice, step by step, after he took power in Germany. Both the future structure and the racial ideological principles of the National Socialist state as well as the main features of his later foreign policy, including the 'necessity' of

wiping Bolshevik Russia from the face of the earth, are anticipated in *Mein Kampf*. Yet sociologically based historiography
refuses to acknowledge this fact, since it reveals the extent to
which an individual was able to determine Germany's path to
catastrophe. Thus, in the face of all the facts, in his biography
of Hitler, Ian Kershaw – trammelled as he is by the dogma of
his academic discipline – asserts that, although Hitler had an
ideology, this only 'amounted to a Utopian vision of national
"redemption"' and 'not a set of middle-range policies'.[53]

In common with many others of his generation of frontline
soldiers, Hitler's starting point for his worldview was a primitive social Darwinism of a kind that he had observed and taken
to heart from his experiences on the battlefield. Hence, Hitler
wrote, all things that happened in the life of a nation (including
wars) were 'not expressions of chance but natural manifestations
of the urge to the self-preservation and growth of a species and
race, even though people are incapable of recognising the innermost mainsprings of their actions'.[54] For him, race was nature,
and it was the duty of humanity to act according to this nature
and its inner necessity – and this necessity meant that only the
strongest would survive.

Central tenets of this ideology for Hitler were the exclusive
identity of each species and racial purity as preconditions for the
self-confidence and strength of a people. Accordingly, he identified 'the most profound and terminal reason for the demise of the
old empire ... in its inability to recognise the racial problem and
its vital importance for the historical advancement of nations'.[55]
The politics of 'compliance' with Versailles and the 'stab in the
back' were therefore merely symptoms for him, the inevitable
consequences of what he saw as the criminally indictable failure
by the Second Empire to 'maintain the purity' of the Aryan race,
the best elements of which had fallen on the battlefields of the
First World War.

Race or 'blood community', which for Hitler was synonymous with the term 'nation', was in his eyes not just an integrative factor but also the ideological underpinning of National Socialism. If everything depended on race, then the human being was not merely the product of certain social circumstances, as 'Jewish Marxism' taught. Instead, race admitted of individuality, which Hitler, who espoused the 'leader principle', saw as a clear point of distinction from Marxist egalitarianism, especially since his conception of race derived more from metaphysics than from biology. The 'superiority of the Aryan race' – provided it kept itself free of 'alien blood' – was therefore in his view also rooted in its idealism, as Houston Stewart Chamberlain had already written and as he had been taught by Eckart.

Basically, none of the ideas that Hitler purveyed about the races in *Mein Kampf* were new. It contained no point or argument that had not already been put forward, albeit in a different context. Primarily, this was of course also true of the trope of the 'soullessly materialistic Jew', whom Hitler characterised as a 'state parasite' and a 'global plague'. For beneath the cloak of the 'Jewish doctrine' of Marxism, Hitler wrote, 'under this cover of social ideas, some truly diabolical aims lie hidden'.[56] He went on: 'By categorically repudiating the role of individual personality and hence of the nation and its racial composition, this doctrine demolishes the fundamental bases of all human civilisation, which essentially depends on these very factors.'[57] From what he had experienced, Hitler claimed that 'one final, great revolution' would ultimately ensue, for:

as the Jew gains political power, so he casts off the last vestiges of disguise he still wears ... Over the course of just a few years, he tries to exterminate all those who represent the nation's intelligentsia, and having thus deprived the people of their natural leaders, he prepares them for their fate as slaves under a perpetual despotism. The most terrible example of this is Russia, where the Jew has killed or starved to death some thirty million people in a round of truly diabolical savagery, and in part through the use of inhuman torture, merely in order that a handful of Jewish literati and stockmarket crooks might keep a great people under their thumb.[58]

His racial ideological impetus crystallised in *Mein Kampf* into the concept of *Lebensraum* ('living space'), thereby creating the economic foundations for a nation whose organisation in terms of its economy would be along the lines of the model proposed by Gottfried Feder. For during the Great War the true implications of what it meant when supplies of food and raw materials were not secured in sufficient quantities had become clear. In solving this problem, Hitler was also influenced by the ideas of the 'geopolitician' Karl Haushofer, one of Rudolf Hess's teachers, who was incarcerated in Landsberg at the same time as Hitler and helped him draft *Mein Kampf*. In Haushofer's view, Germany's resurgence would come about through the formation of a great Euro-Asiatic bloc. The professor saw a vast region, economically and politically unified and extending from the Rhine via the Amur to the islands of Japan with its enormous resources, as the vital prerequisite for Germany's ability to offset the maritime predominance of Britain and the United States.

Yet when Hitler talked about *Lebensraum* in *Mein Kampf*, he had something qualitatively different in mind. He claimed that the National Socialists would 'put a stop to the perpetual Germanic march to the South and West' and instead 'direct our gaze towards the lands of the East'. He went into detail about what he meant by this: 'When we speak of new territory today ... we are thinking primarily of Russia and satellite states that are subject to her.'[59] This was the same Russia that Hitler, on racial ideological grounds, was convinced he had to annihilate. For 'in Russian

Bolshevism we should recognise the attempt that is being made
by the Jew in the twentieth century to secure dominion over the
entire world'.[60]

In Hitler's opinion, this process was already far advanced; in
*Mein Kampf* he wrote that 'the Jew' already saw 'the present European states as weak-willed instruments under his control, be this
indirectly through so-called Western democracy or in the form
of direct domination through Russian Bolshevism'.[61] The same
fate threatened nations in the New World as well: 'Jews control
the financial forces of America on the stock exchange', which
were already planning the conquest of the British Empire.[62] The
destruction of Germany did not serve Britain's interests; instead
it was in the Jewish interest, he stated, and concluded from both
this and the fact that the maritime power Great Britain and the
land power Germany did not have overlapping interests that the
two states were predestined to enter into a future partnership.
Fascist Italy, where the struggle against the 'Jewish world-hydra'
had already been decided in favour of nationalist forces, was
another plus factor in Hitler's calculations.[63]

Hitler's strategy, the basic principles of which he would outline
once more in his so-called 'Second Book' of 1928 (an unedited
transcript of his ideas on foreign policy), foresaw Germany,
Great Britain, and Italy fighting side by side against the 'global
Jewish threat'. Everything ultimately took on an apocalyptic
dimension when Hitler wrote in *Mein Kampf*: 'If the Jew, with
the aid of his Marxist creed, should triumph over the people of
this world, his crown will be mankind's funeral wreath, and this
planet will once again pursue its course through the ether devoid
of any human life, just as it did millions of years ago.'[64]

According to the bizarre logic of this overwrought and fanatical view of the world, saving Western civilisation – and hence, by
the standards of the period, also the world – entailed exterminating the Jews. This belief had steadily matured in Hitler's mind.

Even as early as September 1919, when setting out his position vis-à-vis majority social democracy, he had spoken about 'getting rid of the Jews altogether'. In April 1920, disillusioned by the failure of the Kapp Putsch, he reiterated his 'grim determination ... to tackle the evil at source and to eradicate it root and branch'.[65] The following August, in one of his innumerable speeches in which he launched unbridled attacks on the Jews, he announced:

> And don't think for a moment that you can combat an illness ... without destroying the bacillus, nor should you imagine that you can fight racial tuberculosis without first ensuring that people are free of the pathogen ... Jewish intervention will never come to an end or the poisoning of the people cease as long as the pathogen, the Jew, is not removed from our midst.[66]

A passage from Eckart's final work *Der Bolschewismus von Moses bis Lenin. Zwiegespräch zwischen Adolf Hitler und mir* ('Bolshevism from Moses to Lenin: A dialogue between Adolf Hitler and me'),[67] which was published posthumously, points in much the same direction. In this imagined dialogue, published in 1924 in the form of a pamphlet, Eckart set out his and Hitler's view on the Jews. After the two men have stressed the 'eternally corrosive' role played by the Jews, and the first-person participant in the dialogue (i.e. Eckart) has broached the subject of 'burning down' synagogues and Jewish schools, his third-person interlocutor (Hitler) replies:

> That's the problem, though! Even if a synagogue or a Jewish school or the Old Testament had never existed, the Jewish spirit would still be present, spreading its malign influence. It's been there since the dawn of time; and there has never been a Jew, not a single one, who didn't embody it.[68]

Since spirit and race are inextricably bound up with each other, for both the fictitious and the real Hitler, it follows that the 'evil Jewish spirit' would only vanish from the world if the 'Jewish race' ceased to exist.

This monstrous proposition, which would become a reality with the genocide of Europe's Jews during the Second World War, was already firmly embedded in Hitler's thinking even by the time the first volume of *Mein Kampf* appeared in 1924. It was his response to what he once called the 'worst crime of all time perpetrated against humanity': namely, the ongoing influence, as he saw it, of 'international Jewry' in the form of Bolshevism and the 'stock market'.[69] In other words, the class-based murder conducted by the Bolsheviks was a logical and factual precondition for the racial murder carried out by the National Socialists, just as Nolte maintained. But it wasn't the only precondition. It also required a deep loathing of acquisitive 'Jewish capitalism', which Hitler believed was every bit as destructive as Bolshevism.

# 5

# Hitler's Rise to Power

*How could a racist fanatic become chancellor?*

One of the endlessly recurring questions of German history is how a highly civilised nation, which had produced Goethe and Schiller, could possibly have made a man like Hitler its head of government. How could the Germans have placed the fate of their country in the hands of a deluded racist fanatic? Current historians suggest that the populace was infected with a deep-seated anti-Semitism and a pronounced penchant for authoritarian structures, and that both of these propensities finally found their logical expression in the figure of Hitler. If this were truly the case, however, wouldn't Hitler have been able to exploit the chaos that ensued in the early years of the Weimar Republic, when Versailles and revolution shook the country to its very foundations? Yet at that stage his NSDAP was never anything more than an insignificant splinter group. Why did this all change with the elections of September 1930? The worldwide Great Depression, which hit Germany with full force, cannot on its own explain this occurrence.

When Hitler the failed putschist was released from gaol in Landsberg Fortress in December 1924, times were hard for someone like him. It took a highly developed sense of vocation on his part – indeed, a certain megalomania – to want to proceed with his mission, which he had been forced to curtail the previous year. To be sure, he had the support of loyal acolytes, who

during his term in prison, where he wrote the first volume of
*Mein Kampf*, inculcated in him the idea that he was some kind
of new Messiah. However, this had nothing to do with the actual
situation. In real life, he was a political nobody, a failure who,
even if he wasn't already there, seemed destined to be consigned
to oblivion.

More firmly convinced than ever of his mission, in February
1925 – the same month that Friedrich Ebert, the guardian of
the republic, died aged just fifty-four – Hitler relaunched the
NSDAP. He expressly staked his personal claim to leadership of
the party. He clearly indicated the direction of travel he and his
party would take when he announced his political comeback at
the Bürgerbräukeller in Munich – in other words, quite deliberately choosing the same location where the Beer Hall Putsch
had started two years before. There, he declaimed to his followers: 'Let's take the fight to the Satanic power that has plunged
Germany into this misery, let's declare war on Marxism and the
spiritual sponsor of this global plague and epidemic, the Jew.'[1]

What followed was a root-and-branch reorganisation of the
NSDAP. As an undisciplined, directionless little group, whose
members were poles apart politically and ideologically, it was
urgently in need of reform. In the city of Elberfeld in the Rhineland, a small band of National Socialists from north-west
Germany had established their branch office and were touting
the 'coming dictatorship of socialist ideas'.[2] Their chief spokesman was the editor of the local nationalist newspaper *Völkische
Freiheit* ('National freedom'), Joseph Goebbels, an unemployed
intellectual with a weakness for Russian literature, especially the
works of Fyodor Dostoyevsky. As a 'German communist',[3] to
quote his own description of himself, he was largely instrumental in ensuring that nationalist Bolshevik tendencies prevailed
in Elberfeld. There, they regarded Lenin first and foremost as a
Russian nationalist, while seeing the hated German November

Revolution as the work of an international, and hence Jewish, form of communism.

This was bound to cause conflict with the NSDAP in Munich, and it was duly sparked by the outcome of the meeting at Locarno in October 1925. This international conference, at which the German representatives were chancellor Hans Luther and his foreign minister Gustav Stresemann, set the seal on Germany's renunciation of any attempt to alter by force its western border, which had been set at Versailles, and also confirmed the demilitarisation of the Rhineland enshrined in the treaty. For the West-facing Stresemann, this was a first step towards realising his ambitious goals. Central to these was a definitive solution to the reparations question on favourable terms to the Germans, and a revision of the country's eastern frontier – including regaining the city of Danzig and the Polish Corridor as well as relocating the border in Upper Silesia. He aimed to achieve this through a policy of cooperation with France, the keystone of which would be a close economic interdependence on a European basis.

Meanwhile, the NSDAP working group established by Gregor Strasser in Elberfeld, which brought together all the Nazi Gauleiters from the north and west of Germany, saw Locarno as effectively incorporating Germany into the Western 'battle front' against Russia.[4] However, Strasser insisted that the primary objective of German policy should instead be to regain its freedom, in other words to continue to oppose Versailles and the Western powers. In this struggle, the working group stressed, Russia was the ally that fate had dealt Germany. Furthermore, in accordance with its revolutionary social ideas, in November 1925 and the following January, the Elberfeld group even discussed the possibility of putting forward an alternative to the NSDAP's twenty-five points of principle outlined in February 1920. Its aim was to replace these with a programme with a markedly more socialist policy focus. In Munich, Hitler's close confederate Gottfried Feder complained bitterly that 'even Soviet agents ... could not have been more effective in promoting this pro-Bolshevik course within our ranks'.[5]

At a meeting convened by the Führer in Bamberg in February 1926, by exercising his authority and through the sheer force of his rhetoric, Hitler managed to extract at least a formal assent to his anti-Bolshevik and hence anti-Russian policy direction from the apostates from the 'Mecca of German socialism', as Goebbels had in the meantime taken to calling Elberfeld. This helped strengthen his position as party leader. Goebbels remarked in his diary: 'What sort of Hitler did we see? A reactionary? ... The Russian question is completely beside the point. The prospect of Italy and England as natural allies – horrifying! Our task is to smash Bolshevism. Bolshevism is Jewish eyewash! We must inherit Russia's mantle.'[6]

As foreign policy wasn't a priority for them anyway, the National Socialists from Elberfeld continued to plough their own more socialist furrow where internal affairs were concerned. Ultimately, differences with Munich remained until 1933. Much more momentous, however, was that the party's agenda ceased to be discussed after Bamberg. Accordingly, Hitler's ideological construct of the 'Jewish global conspiracy' was a closed book to the great majority of Nazi functionaries. Least of all did they grasp the true scope of his murderous racial ideology. For the set pieces of this ideology that he constantly trotted out were not understood in their true context. Instead, they were simply dismissed as an anti-Semitic foible of the party leader and attributed to the bad influence of the reactionary, nationalist, and anti-Semitic circles he moved in. For a long time, Hitler had Goebbels' split personality to thank for the opposing positions within the NSDAP not causing a schism. He would soon appoint Goebbels as Gauleiter (Nazi regional governor) of Berlin. The

Rhinelander had remained a socialist at heart, while at the same time displaying a doglike devotion to Hitler.

As long as his leadership was not questioned, Hitler largely let matters within the NSDAP take their own course. He was focused on his own obsession and not the direction of his deputies around the country. He made the Jewish conspiracy the repeated subject of his speeches but also treated the subject at length in the second volume of *Mein Kampf,* which appeared in December 1926, eighteen months after the first. There, he once again conjured up the image of a 'global struggle' between the races, when he wrote:

> The Bolshevisation of Germany – that is to say, the extermination of the nationalistically and patriotically minded German intelligentsia, paving the way for the oppression of the German workforce beneath the yoke of international Jewish finance – is only intended as a prelude to a further expansion of Jewish power aimed at bringing the whole world under its dominion. As has so often been the case in history, Germany is the main pivotal point of this formidable struggle. If our people and our state should fall victim to these oppressors of nations, who lust after blood and money, then the entire earth will become ensnared by that hydra.[7]

It is a myth that the chaotically structured volumes of Hitler's autobiography, with their apocalyptic scenarios of global conspiracy that were presently combined into a single book, instantly found a large readership and a corresponding resonance among the German public. To begin with, its impact was minimal, as was support for the party of a man who had only ever come to the attention of the wider German public on one brief occasion, when he appeared in the dock of the courthouse in Munich and defended his attempted Beer Hall Putsch. As a result, membership of the NSDAP flatlined. Likewise, there was no question of the NSDAP enjoying success at the ballot box. In the first round of the presidential election of March 1925, Hitler's candidate Erich von Ludendorff suffered an embarrassing defeat by winning just over 1 per cent of the vote. (Hitler was able to hush this up to some extent by throwing his support behind Paul von Hindenburg, who made the running in the second round.) The party had an equally dismal showing in the state elections later the same year, achieving 2.5 per cent in Oldenburg and only 1.2 per cent in Baden.

If hardly anyone was interested in Hitler and the NSDAP, then this was due to a recent upturn in Germany's fortunes. Since the signing of the Locarno Pact, the country had been positively basking in a sense of euphoria. After all the years of national humiliation, Germany had returned to the world political stage. In 1926, it joined the League of Nations. Then came a Nobel Peace Prize for foreign minister Stresemann, who received the award jointly with his French counterpart Aristide Briand. The talk now was increasingly of a new, peaceful Europe, in which the trenches of the First World War would finally be consigned to history. The old dreams that many a majority Social Democrat politician had dreamt in early 1919 now seemed to be within the realms of the possible.

This was a period of self-delusion in Germany. Enthusiasm was unbounded when Briand unveiled his plan for a 'European Federal Union'. Yet in the end, all the French statesman was aiming at with this proposal was to cement the territorial status quo established at Versailles and thwart any German attempt to revise the treaty. Paris duly rejected Stresemann's demand that Eupen and Malmedy be returned to Germany as well as his call for the plebiscite in the Saarland, which at Versailles had been set for 1935, to be brought forward. It was only in June 1930 that the French occupying force withdrew from the Rhineland, whereupon the region became a demilitarised zone. As far as the question of Germany's eastern borders was concerned, the French government threw its weight behind Warsaw, which refused to countenance any modifications whatsoever. Stresemann's economically liberal policy of revision, which had been so fêted at the outset, was thus doomed to failure. In 1929, he glumly told a British interlocutor: 'You gave away practically nothing, and the tiny concessions you did finally grant came too late. We've lost an entire generation of German youth. That's my tragedy and your fault.'[8]

Yet in 1926–7, none of this could have been foreseen. A mood of unbridled optimism prevailed in Germany. The hardship and misery of the post-war period were things of the past. The country's standard of living rose as normality gradually returned. Instilled with a new zest for life, and after many years of privations, people now caught up on all the amusements and entertainment they had been missing for so long. It was not for nothing that the ensuing years became known as the 'Roaring Twenties'. Yet the glittering facades of this breathless period hid a German society that was as ruptured as ever. While some people shunned all traditional values and norms, others yearned for the return of a bygone era; but looming over all of this was the country's rankling defeat in the Great War.

The glitter of this period outshone the dour propaganda put out by the Nazi Party. Regional elections over these two years brought little in the way of success for the National Socialists. It says a great deal that the party celebrated winning a mere 5 per cent of the votes in the small, rural region of Mecklenburg-Strelitz. Its share of the vote was well below this in other election contests. One reason for this was the parlous public image of division presented by the NSDAP, where, in the eyes of its 'strategist' Gottfried Feder, discord, strife, and dilettantism reigned supreme. The only person in the party to remain unaffected was

Adolf Hitler, who – whether in his public speaking engagements or the annual 'spectaculars' staged by the movement, such as the memorial march held to honour the victims of the putsch outside the Feldherrnhalle in Munich or the Nuremberg party congresses, where the party and its stormtroopers put on a show of strength – continued to style himself as an 'instrument of destiny'.

In light of the major differences of opinion within the party, in the campaign for the general election of 1928 Hitler set the guidelines for the NSDAP's propaganda drive. In addition to Versailles and Marxism, his major themes now also included the Locarno Pact and Stresemann's policies as well as criticism of the government's export-driven economic policy, which was incapable of resolving the contradiction between population numbers and *Lebensraum*. These guidelines did not win the party any new supporters, as everyone wanted to revise Versailles, Bolshevism (whether perceived as 'Jewish' or not) no longer seemed to pose a threat, and talk of 'living space' sounded rather esoteric. What's more, Hitler's intemperate anti-Semitic diatribes tended to put voters off, as for example at the end of February 1928 when he proclaimed that the National Socialists would never allow 'our German nation to come completely under the control of a foreign agency ... let the blood that the Lord God gave us be bastardised ... permit our whole civilisation to fall prey to Negro influence ... or allow all our elite intellectual posts to be filled by an alien people'. In his peroration, Hitler invoked Our Saviour, who, he claimed, had described 'those very same Jews ... [as] vipers, sons of Satan, and devils' and refused to make peace with them.[9]

The general election of May 1928 ended in fiasco for Hitler, with his party gaining just 2.6 per cent of the vote. Nor was that the worst of it: in the regional elections held at the same time, the Nazis won only 1.8 per cent in Prussia, while in Berlin, where the fanatical Goebbels had been agitating for over two years, they attracted a paltry 1.5 per cent. In Bavaria, however, Hitler's party did manage 6.1 per cent. The other big loser in the general election was the conservative, nationalist DNVP, which was forsaken by a quarter of its former voters. This was in marked contrast to the SPD, which with more than nine million votes (or 29.8 per cent of the electorate) enjoyed its biggest success since 1919. The KPD also had an improved showing, ending up with 10.6 per cent. SPD-led centre-left administrations under Hermann Müller and Otto Braun took office in the country as a whole and Prussia, respectively; these appeared to guarantee a continuation of the relative stability of the recent past.

The 1928 elections showed that there was no place in the political landscape of the Weimar Republic for a racist like Hitler. They also seemed to suggest that there could be no talk of anti-Semitism taking hold in the country. Indeed, the very opposite appeared to be the case, for the number of anti-Semitic organisations and groups also declined. Even the notorious Thule Society had disbanded in 1925. Jews were part of this Germany just like everyone else. Fewer and fewer people were bothered that Jews were especially well represented in cultural life or the academic sector. After all, figures like the physicians Otto Meyerhof and Paul Ehrlich and the physicist Albert Einstein, to name just a handful of luminaries, had enhanced the country's reputation abroad.

That Hitler nonetheless made it onto the great national stage was facilitated by an event over which neither he nor indeed German politics as a whole had any influence: the Great Depression. There had been a downturn in economic activity as early as the autumn of 1928, leading to an uncommonly sharp rise in unemployment. Whereas the number of those out of work was still below the million mark in October 1927, by December 1928 almost two million people were without a job. In February 1929, there were 3.2 million unemployed. And there was no end in sight. For the great economic crisis, which began with the Wall Street Crash as a result of a speculation bubble on the massively overheated American stock market and led to the collapse of stock markets worldwide, hit Germany especially hard, thanks to its high level of borrowing from the United States. American investors withdrew their funds from Germany, spelling bankruptcy for countless German companies and bringing about the collapse of large banks. Like some bad omen, Stresemann's death in October 1929 seemed to foretell the catastrophe into which the country was now slipping.

The hardship of the immediate post-war period now returned to Germany with breakneck speed. Unemployment meant destitution. The situation was exacerbated by a persistent rise in the cost of living that even made life more difficult for those who were still in gainful employment. Against this background, the negotiations about the Young Plan, the latest attempt to restructure reparations payments, struck most Germans as an absurd and cynical game with figures running into the billions. When the conference of experts convened in Paris in 1929, the creditor countries set their annual estimated payment demands at around 2.7 million gold marks, which was rapidly scaled down to 2.3 million.

The internal enemies of the Weimar Republic had no need to generate any propaganda to establish a link between the incipient mass destitution and the excessive demands of the victorious nations, as a simple cause-and-effect relationship between the two seemed perfectly self-evident from the outset. Some critics castigated capitalism, while others blamed the 'vicarious agents' of the policy of entente in the form of the Social Democrat-led government in Berlin, pointing out that chancellor Hermann Müller had, in his previous role as foreign minister, been part of the German delegation that had travelled to Versailles in the summer of 1919 to sign the humiliating treaty. The swift reduction by the Western powers of the total sum still owing in reparations to 112 billion Reichsmarks did nothing to alter the situation.

In these circumstances, Hitler decided on a step that reawakened with new ferocity the ideological conflict between the Munich headquarters and the Strasser wing of the party. He formed an alliance with the leading representative of the hated 'forces of reaction'. Together with the leader of the DNVP Alfred Hugenberg, the *Stahlhelm* (the foremost ex-servicemen's association representing former frontline soldiers) and other far-right organisations, the NSDAP now became involved in an official commission to organise a popular referendum against the Young Plan. This undertaking ended in December 1929 with a heavy defeat in the vote. All the same, it was a success for Hitler and his party as it put him in the public eye and even raised his profile as the main spokesman of the 'national opposition'. This duly paid dividends in local elections in liberal Baden and in Thuringia, a former stronghold of the Left, where the NSDAP gained 11.3 per cent. Wilhelm Frick, later Reich minister of the interior under Hitler, thus became the first Nazi to hold a ministerial post in a regional administration.

Not least in the light of these gains, Hitler continued to invest all his hopes in a crisis breaking out. Developments were to prove him right. Although the Young Plan was passed by the German parliament on 12 March 1930 by a majority of 270 to 192, it was only the SPD that stood four-square behind the treaty. The vote on the revision of reparations payments and the agreements reached in parallel had shown how flimsy the ties that bound together the governing parties now were. Indeed, they were to finally snap when a row broke out shortly afterwards over whether contributions to the unemployment insurance fund should be raised by half a per cent or not. The parties failed to reach a minimal consensus, given that the SPD was under pressure from the trades unions, and was also fearful of losing too many voters to the communists if it agreed to this measure. Müller's administration stepped down at the end of March 1930. The last Grand Coalition government of the Weimar Republic was no longer equal to the task of tackling the growing international economic crisis against the background of the psychological and material burdens caused by defeat in the First World War.

German society drifted apart and became polarised. Faced with these enormous, obvious, and irreconcilable differences, the country increasingly lost its 'internal compass'. Special interests, egotisms, and resentments triumphed over the common good. Speaking from a conservative perspective, the future president of the senate of the Free City of Danzig, Hermann Rauschning, observed that 'the last standards and certainties of a spiritual and moral order' had been abandoned. In his book *Die Revolution des Nihilismus* ('The revolution of nihilism'), Rauschning went on to explain: 'The tension within a deeply unsettled system created an atmosphere of mistrust and ever-present violence … the nation was in a state of flux that had not been imposed from outside but which had arisen from profound changes in the spiritual and social fabric.'[10]

The chancellorship of the centrist politician Heinrich Brüning was now meant to steer a course out of this debacle. This former officer from the Great War, who was of the best repute, was recommended to President Hindenburg by General Kurt von Schleicher, the head of the armed forces ministry and a personal friend of the Hindenburg household. Brüning now governed with shifting majorities of the Centre Party, DVP, DDP, BVP, and DNVP, as well as the Reich Party of the German Middle Class and the Popular Conservative Alliance. His big idea to overcome the crisis was deflation, which he aimed to bring about through consistent budgetary consolidation and state-imposed low wages and price cuts. Germany was to shrink its way to good fiscal health in order to become more competitive again in the global marketplace. Brüning also took the view that this economic policy of his would render the question of reparations payments an absurd irrelevance because it would be in nobody's commercial interests to see Germany completely collapse. However, the price of such a policy was high. Unemployment soared in Germany to reach a peak of 6.14 million in February 1932. The common image of German cities became one of endless lines of people queuing outside labour exchanges for dole payments that didn't even allow them to subsist. The desperate hardship being suffered by millions created a social powder keg and radicalised political debate.

It was at this point that the KPD declared open warfare on those whom they called the 'oppressors of the proletariat' in Germany and decried as 'Social Fascists': namely, the Social Democrats. The communists accused the SPD of being the 'main organiser of a united capitalist and anti-Soviet front'.[11] The KPD attack was orchestrated by Moscow – the same Moscow that, at Rapallo in 1922, had agreed among other things to a secret collaboration between the Red Army and the Reichswehr, and in Berlin in 1926 had concluded a treaty of friendship and cooperation with Germany. Following the failure of the attempted coup of October 1923, Stalin had been forced to abandon his far-reaching revolutionary objectives regarding Germany, but now the new party line called for the further Sovietisation of the KPD, thereby creating a powerful political force to promote the foreign-policy interests of the Soviet Union. After the German section of the Comintern identified a 'pre-revolutionary climate' in Germany in early 1929,[12] the intention was that the KPD should start to dismantle the Weimar Republic. All means to achieve this were considered legitimate, even partial alliances with Hitler's party, as happened during the strike on the Berlin transport network in 1932.

The KPD's activities began in the capital on 1 May 1929, the 'Working Class Day of Struggle', when it called for banned demonstrations to be held in many parts of the city. Several days of pitched street battles ensued between the 'Red Frontline Soldiers' League' (RFB) of the KPD and the police. The result of 'Bloody May' was thirty-three dead, 198 non-fatal casualties among civilians, forty-seven policemen wounded, and 1,228 arrests. The following months descended into a 'limited civil war'. This period witnessed targeted political assassinations, such as those of the Social Democrat Berlin police captains Paul Anlauf and Franz Lenk, carried out by a group of Red Front fighters that included one Erich Mielke. After the Second World War, Mielke became the state security minister of the German Democratic Republic (East Germany).

Despite the determined opposition shown to the communists by the SPD, it was increasingly the party of Adolf Hitler, with its radical brand of anti-Bolshevism, that captured the popular imagination as the KPD's true adversary. People gradually began to take the NSDAP seriously. After Heinz Neumann, the editor-in-chief of the *Rote Fahne* newspaper coined the slogan 'Smash the Fascists wherever you find them!' in August 1929,[13] violent clashes escalated between gangs of thugs from the banned Red Front and Nazi Brownshirts of the *Sturmabteilung* (SA), which at times was also a proscribed organisation. Acts of murder and homicide were glorified as 'fighting for a better world'. Those who were engaged in the brawls saw themselves as the vanguard of the movements they represented. For instance, on the National Socialist side, the Berlin SA stormtrooper leader Horst Wessel wrote the words for a battle song entitled *Die Fahne hoch* ('Raise your banner!') in the summer of 1929. Not least as a result of his 'martyr's death' at the hands of communists in February 1930, Nazi propaganda subsequently turned the 'Horst Wessel Song' into a second national anthem.

The parliamentary elections of September 1930 saw the 'Brownshirt battalions' of the SA out in force on the streets. At a stroke, the ballot catapulted the NSDAP to within touching distance of power. The party won a sensational 18.3 per cent of the vote – a political earthquake. Overnight, Hitler's party had become the second strongest political force in the country, behind the SPD (who still commanded 24.5 per cent) but ahead of the communists, who polled 13.1 per cent. What had happened? How had the NSDAP now succeeded in making political capital out of a national crisis, something that had eluded them in the early days of the Republic? Admittedly, Hitler's party was an increasingly visible presence on the streets, and it had in the intervening years built up a modern, efficient party apparatus. It exploited new ways and means of spreading propaganda, such as the radio. It insistently intoned the mantra of wanting to come to power solely through legal means. Moreover, by standing shoulder to shoulder with Alfred Hugenberg's DNVP and by combatting the KPD, it had also made a name for itself among right-wing voters. Above and beyond all this, there was another element that cleared a crucial obstacle out of Hitler's path to power. For Hitler had by this stage realised that he was not going to make any headway with the general populace by continuing to air his positively manic obsession with racial ideology. It had become clear to him that he would not succeed in mobilising the broad mass of the people (whom he regarded as 'lumpen') behind himself and his party by harping on about his special 'sovereign knowledge' on this matter, so he instructed his party to soft-pedal its anti-Semitic propaganda. For the same reason, he held back from publishing his 'Second Book', which he completed in the summer of 1928 and in which he programmatically outlined a future National Socialist foreign policy. Thus, it was at most only his immediate circle in Munich who knew that he continued to be driven by an ardent desire to annihilate the 'Jewish-Bolshevik

Soviet Union' and to cover his back strategically in the West for
a war in the East by negotiating a reconciliation of interests with
Britain – or that, with an eye to forming an alliance with Fascist
Italy, he had resolved to let the South Tyrol region, which had
been ceded to Italy by the Treaty of St Germain, remain Italian.

To be sure, Hitler had already aired most of his views in *Mein
Kampf* or piecemeal over the course of countless earlier speeches.
Now he deliberately refrained from doing so – in the knowledge
that things he had once written or said would quickly be dis-
missed as 'all water under the bridge' in these fast-moving times.
He no longer spoke of a 'Jewish global conspiracy' in public.
Whenever he did publicly attack the Jews, it was only in the form
of brief asides and allusions, as a more restrained form of anti-
Semitism seemed to play well. Admittedly, things were different
whenever he spoke to the smaller circle of his close followers in
Munich, in other words insiders who were fully conversant with
his racial ideology. There, he did not hold back from castigating
'global Jewish Marxism', since this seemed to him to be on the
rise throughout the world, be it in far-off China or in Nicaragua
in Central America. In the Soviet Union, where Hitler followed
developments closely, he believed that 'Jewish hegemony' was
nearing 'completion'. Time and again when addressing his inner
circle, he would invoke the apocalyptic scenario of Russia's fate
being repeated in Germany, only under 'even more nightmarish
circumstances ... the fate that Russia suffered is as nothing compared to what will happen in Germany'.[14]

As for the NSDAP as a whole, the level of anti-Semitic agitation depended on the personal attitude of whichever of Hitler's
deputies was involved. Unlike Julius Streicher in Franconia or
Robert Ley in the Rhineland, Gauleiters such as Wilhelm Murr
in Württemberg or Albert Krebs in Hamburg were completely
indifferent on the question of anti-Semitism. The North German
faction of the NSDAP around the brothers Gregor and Otto

Strasser, for example, had no truck with a 'collective' anti-Sem-itism and considered the idea of a 'Jewish global conspiracy' complete nonsense. A review of Nazi literature conducted by the 'Central Association of German Citizens of the Jewish Faith' in 1932 even concluded that although there were plenty of instances of anti-Semitism – especially in areas and groups that saw them-selves threatened by Jewish competition – there was nothing to suggest that the NSDAP took a consistent anti-Semitic line.[15]

In general, the image presented by Hitler's party was so multi-faceted that contemporaries found it almost impossible to ascribe a clear ideological direction to it. The North German Strasser wing was on the Left, as it always had been, while Hitler and his South German party were perceived as being on the Right. Consequently, the agitation of the party as a whole was directed in populist fashion against practically everything: the Weimar system that had allowed Versailles to happen, the so-called regime parties such as the Conservatives, Liberals, or Social Democrats, but above all against the communists and their Moscow backers. However, the Jewish component in its anti-Soviet propaganda now played a far less significant part than previously.

Leaving aside campaigning for revision of the Versailles Treaty, in which Hitler had made common cause with Hugen-berg, the political programme put forward by Hitler and the NSDAP came across as extremely vague – as is often the case with populist and protest parties. There was little there by way of a constructive agenda. Instead, it was a mish-mash of polem-ics and pseudo-truths, and no end of emotive appeals, with Hitler making repeated references to 'providence' and citing inappropriate analogies with German history. In October 1930 Thomas Mann, reacting to the election results of the previous month, remarked that the way voters had flocked to the 'mass emotional appeal' of National Socialism could not simply be explained by the economic crisis. Instead, he claimed, it also fed off people renouncing their 'belief in reason; fully in keeping with the wayward mental state of a populace that has taken leave of its senses is a grotesque style of politics that employs Salvation Army methods like mass knee-jerk responses, bell-ringing, hallelujahs, and the dervish-like repetition of monotonous slogans until everyone is frothing at the mouth.'[16]

In the eyes of many people, Hitler had become a blank slate onto which they projected all their wishes and hopes for a better future. Thus, he appeared the ideal man to millions from across the political spectrum who were suffering joblessness and a lack of focus and who longed for a proactive state to tackle the great economic crisis, unlike governments that represented the 'system'. He was also the man of choice for all those who still felt at home in the authoritarian society of the imperial age and who had no time for the diversity of a republic that seemed in terminal decline, yearning instead for order and discipline. He was the man for First World War veterans, who struggled to come to terms with the idea that all their sacrifices had been in vain – the unequivocal message conveyed by Erich Maria Remarque's novel *All Quiet on the Western Front*, which had sold in millions. Hitler was also the man of choice for millions of Germans living in regions that had been ceded to or occupied by the victorious nations, who placed their trust in him alone to bring them 'home to the Reich'.

Hitler was able to score highly for his fight against Bolshevism that, as he repeatedly stressed, he intended to see through to the bitter end. For the paramilitary wing of the KPD was continuing to spread terror throughout the country, allowing the SA to cast itself in the role of saviour of the fatherland by opposing it, in the process of which it paid a far higher price than its adversaries. This failure was reflected in the statistics, which showed that in 1931 in the Berlin region alone, 1,228 communists fell victim to political violence, whereas the number of National Socialists killed was 4,699.[17] Thanks to the experiences of the revolutionary period, anyone in Germany at this time who was not a communist or a KPD sympathiser saw the main threat to democracy as coming from the communists. The KPD, which in the final days of the Weimar Republic commanded 16.9 per cent of votes, was not unreasonably regarded as Moscow's 'fifth column'. It was the party of a foreign power, as revealed not least by the fact that members of the Red Front Fighting League were required to swear allegiance to the Soviet Union.

The situation resembled that in the early days of the republic, except that it was now Hitler's NSDAP and not the majority SPD that was at the forefront in battling the communists or the Bolsheviks. This factor caused the NSDAP to be seen as more acceptable, even within the ranks of the SPD. The Social Democrat Berlin chief of police Albert Grzesinski voiced a widely held view when he declared in the autumn of 1930: 'I don't regard the National Socialists as the threat that they are seen as in some quarters; the communists represent a far greater danger.'[18] After being forced to flee Germany, the very same Grzesinski later claimed to have said the exact opposite. He was just one of many who saw things quite differently with the benefit of hindsight.

Certainly, the repercussions of economic crisis, which had brought the terrorism-plagued country close to collapse, and of the shift in the political balance of power, were felt in the German parliament. One by one, the parties that supported Brüning's chancellorship fell away, leaving him with no choice but to tender his resignation in October 1931. As any attempt to form a new government on the basis of a parliamentary major-ity seemed a hopeless proposition, Brüning and the president agreed that a cabinet should be formed that was reliant not on a majority in parliament but solely on Hindenburg's exercise of emergency powers, and derived its legitimacy indirectly from the fact that the president had been democratically elected.

Brüning thus wielded sufficient power to govern, especially

since he and his defence minister Wilhelm Groener jointly took control of the internal affairs portfolio, and the German army, the *Reichswehr* – primarily through the figure of Hindenburg as commander in chief – was also brought on side. The only qualification to this arrangement, albeit a crucial one, was that Brüning was now wholly dependent upon Hindenburg; he was the president's chancellor, indeed the chancellor by presidential decree. Henceforth, the key person on whom the weal and woe of the republic depended, was therefore an eighty-four-year-old who could hire and fire the chancellor, dissolve parliament, and interfere in the legislative process by issuing emergency decrees in accordance with Article 48 of the Imperial Constitution. In his heart of hearts, Hindenburg had remained a monarchist, yet impelled by his innate sense of duty still attempted to satisfy the demands of a parliamentary democracy. As long as the field marshal from the Great War – who was still revered by large sections of the populace, who saw him as a new version of the former Kaiser – did not waver, the country had good prospects of making it through the vale of tears.

In order to steer matters in the right direction, notwithstanding his advanced age, Hindenburg even decided to run for the highest state office once more in the forthcoming presidential elections in March. Meanwhile, Hitler, who had been busy wooing all manner of potential allies – much to the annoyance of many in his party, he even spoke at the Industrialists' Club in Düsseldorf – resolved to make a direct bid for power himself. Knowing that he was in a blind alley with no clear way forward, the First World War private threw down the gauntlet to the field marshal. Despite running a huge propaganda campaign, in which he shuttled around by aircraft for the first time to deliver speeches in several cities on the same day, Hitler lost the presidential election. He gained 36.8 per cent in the second round of voting in mid-April, compared to Hindenburg's 53.1 per cent.

Hindenburg's re-election temporarily strengthened Brüning's position but did nothing to alter the trend that had become apparent in regional elections in Prussia and other provinces like Bavaria, Württemberg, Braunschweig, Hamburg, and Anhalt – a trend that threatened to gradually squeeze the life out of the middle ground of politics. Everywhere the political extremes grew stronger, in spite of all the proscriptions, restrictions, and conditions that the state had imposed on them. Evidently, fewer and fewer Germans had any faith that the democratic system was capable of surmounting the crisis. In the Prussian regional parliament, Hitler's party now no longer held a mere six seats but 162, while Ernst Thälmann's KPD returned fifty-seven delegates. The Prussian administration of the Social Democrat Otto Braun that had been kept in power by a coalition of the SPD, the Centre Party, and the German State Party (DStP: a party created by the merger of the former DDP and two other smaller organisations) thereby lost its parliamentary majority. It stepped down but continued to conduct the business of government as the absolute majority required for a new president of the Prussian parliament to be elected had not been achieved. Despite such successes, however, Hitler had not moved a single step closer to his goal. Goebbels reflected the sombre mood among the NSDAP leadership when he noted in his diary that they would have to gain power within the foreseeable future, 'otherwise we'll win all the electoral battles but lose the war'.[19]

It was now that pure chance came to Hitler's aid. A row over agricultural reforms put forward by Brüning that ran counter to the interests of the Prussian landowner Hindenburg lost the chancellor the president's favour. Angered and prone to being manipulated as a result of his growing senility, the president fell completely under the spell of Schleicher, who was well informed about events and already had in mind a new candidate for the chancellorship. Schleicher made the general's 'concerns' about the 'indecisive and vacillating policies of the chancellor' – whom Hindenburg claimed was refusing to do what was necessary and pursue a clear right-leaning course – his own and resolved to drop Brüning as his protégé.[20]

This was a moment of destiny for the Weimar Republic, heralding as it did the end of a relatively stable period of presidential rule. What ensued was a morass of intrigues in which the geriatric president, whose mind was failing, increasingly became the hapless puppet of those around him – all at a time when, by Brüning's own account, he was agonisingly close to achieving his aims. Bit by bit, the danger of a complete collapse of the state had been averted and a state of calm restored to the economy and the financial markets. At the preliminary negotiations for the Lausanne–Ouchy conference of June–July 1932, it now emerged that even France, which had been presented by the Americans with the prospect of having all its war debts to the United States written off, would finally renounce the economic 'scorched earth' policy it had hitherto pursued towards the German Reich. A few weeks later, the conference delegates agreed on a final German payment of three billion gold marks, thus ending the round of reparations that had begun thirteen years earlier in Versailles. Consequently, job creation schemes, which had been delayed up till now, could finally be implemented in Germany. Some progress had also been made on the restrictions to German rearmament.

Instead of being able to continue to pursue his course of economic consolidation on this basis and to finally lead Germany out of crisis, Brüning was now forced to go. On the warmest of recommendations from Schleicher, Hindenburg invited Schleicher's close acquaintance Franz von Papen, a backbencher from the Centre Party, to form a new government. Schleicher had once called Papen 'a hat with no head in it', when conceding that he was no great thinker but added, 'Then again, he was never meant to be that.'[21] Papen now led a 'cabinet of barons' consisting exclusively of DNVP members or people with no political affiliation, and without any backing in parliament but once again relying solely on the emergency powers of an aging president.

Hindenburg sanctioned Papen to dissolve parliament in June 1932 and to set new elections for July. One again, a Nazi propaganda wave swept through Germany, with the ever-present Hitler criss-crossing the country by aircraft. The election campaign was accompanied by an unprecedented surge of violence, for 1932 was to be the year of reckoning for the communists as well. A grim struggle ensued, against 'the bourgeoisie' and 'fascism' on the one side, and against the 'global scourge of Bolshevism' on the other. In Prussia alone, the months of June and July brought a hundred political murders. Count Harry Kessler wrote: 'There are bitter armed clashes between two ideologies that spurn any thought of compromise … it's like the St Bartholomew Day's Massacre on a daily basis.'[22]

When eighteen people were killed in Altona, near Hamburg, on a single 'Bloody Sunday', Papen used this as an excuse to get rid of the last and most significant bastion of a dependable republican legislature and executive in Germany, under the pretext that the Prussian government was no longer capable of keeping order. Otto Braun, the Social Democrat caretaker prime minister, was forced to step down. The power to govern as Reich administrator was transferred to Franz Bracht, a trusted ally of Papen. With this so-called Prussian Coup, which ultimately met with no resistance, Schleicher and Papen hoped to take the wind out of the sails of Nazi agitation.

However, that remained just a pipe dream. In the sixth parliamentary election to be held since the end of the war, the NSDAP gained 37.4 per cent and became the strongest party. The communists won 14.3 per cent, meaning that parties that wanted to abolish the republic now commanded a parliamentary

majority. On the strength of these results, Hitler, who held fast
to his policy of all or nothing, since only this would enable him
to pursue his insane racial ideological objectives, laid claim to
the chancellorship. Hindenburg and Papen, however, refused
and offered him the post of vice-chancellor instead. In revenge
for this snub, the National Socialists inflicted a serious defeat
on Papen. Hermann Goering of the NSDAP, who had become
president of the Reichstag, pulled off a procedural trick which
ensured that the new presidentially appointed chancellor lost a
vote of no confidence. The upshot was another round of elections scheduled for November 1932.

Yet Hitler's gamble that he would now come to power through
the votes of the German electorate did not pay off. Most people
did not want him as chancellor. Alongside a general weariness
with the voting process, it was primarily his untenable rejection-
ist attitude that caused more than two million voters to turn
away from the NSDAP, translating into a fall in its share of the
vote from 37.4 to 33.1 per cent. Coupled with this dwindling
popular support, Hitler's bid for power appeared to have been
thwarted above all by a plan hatched by Hindenburg's confidant
Schleicher. This socially-minded general with strong Prussian
nationalist leanings was in the process of forging an alliance –
a 'third position' (*Querfront*) – that would bring together the
trade unions, the leftist Strasser wing of the NSDAP, and the
military, but Schleicher no longer regarded the dilettante patri-
cian Papen as being equal to this task. Speaking as one military
man to another, he persuaded Hindenburg to remove 'Little
Franz' and install him as chancellor instead.

Schleicher's plans to create a 'third position' resonated not
only with Strasser and the left wing of the NSDAP but also with
men like Gottfried Feder, leaving Hitler in a very difficult position. His party, with its deep, unresolved internal fault lines, now
threatened to break apart. This would inevitably have spelt the

end for Hitler's grand plans. The crisis in the NSDAP was played out for all to see and Hitler's star began to wane rapidly. In addition, a general feeling was slowly spreading in the country that a turning point had now been reached in the economic crisis, although the unemployment figures remained stubbornly around the six million mark. In its leader article on New Year's Day 1933, the economically liberal *Frankfurter Zeitung* confidently announced: 'The fierce National Socialist assault on the democratic state has been defeated'[23] – but in this, the leader writer miscalculated, as did most of his compatriots.

A sense of wounded vanity, the mental debility of an old man, and an absolute will to power would conspire to turn the tables once more. The final chapter in Hitler's route to power on 30 January 1933 began at the house of the Cologne banker Baron Kurt von Schröder. Having just managed to avoid a split in his party as a result of hesitancy on the part of the dissenters, Hitler had come there to a meeting with Papen arranged by their host. Papen, still smarting from his dismissal as chancellor, was now intent on regaining power with the help of the NSDAP leader. A combination of events in January 1933 – a regional election in the small state of Lippe that saw the NSDAP gain 40 per cent of the vote, a result loudly trumpeted by its propaganda machine as 'the will of the people', and further clandestine evening meetings between Papen and Hitler at the Berlin villa of Joachim von Ribbentrop, a champagne merchant who would later become Hitler's foreign minister – ultimately saw a revenge-obsessed Papen forego the chancellorship in favour of Hitler and seek an audience with Hindenburg, where he convinced the president to drop Schleicher and install a Hitler–Papen administration.

Papen's intention was to 'contain' Hitler within a cabinet of 'national concentration'. Within two months, he is reputed to have said, Hitler would be so boxed in 'that he'll squeak'.[24] Papen went to see Hindenburg to tell him about his plan. Papen and his fellow conservatives clearly genuinely believed that they would be able to exploit Hitler for their own ends. They regarded him as an upstart. Hindenburg spoke dismissively about the 'Bohemian private'* whom he had long sought to keep from becoming chancellor. Once Hitler was seated at the top table and endowed with the same outward signs and privileges of power as the good and the great, he would soon resile from his inflammatory rabble-rousing – or so they assumed. They measured Hitler by their own criteria, with a mixture of condescension, arrogance, and ignorance. As a result, they believed that Hitler was pursuing the same goals that they had – the eradication of Bolshevism, a foreign policy aimed at revising the Versailles Treaty, and hence a restoration of Germany's former might – only more aggressively and forcefully.

Certainly, the 'barons' should have realised what Hitler's true intention was, but no one was inclined any more to take seriously the agenda that he had set forth in *Mein Kampf*. Indeed, how could anyone have been expected to pay any heed to the ideological racist nonsense about the 'Jewish global conspiracy' and the supposedly existential race war to ensure the survival of humanity? All this sounded just too bizarre; so when those who imagined they would be able to 'manipulate' Hitler read his book, all it prompted was a wry smile at best. Insofar as they read it at all, that is, which for most of them was not the case, even though by 1933 *Mein Kampf* had, in line with Hitler's growing public profile, sold 214,000 copies. In any event, that he was an anti-Semite troubled nobody, for such people were thick on the ground – in Germany, in Europe, and throughout the world, not least thanks to the global economic crisis.

On 30 January 1933, Hitler received his letter of appointment as chancellor of Germany, once Papen and his allies had talked Hindenburg out of his antipathy towards the subaltern by assuring him that Hitler wanted to restore the monarchy. What

happened then was not a seizure of power but rather a trans-
fer of power to a party leader who already appeared to have
passed his peak. That Hitler was nonetheless made chancellor is explained by a fixation on political power games and the
idea of a powerful conservative state to supplant the wretched
Weimar Republic. To begin with, it seemed as if Hitler might
fulfil the expectations that had been placed upon him. In the
end, however, everything turned out to be a huge deception on
the part of a man possessed, who thought that any means were
legitimate to achieve his goal, a man who operated outside any
norms of behaviour, and whose worldview and programmatic
aims went far beyond anything hitherto imaginable. Yet hardly
anyone had realised this.

* *Translator's note*: In the Bavarian army, Hitler was a *Gefreiter*,
which has often been mistranslated as 'corporal' or 'lance corporal'. Military ranks are a problematic area of translation, since
there are not always direct equivalents, but the most accurate
rendering of *Gefreiter* is 'private first class'. As Thomas Weber
(*Hitler's First War*) has pointed out, any suggestion that Hitler
was an NCO in the First World War is quite wrong, since he 'had
no line of command over anyone else'.

The eighty-four-year-old Hindenburg's description of Hitler
as 'Bohemian' was based on the misapprehension that he came
from Braunau in the Sudetenland (now Broumov in the Czech
Republic) rather than Braunau am Inn in Austria.

# 6

# Chancellor and Führer

*Did Germans realise what Hitler's real aims were?*

Hitler gained an enthusiastic following among the German people. Granted, he had never won an outright majority in a democratic ballot, but in the years when he set about revising the Versailles Treaty, he would surely have achieved one if free elections had still been held. His triumphs, especially the annexation of Austria, caused his approval ratings to soar and, in the light of past humiliations, turned him into a Messianic leader figure, a shining beacon of hope for Germans, thereby making it easier for them to overlook the brutal elimination of his political enemies and his inhumane racial policies. They adapted to the prevailing circumstances, fell in line, and went along with things, as has always happened, and still happens, in every dictatorship. In this respect, there will always be 'willing executioners'[1] among the general populace – to quote the blanket term that the US sociologist Daniel Jonah Goldhagen applied to Germans during the Third Reich. This label is not without some justification, given that they knew full well about Hitler's criminal objectives, which he had outlined during the so-called period of struggle (i.e. the years from the formation of the NSDAP to 1933), and so had de facto condoned race war and genocide. Indeed, Volker Ullrich, who between 2013 and 2018 wrote a two-volume biography of Hitler, implies precisely this when he concludes that although Hitler may be accused of many things, 'we can exonerate him on one count: namely, that he never sought to conceal his true intentions'.[2]

To begin with, at the start of Hitler's chancellorship, there were people in all political camps who were convinced that he would spark a new war – for his stated aim was to revise Versailles. In other respects, the image that Germans had of him was extremely varied. Nationalist conservatives saw him as the barons' attack dog, who could now be unleashed on the communists and other leftists. On the Left, Hitler was feared as the most radical henchman of 'monopoly capital', while his appointment as chancellor was regarded as a declaration of war against the working class. For the liberal, educated middle class, he represented the end of the constitutional state and the beginning of despotism and intolerance. In contrast, for his supporters (the largest group), he was the 'saviour of the Fatherland'. Yet what none of them spotted at first was his irrationality, specifically his mania about a 'global struggle' between the races that he had carried with him from the revolutionary period into the office of chancellor.

As if he were expressing the innermost feelings of most Germans, in the very first speech he gave in his new role Hitler declared his most pressing task to be the eradication of Marxism, which he claimed had ruined Germany over the past fourteen years. He also announced that he would 'restore the unity of our nation' and defend 'Christianity as the basis of general morality' and 'the family as the nucleus of our nation and body politic'. As for the economy, his intention was to kickstart it into life again 'with two grand four-year plans'. He ended his speech by reassuring Germans that he would stand up for 'the preservation and consolidation of peace'.[3] His words, which were broadcast to the country on national radio, had nothing in common with his aggressive rhetoric of the previous year. They met with widespread approval, even among the centre parties, and lulled

Hitler's coalition partners into believing that they were correct in their assumption that they would be able to rein him in.

Likewise, the leadership of the German army under defence minister Werner von Blomberg was impressed by this Hitler. He was making all the right noises about the 'militarisation' – in other words rearmament – of Germany, a cause that he promoted from the moment he took office as chancellor. He also mapped out his foreign-policy aims to the generals. When he spoke about *Lebensraum* in the East and his plans for 'Germanisation',[4] they took it as read that he meant a war against the universally hated state of Poland, which had been awarded sizable portions of German territory in the Versailles Treaty. It pleased the military that this chancellor seemed determined to revise Versailles by launching another armed offensive if necessary and to restore the Reich to its former extent prior to the ignominy of 1918. War was their stock-in-trade, and in this instance war was perfectly justified, not only in their view, since it was about safeguarding the nation's future. Hitler flattered the generals, while keeping to himself his desire to achieve absolute power and to use this offensive to launch a campaign against 'World Jewry' and its alleged exponents in the vast expanses of Russia. He did so in the knowledge that the aristocratic German army high command, for whom he actually felt a deep loathing, would not know where to begin with his racial ideology anyway. In this way, the medal-bedecked monocle-wearers with the red stripe running down the outseam of their trousers were gradually cajoled into abandoning the resentment they felt towards this erstwhile private from the Great War.

Hitler was intent on getting people to believe that he was wholly committed, in his role of Reich chancellor, to the principle of legality. Therefore, at the beginning of February 1933 – as agreed – parliament was dissolved and new elections set for 5 March. While the new head of the government, who expected to be able to use the dividend of the chancellorship to secure an outright majority for the NSDAP, ordered Goebbels to crank up the propaganda machine once more, Hermann Goering, in his capacity as acting Prussian interior minister, began to implement a policy of Nazification (a programme known as *Gleichschaltung*, or enforced coordination) within the Prussian security apparatus. He placed SA leaders in charge of police departments and, to 'ease the burden' on the regular police, ordered the formation of a 50,000-strong auxiliary police force consisting primarily of SA stormtroopers and SS men. In addition, he set up a secret police department for Prussia. These measures amounted to a kind of mobilisation for the final showdown with the Left in Germany.

In the KPD, meanwhile, the general supposition was that a signal from the Moscow Comintern to stage an armed uprising would not be long in coming. This surmise was stoked by regular reports to this effect in the *Rote Fahne* newspaper. Yet the signal never came. The German comrades failed to grasp that Stalin was actually perfectly content for Hitler to be chancellor, since the latter's aggressive rhetoric on Versailles led Stalin to believe that a war between Germany and the West was imminent. Or perhaps the KPD simply did not want to admit to itself that global revolution was one thing and Russian national strategic interests quite another. Thus, it was more an expression of helplessness when far-left groups – off their own bat, so to speak – undertook isolated terrorist attacks. As the SA also thought the great moment of reckoning had finally come, a new wave of violence swept across the country.

As was his way, Goering put his money where his mouth was. He ordered the police to occupy the KPD headquarters in Berlin and circulated in the press that 'several hundredweight of treasonable printed matter' had been found in the underground catacombs of Karl Liebknecht House, inciting 'armed insurrection' and 'bloody revolution'.[5] The parallels with November

1918 were obvious. Yet Hitler, pointing once more to his concern to act within the bounds of legality, still considered it premature to 'cleanse' Germany of the 'bloody scourge of Moscow's foreign legion'. 'Red terror', he argued, first needed to 'flare up' again.[6] Then an incident came that played right into his hands, prompting a controversy that has rumbled on for decades among post-war historians and self-appointed experts but has never been satisfactorily resolved: the Reichstag fire.

There is much evidence to suggest that Hitler was taken by surprise when, on the night of 27–28 February 1933, the German parliament building, designed by architect Johann Paul Wallot in 1884, went up in flames. The person arrested as the culprit was a mentally disturbed Dutchman, a vagrant with a string of previous convictions by the name of Marinus van der Lubbe. The authorities lost no time in alleging that he had a communist past. He is thought to have acted alone, although even that has never been verified. The only sure thing was that, from the very beginning, the National Socialists and the great majority of Germans were in no doubt that the fire had been set by the communists to signal the start of an armed uprising. The Reichstag fire thus provided Hitler with a welcome pretext to begin his great purge. To facilitate this, the cabinet immediately issued a 'Decree for the Protection of the People and State'. Shaken by events, Hindenburg signed this provision, which at a stroke annulled seven articles of the constitution and the fundamental political rights they enshrined. This decree, which was soon supplemented by another 'for the prevention of treacherous attacks against the government of national renewal', effectively imposed a state of emergency, which lent a veneer of legality to the National Socialists' ensuing systematic terror campaign against their political opponents.

Although the steps taken against the KPD were broadly welcomed by most Germans, many were still appalled by the SA's violent, loutish behaviour that not even the most elaborate National Socialist propaganda of the kind produced by Goebbels could offset. The parliamentary election of 5 March 1933 was a disappointment for Hitler, with the 43.9 per cent won by the NSDAP falling short of an absolute majority, but just a few days later, with the celebrations in Potsdam to mark the opening of the new parliament on 21 March, he pulled off a propaganda coup that dispelled the gloom of the election result.

With parades through the festively flag-bedecked city and speeches by Hindenburg and Hitler in the Garrison Church – the site of Frederick the Great's tomb – the so-called Day of National Renewal was designed to show the nation how the new National Socialist regime stood shoulder-to-shoulder with the old Germany. The racist fanatic Hitler consciously aligned himself with Prussian-German tradition by dressing for the occasion in a morning coat and top hat. He also quite calculatedly co-opted Hindenburg for his purposes by hailing the popular old field marshal as the 'patron ... of our nation's resurgence' and in the name of Germany's youth thanked him for lending his support to 'the task of national renewal', a seal of approval that he deemed 'a blessing'.[7]

Millions of Germans listened to the radio broadcast of the festivities on 21 March 1933 – which would go down in history as the 'Day of Potsdam' – or watched the *Deutsche Wochenschau* newsreel footage of the event in cinemas. Millions of others participated in celebrations the length and breadth of the country. They too contributed to the triumph of the 'spirit of Potsdam', as it was now being called. Images of Frederick the Great, Bismarck, Hindenburg, and Hitler side-by-side were even reproduced on beer mugs and picture postcards, and beneath them the words: 'What the King conquered, the Prince shaped and the Field Marshal defended, the Soldier has now rescued and united.'

After all the years of revolution and revolt, the great humiliation of Versailles and the economic slump, National Socialist propaganda now tapped into a profound longing for better, more stable times. Times such as these were characterised by both an affirmation of German greatness and a desire for a new clarity in political life. In his work *The Years of Decision*, which appeared in 1933, Oswald Spengler wrote: 'something was bound to come, in some form or another'. Taken in by the illusion, the historian and philosopher praised the 'national revolution' as 'something powerful ... and, by virtue of the elemental, universal force with which it occurred, something enduring too'.[8] This illusion, which only assumed tangible form through Hindenburg's symbolic handshake with Hitler in the Garrison Church, enabled people to believe all too readily in Hitler's pronouncements about the unity of the people, welfare, and peace.

As the German public became conscious of living through a period of national rebirth, they began to treat the accompanying violence as a trifling matter. Protestant churchmen played it down: for instance the general superintendent of the Kurmark, Otto Dibelius, who declared that 'a new chapter in a nation's history ... always somehow unfolds amidst violence'.[9] Unlike the Catholic Church, which took a rather reserved and dismissive attitude towards Hitler and had called upon voters to cast their ballots for the Centre Party or the Bavarian People's Party. Protestantism, mindful of its traditional closeness to the Hohenzollern monarchy as a pillar of the state, and encouraged by the apparent reconciliation between National Socialism and the old Prussia, swung decisively behind Hitler. The exception to this general rule was a small group of liberal theologians like Dietrich Bonhoeffer of the 'Confessing Church', who after Hitler's accession to power took a public stand against the policies espoused by the National Socialists.

The actual death of the Weimar Republic occurred on 23

March 1933. On that day, while Germany was still basking in the glow of the Potsdam spectacle, Hitler brought before parliament, which for the time being was sitting in the Kroll Opera House, the 'Law to Alleviate the Distress of the People and the Reich'. By approving this bill, parliament would be voting itself out of existence, since this 'Enabling Act' empowered the government to pass laws for a period of four years without involving parliament or the imperial council. According to the constitution of the Weimar Republic, a two-thirds majority was required for the bill to pass into law. Since the NSDAP and the DNVP combined only accounted for 51.9 per cent of the delegates, it would therefore need the approval of the Centre Party as well.

Of course, the National Socialists had made sure to put on an impressive and threatening display of martial might to accompany this session of parliament, with units of the SA and SS parading outside the Kroll Opera House. However, the parties in the political middle ground – namely the Centre and other smaller groupings like the BVP and the Christian-Social People's Service, which had long kept the banner of the republic flying – now got caught up in the slipstream of the times and chose to turn a blind eye to this blatant intimidation. They wanted to be in on the act rather than withhold their support, especially since Hitler, in an official government address to the churches, had recently praised them for being 'the most important factors in maintaining our national identity'. Even the delegates from the German State Party, a secular grouping, voted in favour of the Enabling Act.

The SPD was the only political force that continued to stand up to the new chancellor. In this, they were 'far from being a united front', as the parliamentarian Wilhelm Hoegner, who was later to become prime minister of Bavaria, recalled after the Second World War.[10] Finally, the party chairman Otto Wels rose to speak in the plenary session of the house. It was a brave statement, which spoke to the stature of the man, when Wels, in the face of a howling mob of National Socialists, declared: 'You can take our freedom and our lives, but you can't take our honour ... At this historic moment, we solemnly proclaim our allegiance to the basic principles of humanity and justice, freedom and socialism.'[11] After many years of mediocrity, this was once more a great moment for German social democracy in the darkest of times.

Following his memorable performance in parliament, Wels was forced to go underground. In Prague he was instrumental in setting up the 'Sopade', the exile organisation of the German Social Democratic Party. Other notable Social Democrats such as the former chancellor Gustav Bauer and the president of the Reichstag Paul Löbe suffered periodic spells of imprisonment. Others were mistreated, and some even murdered, like Johannes Stelling, the acting chairman of the banned Reichsbanner organisation, the defence league of the SPD. A band of marauding SA stormtroopers tortured and then shot him dead during 'Köpenick's week of bloodshed', a crescendo of Nazi violence that swept through a south-eastern suburb of Berlin in late June 1933.

German communists suffered immeasurably worse treatment, being hunted down like wild animals. KPD leader Ernst Thälmann was arrested and vanished into one of the newly established concentration camps. After eleven years' solitary confinement he was executed in Buchenwald – presumably on Hitler's orders. He was just one of many communists to perish at the hands of their National Socialist persecutors. However, most of the KPD leadership – like Walter Ulbricht, Wilhelm Pieck, or Willi Münzenberg – were able to escape to pre-prepared hideouts, cross the border to France, or to make it to Moscow by circuitous routes. They sometimes needed to be made of stern stuff to remain true to their cause, given that many of them felt betrayed by Stalin. It was nothing short of a trauma – a trauma that was to be repeated for a later generation of German communists when another Soviet leader, Mikhail Gorbachev, 'sold out' their republic to the West. Egon Krenz, the very last secretary-general of the GDR's Socialist Unity Party (SED) openly confessed as much to the author of this book.[12]

What steps did Hitler take against Germany's Jews after coming to power? They now found themselves in a desperate situation, only made worse by the reaction from abroad. American and European Jewish organisations had called for a boycott of German export goods that would entail serious losses for a German economy only now slowly recovering. At the forefront of this campaign was the American Jewish Congress, which advocated a 'Bellum Judaicum' and prophesied that the German Reich would suffer 'downfall and ruin'.[13] Yet this activity only served to corroborate Hitler's own racial ideological worldview. Nonetheless, with an eye to his conservative coalition partners, he at first reacted with genuine restraint, even curbing the excesses of those in his party who called for a tough response. When the public backlash to the Jewish embargo duly came, he knew that he could count on the support of most Germans, who were outraged at this intervention by foreign Jews. At the beginning of April 1933, a nationwide boycott of Jewish businesses began.

Not long afterwards, a law was passed debarring civil servants and other public employees who professed the Jewish faith from state service, although the Reich president demanded that people who had done military service during the Great War should be exempted. Soon, the 'protagonists of decline' and 'supporters of revolution' were also excluded from all academic and cultural positions. The whole enterprise was lent additional momentum by mediocre individuals weighing in, since the dismissal of

Jews from their posts gave less well-qualified people a chance of moving up in the world. Although these actions satisfied many people's basest instincts, they were also seen as a justified check against Jewish influence in Germany. Thus, when bonfires blazed up in university towns, and works by authors such as Egon Erwin Kisch, Thomas and Heinrich Mann, Stefan Zweig, and many other writers defamed as providing the 'intellectual basis for the November revolution', were cast into the flames, no general outcry ensued. Most Germans did not recognise these measures as the start of a systematic 'removal' of all things Jewish from the 'body of the German nation' – which had been unequivocally set out as a key objective of National Socialist policies. How could they have been expected to recognise them? After all, despite the general concern, even most Jews assumed that this sudden surge of anti-Semitism would soon abate. However, some 37,000 Jews left Germany in 1933.

In the final analysis, in the eyes of most German citizens the fate of the country's small Jewish minority was of little consequence against the recognition that millions of Germans had found gainful employment once more. Putting food on the table takes precedence over everything else, and Hitler was well aware of this pragmatic reality. As a result, no sooner had he become chancellor than he implemented a series of unorthodox programmes involving mass public participation that, helped by the incipient economic upturn, would soon bear fruit. He also brought on side the country's captains of industry, who had for a long time taken a sceptical view of him. Even workers whose sympathies had originally been with the Left boldly switched their allegiance. Before long, former Red Front fighters and SA stormtroopers, who until recently had fought pitched street battles against one another, were marching side by side, with spades on their shoulders, to take part in road construction projects that had been introduced as job creation schemes throughout the country. Adolf Hitler became their champion, and it was a highly symbolic moment when he formally named 1 May the German 'Day of Labour' and declared it a public bank holiday. The festivities surrounding the inaugural May Day in Berlin were directed with great pomp and circumstance by a young architect named Albert Speer.

The new German state did not merely provide its citizens with bread and work. In parallel with a ban on all rival political parties to the NSDAP, trade unions, and a host of other organisations, the new state soon permeated and organised all aspects of life – from the Hitler Youth to the National Socialist Women's Organisation and the NS Drivers' Corps. This highly synchronised society, which the agitation of new Reich minister for propaganda Joseph Goebbels had whipped into line, took people by the hand and regulated their lives. Presently, even the holidays taken by 'national comrades' were being organised by the German Labour Front, as the new unitary state trade union was called, under the slogan 'Strength through Joy' ('Kraft durch Freude'). Even those who still believed that they answered to a higher authority, such as devout Roman Catholics, were mollified when a Concordat between the Holy See and the German Reich, signed in July 1933, appeared to safeguard the Church's continuing existence in the new Germany.

The people who marched headlong into catastrophe thought that they were progressing towards a better, peaceful future under the swastika. The non-aggression pact signed with the hated Poles in January 1934 strengthened such hopes, since it brought to an end tensions with Germany's neighbours to the east over the Free City of Danzig, which had been governed since the Versailles Treaty by a League of Nations mandate. The previous year, National Socialist Germany had quit its membership of this organisation and the affiliated Geneva Conference for the Reduction and Limitation of Armaments in order to give itself free rein to rearm. Although rearmament contravened the provisions of the Versailles agreement, it was welcomed by the German people, the vast majority of whom regarded an army limited to just 100,000 men as a humiliation in and of itself.

However, like all dynamic phenomena, the dynamism of the National Socialist revolution ran out of steam. In early 1934 – a year that began with a defeat for the party when the Leipzig High Court sent the Reichstag arsonist Marinus van der Lubbe to the gallows but at the same time ruled that he had acted alone and was not part of a wider communist conspiracy – disappointing trade figures suggested that the economy was not growing as fast as people had hoped. The popular mood was further darkened by reductions in working hours and falling wages, coupled with a rise in the cost of living. The spectacle of fat-cat greed, nepotism, corruption, and sometimes naked profiteering on the part of local Nazi officials who were taking every opportunity to feed at the trough also played its part, with the result that discontent and defeatism began to grow in many places. Evidence of this came from reports prepared by the Gestapo; the problem was especially acute in regions that had been badly hit by the recession, such as the Ruhr, the Rhineland, Silesia, and Saxony.

The mood was even sombre within the mass organisations. Seething discontent of a kind that had not been seen for a long time became apparent in the now largely redundant *Sturmabteilung*. Many of the 'old fighters' felt that they had been robbed of the fruits of victory by party bigwigs who were now in league with the hated forces of reaction. In spite of the state ordering preferential treatment and placing liaison officers in the labour exchanges, the programme to reintegrate SA stormtroopers into the workforce was not going well. All attempts to keep the huge army of party supporters occupied with training exercises and other activities could do nothing to prevent calls for a 'second revolution' becoming ever louder from within their ranks. The agreements that Hitler reached with the high command of the Reichswehr, making the SA into a subordinate auxiliary unit of the army, further fuelled unrest. The SA leader Ernst Röhm's far-reaching plans to create a huge militia army were now off the table, and the disillusionment with Hitler felt in the SA knew no bounds. He had come down on the side of the conventional forces because it was only with their help that he could realise his goals.

The discontent among the coterie of conservatives around Papen was no less acute. They had been forced to acknowledge that it was not they who were manipulating Hitler, but that he had in fact callously exploited them. Chastened, they had looked on impotently while, with breathtaking speed, he shaped the state according to his will. While applauding his drive to expel communists and possibly also Social Democrats, they were appalled by his proscription of the DNVP and other right-wing organisations at the same time. Egged on by a nationalist-Catholic circle around the journalist and political consultant Edgar Jung, who had been an advocate of a 'conservative revolution' in the Weimar Republic, Papen was finally moved to voice his opposition to Hitler's course towards total dictatorship.

In a speech to the Marburg University League on 17 June 1934 that had been drafted for him by Jung, the German vice-chancellor launched a full-frontal attack on the chancellor, declaring that domination by a single party could only ever be a transitional phase. He warned of a 'class struggle by any other name' and against 'confusing vitality with brutality', and complained that 'self-interest, lack of character, mendacity, a lack of chivalry and arrogance' were spreading under the guise of the National Socialist revolution. The rich fund of trust that the German people had placed in it was under threat, Papen went on, and called for all talk of a 'second revolution' to cease.[14] All this was powerful stuff and created quite a stir in conservative circles, despite the fact that Goebbels did not broadcast the speech on national radio.

Papen, whom no one had thought capable of such a bold move, now planned a meeting with Hindenburg at the president's estate at Neudeck to try and bring him onside against Hitler. This meeting took place on 21 June 1934. In view of his failing faculties, Hindenburg had asked Blomberg, the army minister, to attend and left most of the talking to him. Blomberg, whose sympathies lay with Hitler, presented the role of the army as a decisive factor in maintaining the balance of power in the country, and demanded that the SA's activities be terminated once and for all, effectively painting Hitler into a corner. His chosen way out of it was to stage a treacherous coup, a violent and perfect feint on his part. To achieve his aim of wresting absolute power over Germany and then embarking on the main struggle against 'World Jewry', he prepared to launch a decapitation strike against the SA – his own party's paramilitary force that had been instrumental in bringing him to power.

His aim in doing this was to muzzle his critics in the conservative camp and secure the support of the army. For in the eyes of the Reichswehr, the proletarian SA units, with their vulgar anti-Semitism and their talk of a second (socialist) revolution, epitomised the abhorrent face of the National Socialist movement. For the army's elite officer corps, the immeasurably larger party militia had long since become a rival organisation that was despised and feared in equal measure. After Blomberg was shown fake reports suggesting that the SA was plotting a coup and hence a strike against the army, he was all the more keen to make common cause with Hitler.

There now ensued a series of brutal nationwide raids by the SS and its security service, the SD (*Sicherheitsdienst*), coordinated by Hitler and Goering. These ended with the assassination of Röhm and the rest of the SA leadership. The so-called 'Night of the Long Knives' also targeted the conservative group behind Papen, including men like Jung, Erich Klausener, and Herbert von Bose. Hitler spared the life of the vice-chancellor, no doubt because he considered him a lightweight and because he owed his chancellorship to him. Hitler also took the opportunity to settle some 'old scores'. Thus, the assassins' bullets also cut down the former Bavarian state commissioner Gustav Kahr, whom Hitler blamed for the failure of the Beer Hall Putsch in 1923, as well as Kurt von Schleicher and Gregor Strasser, who had come so close to thwarting Hitler's bid to become chancellor. By the time Hitler declared the 'cleansings' over on 2 July 1934 – which by then had started to acquire a momentum of their own – more than 150 people had been killed.

National Socialist propaganda moved swiftly to nip in the bud any potential unrest in the general populace over what had happened. On all national radio stations, Goebbels informed the German people about a revolution that had been foiled at the eleventh hour by the decisive actions of the Führer. He and his 'trusted lieutenants', Goebbels maintained, could not possibly have let their 'work of renewal, begun by the whole nation amid untold sacrifices' be jeopardised by a 'small clique of criminals', who had supposedly been in league with the 'forces of reaction' and an unnamed foreign power.[15] Most people in Germany allowed themselves to be bamboozled by these lies about a clique of criminals – peddled by far bigger criminals – and chose to believe the story of the alleged 'Röhm Putsch'. The general view was that the 'forces of good' in the National Socialist movement embodied by Adolf Hitler and his inner circle had triumphed. This was the beginning of the myth about Hitler being sacrosanct. It was not long before 'national comrades' began to respond to any perceived failings in the system with the mantra: 'If only the Führer knew about this!'

As regards the trust that Hitler enjoyed among the general

public, this was now stronger than ever. An SD report on public opinion in Bavaria, representative of many written at this time, found that the suppression of the 'Röhm Revolt' had had the effect of a 'cleansing thunderstorm' that allowed the populace to breathe a collective sigh of relief.[16] The delusion was so complete that in conservative intellectual circles Hitler's orgy of violence was celebrated as a 'coup for the nation'. For example, the constitutional lawyer Carl Schmitt hailed it by claiming 'The Führer is protecting the rule of law.'[17] Even the *Frankfurter Zeitung*, which had hitherto retained some measure of independence, wrote at the beginning of July 1934: 'The National Socialist leader's authority has never been greater than at this moment, when he decided to sort the wheat from the chaff.'[18]

If Hitler was now to make a bid for absolute power, then – just as in January 1933 – a handful of opportunists from the entourage of the president, who by this time was declining rapidly, would play a part. They helped create the impression that Hindenburg unreservedly supported Hitler's strike against the leaders of the SA, Schleicher, and the rest. They fabricated telegrams by Hindenburg congratulating Hitler and Goering, and then leaked them to the press. On 1 August 1934 – with the news from Neudeck signalling the imminent demise of the almost eighty-seven-year-old president – Hitler presented his cabinet with a draft bill concerning the succession, according to which the office of Reich president would be merged with that of the 'Führer and Reich Chancellor'. The very next day, 2 August, after Paul von Beneckendorff und von Hindenburg had departed this life in the early hours of the morning, the legislation came into force.

As the whole of Germany paid its respects to the deceased field marshal, in an act of subservience Blomberg ordered the troops of the Reichswehr to swear allegiance to the new head of state, Hitler. The army minister was convinced that in putting down the 'Röhm Putsch' Hitler had preserved the Reichswehr's fundamental role and saved Germany from a new civil war. Instead of pledging allegiance to the constitution, which obliged them to faithfully serve the people and the Fatherland, soldiers in barracks throughout the country now swore a 'sacred oath' to 'give unquestioning obedience to the Führer of the German Reich and people Adolf Hitler, supreme commander of the German army' and to commit their lives to fulfilling this oath at all times.[19] In swearing this outrageous form of oath, the army, with its steadfast notions of soldierly loyalty, became a tool in the hands of a person driven by irrational concepts of racial ideology.

Hitler now wielded absolute power in Germany. In turn, he took the merging in his person of the offices of chancellor and president as a pretext to uphold the semblance of legitimacy. He organised a plebiscite, which once again saw the country swamped by a mighty wave of propaganda. In mid-August, on a turn-out of 95.7 per cent, 89.9 per cent voted 'Yes'. Admittedly, like the referendum held to confirm the country's exit from the League of Nations the previous year, this was not a free vote. The results were subject to manipulation. Even so, the level of approval shown by the German people to their Führer, whose decisive action had, they believed, averted a worse outcome for the Fatherland, had undoubtedly reached a new high. For Germans it was only right and proper that Hitler should now have absolute power vested in him, especially as most of them only had bad memories of the country's fourteen years of democracy. To many, his dictatorship seemed a viable modern alternative.

Hitler himself now began to increasingly style himself as a man with a special calling. The 'shield of providence' that Goebbels 'knew' protected the Führer was a metaphor that he himself started to use more and more. Generally speaking, Hitler and his propaganda minister were wont to raise everything to a pseudo-religious sphere. Faith was transfigured into the driving force behind the movement. Goebbels once declared: 'For us, politics is the miracle of the impossible.'[20] The real nub of Hitler's movement as a form of political religion lay in that irrational aspect, in those metaphysics of blind faith. The disconnect from reason in favour of this blind faith and the resulting unconditional allegiance to Hitler became National Socialism's most potent weapons. This allegiance was there for all to witness at the party's annual Nuremberg Rallies – the 1934 meeting was officially known as the Reich Party Congress of the Will ('Reichspartei-tag des Willens') and director Leni Riefenstahl's documentary *Triumph des Willens* ('Triumph of the will') was filmed at this event. Those present spoke of the powerful emotions that took hold of them when they gathered in their hundreds of thousands and the Führer strode down the serried ranks of the party faithful with his cloak billowing behind him on his way to the speakers' rostrum. It was like a religious service, they recounted, and no one doubted that they were pursuing the right path.

Such emotions also gripped the entire nation in mid-January 1935, when the results of the plebiscite on the future of the Saarland became known. Until then, the region had been under the jurisdiction of the League of Nations, in line with the provisions of the Versailles Treaty. No less than 90.5 per cent of inhabitants of the Saarland voted for their homeland to be reincorporated into the German Empire. In the eyes of the overjoyed nation, it was Hitler who had brought the Saar 'back home to the empire'. It was no longer of any significance that, in truth, all this had very little to do with him or with National Socialist convictions, and much more that the Saarland simply saw itself as German, regardless of Hitler. Hitler's deputy Rudolf Hess summed up the prevailing mood of euphoria when he proclaimed ecstatically: 'The party is Hitler. Hitler is Germany, just as Germany is Hitler!'[21]

Hitler also won great approval when he announced the

reintroduction of universal conscription and set the future strength of the German army at 550,000 men. Because the parliament in Paris had recently voted in favour of prolonging compulsory military service, it was easy for Hitler to defy Versailles and its stipulation of 100,000 men while continuing to masquerade as the frustrated man of peace, who had simply been forced to respond. Accordingly, the German government gave an assurance that it would 'never go beyond the bounds of safeguarding German honour and the peace of the empire and in particular, with regard to national German rearmament, would never seek to create any instrument of belligerent aggression but rather one exclusively aimed at defence and the preservation of peace'.[22] Where the general populace was concerned, another pointer in this direction was the Anglo-German Naval Treaty of June 1935, which confirmed the relative strengths of the German and British fleets at a ratio of one to three.

At the Nuremberg 'Reich Party Congress of Freedom' in mid-September 1935, the chief topic of concern was the 'Bolshevik Jew in Moscow', who, according to Hitler, was 'preaching destruction to the world in a new declaration of war'.[23] From the perspective of the 'national comrades', this topic was merely the political rhetoric of an annual ritual. Hardly anyone suspected that their Führer was determined, once conditions were favourable, to set off on a 'Great Teutonic march' eastwards: to set in train the destruction of the Soviet Union. Nor, indeed, that the growing external threat from Bolshevism that Hitler claimed to have identified was for him of a piece with the domestic anti-Jewish measures he had put in place. The particular legislation in question here was the 'Reich Citizenship Law' and the 'Law for the Protection of German Blood and German Honour' (collectively known as the 'Nuremberg Laws'). In practical terms, these laws defined a citizen of the Reich as a person of 'German or related blood', who was willing and able 'to loyally serve the

German people and the Reich'.[24] Since such a status was categorically denied to Jews, they were de facto stripped of all civil rights. They were further isolated when 'marriages between Jews and citizens of German or related blood' were proscribed, as was extramarital intercourse between the two.

For as long as they could, German Jews tried to preserve themselves from this social isolation and disenfranchisement, which came on top of their enforced exclusion from public and business life. Those who did not simply emigrate, and who were excluded from the national community, attempted to refute the National Socialist racial mania by emphasising above all the contribution they had made to their German homeland down the ages. The great majority of German Jews still refused to believe what was happening and had no inkling of what was to come. They clung to the idea that the German-Jewish community would ultimately survive. Some of them disappeared into the communist or Social Democrat underground or even proffered their services to the National Socialists, presenting themselves as comrades-in-arms in the fight 'against all hate-filled parasites on the German people, Jews from the East and internationalists'.[25] Not so the Zionists. They saw their old arguments vindicated: namely, that the Jews would never prosper in a non-Jewish country, and so propagandised for a 'commitment to the Jewish nation and the Jewish race' as the basis for their own state on the site where their historic roots lay – in Palestine.[26]

The Jews did not receive any systematic support from non-Jewish Germans. Indeed, how could such help have been forthcoming in the conformist 'Nazified' state? Instead, aid was confined to a large number of individual initiatives, though these could not disguise the fact that Germans were either indifferent to their plight or were divided over the question of the Nazi race laws. Gestapo reports even state that this legislation was received 'for the most part with satisfaction' by the populace at large. In Catholic circles, however, it was 'not welcomed'.[27] Many others who took a rather dim view of the matter may well ultimately have convinced themselves that everything was rosy by considering the negative and positive aspects of the new age and concluding that the latter far outweighed the former.

The year 1936 appeared to offer 'national comrades' much in the way of positivity. At the beginning of March, the Wehrmacht (as the Reichswehr was now known) marched into the demilitarised zone of the Rhineland amid much fanfare and to the delight of the jubilant local population. Since the victorious powers from the First World War did nothing more than issue diplomatic notes of protest, and because the German people remained unaware of the chaos that Hitler's high-risk gamble sowed among Reich officials, the occupation of the Rhineland was widely received as the coolly calculated act of a great statesman. Hitler was concerned to convey just such an impression when he declared that he was treading the path that 'providence' had laid out for him 'with all the sure-footedness of a sleepwalker'.[28] The Germans invested ever more trust in their Führer, especially now that there was much talk of peace again. It was not only the man or woman in the street who was completely unaware that Hitler was striving towards war.

Hitler used his public relations coup in the Rhineland to once again have his leadership 'legitimised' by the people. Wherever he appeared in public, he was greeted with a rapturous reception by crowds numbering in their thousands. The result of the plebiscite was thus a foregone conclusion, with 99 per cent approval in the country as a whole, rising to 99.7 in the Saarland Palatinate and even 99.9 in East Prussia. 'Adolf Hitler and Germany are as one', ran the jubilant headline that was fed to the compliant German press[29] – not without some justification, however, since public approval of Hitler was genuinely overwhelming, now that he had not only regained full sovereignty for the empire but also,

most importantly, restored some of its lost honour. The demilitarised Rhineland had been a particularly sore thorn in the
nation's flesh, associated with painful memories. All that was
now in the past. Even those who did not condone such actions
magnanimously chose to connive at them – a tendency that was
lent greater impetus in the summer of 1936, when the world's
youth came to the capital of National Socialist Germany to take
part in the Olympic Games.

In the meantime, the attitude of the outside world to this state
had changed fundamentally. Among other factors, this had to do
with developments in Europe. National Socialist or fascist ideologies had long since spread across the whole continent. With
the rise of communist and internationalist ideas in the wake of
the Great War, as a kind of countermovement, large numbers of
adherents of nationalist ideologies had formed themselves into
various organisations and splinter groups, not only in Germany
and Italy. In many cases, these simply emulated the NSDAP: for
example, the Belgian Rexists founded by Léon Degrelle or Frits
Clausen's Danish National Socialist Party. Yet often they had
their own roots, like the Iron Guard in Romania or the Arrow
Cross movement in Hungary. Fascist groups were especially
widespread in Western democracies, such as in Great Britain,
where Oswald Mosley's British Union of Fascists attracted well
over half a million members. Similarly, French groups like François de la Rocque's Croix-de-Feu, Pierre Taittinger's Jeunesses
Patriotes, or Jacques Doriot's Parti Populaire Français, set up to
counter the supposed pre-eminence of the Left in France, also
enjoyed great popularity. In the mid-1930s, this trend led the
Italian 'Duce' Benito Mussolini to proclaim that fascist ideas
were the ideas of the age, and that within a few years the whole
of Europe would be fascist.[30]

Prompted by a widespread feeling that the world was at a historical crossroads and on the cusp of a new era, many people saw

National Socialism or fascism as a modern alternative to the crisis of European society. Thus in Germany, people could experience at first hand Hitler's 'national community' led by the 'new elite'. Since 1933, snobbery and class consciousness had been systematically dismantled. A social mobility was present that had never existed before, and generally speaking people who worked with their hands were regarded more highly than those who worked with their heads. The 'National Socialist model enterprise', which was pushed through by Hitler and Robert Ley's 'German Labour Front' in the face of opposition from employers, was the kind of workplace that could boast real sociopolitical benefits that had no counterpart in Europe at that time. The entertainment industry also boomed, with feature films and radio providing diversions for the citizens of the National Socialist state. Indeed, in the German Reich people identified all too readily with this national community and its achievements.

Yet that only held good for members of that community – those who were of 'German blood'. Often, there were other reasons why people chose to turn a blind eye to the regime's aggressive racial policies towards the Jews, of whom there were still some 400,000 living in Germany in 1936. Even in Western democracies, it was argued, racial minorities were marginalised, as were, for example, the 'Negroes' in the United States, as the discrimination suffered by Black members of the US Olympic team seemed seemingly proved. The American field and track legend Jesse Owens – who had a longstanding friendship with his great rival in the long jump, the German athlete Luz Long – actually found Nazi Germany to be less racist than his own country, for which he won three gold medals. And what about the British and the French, both of whose squads gave Hitler the straight-armed salute on entering the Berlin Olympic Stadium for the opening ceremony? They, too, apparently had no problems with this National Socialist Germany.

To be sure, these reactions could be explained in part because the regime quite deliberately sought to give the impression to the outside world that the situation in Germany regarding anti-Semitism was really not so bad. Accordingly, the signs on Berlin park benches reading 'No Jews Allowed' were removed for the duration of the Games, and the publication of anti-Jewish magazines was suspended. At the Games themselves, German 'token Jews', such as the fencer Helene Mayer, were allowed to compete. Likewise, the sports official Theodor Lewald, who was of Jewish extraction and who as a member of the IOC executive committee in the Weimar period had been instrumental in bringing the Games to Germany, was left in post by the National Socialists. Drunken SA stormtroopers made it clear that things wouldn't go on in this vein when they chanted: 'Once the Games are over, we'll beat the Jews to a pulp.'[31]

However, for the most part, guests from abroad failed to notice. They experienced an Olympiad of superlative performances held in the capital of a Germany that was open and welcoming to the world. They saw nothing of the concentration camps filled with political opponents of the Nazis and other dissidents that the SS had by this time expanded into an entire network. Thus it was that the former British prime minister David Lloyd George, who after attending the Berlin Games embarked on a tour of Germany in September 1936, was able to write:

I have just returned from a visit to Germany ... I have now seen the famous German leader and also something of the great change he has effected. Whatever one may think of his methods – and they are certainly not those of a parliamentary country – there can be no doubt that he has achieved a marvellous transformation in the spirit of the people, in their attitude towards each other, and in their social and economic outlook ... The people are more cheerful. There is a greater sense of general gaiety of spirit throughout the land. It is a happier Germany. I saw it everywhere.[32]

From the standpoint of many people in neighbouring countries, it was above all the internal stability of this country, which even offered ordinary workers the opportunity to holiday aboard cruise ships, that enabled it to become something of a bastion against communism. This impression was heightened when a coup led by General Francisco Franco set in motion the Spanish Civil War in July 1936, and it soon became clear that Stalin was attempting to gain a foothold on the Iberian Peninsula by lending his support to the Popular Front Spanish Republic. These events were of little consequence to the German public in the summer of 1936. They were more concerned about their holidays on the German coast or at Wannsee Lake in Berlin. Their everyday reality was far removed from the grim world of their Führer, who spoke of a deadly encirclement of Germany and wrote a memorandum in which he noted, almost in panic, that the world was heading 'with gathering speed' towards a new conflict, 'whose most extreme outcome is Bolshevism, but whose real substance and aim is to eliminate those echelons of society that have hitherto been in charge and replace them with international Jewry'.

Hitler sent a combined force of aircraft and tanks – the 'Condor Legion' – to Spain. No one at the time could have imagined that Spain would become a proving ground for the new German Luftwaffe for the coming world war. When Hitler's air force obliterated the Basque cities of Durango and Guernica, inflicting many civilian casualties, the ensuing international outcry barely reached the ears of the German public, very few of whom were listening to, or could understand, the radio broadcasts of the BBC. In any event, deaths had also resulted from offensives by the 'Reds', whose barbaric cruelty when waging war Germans were regularly 'informed' about by Goebbels' propaganda.

According to the Four-Year Plan of 1936, the Wehrmacht was to be fully ready for war by 1940. At the same time 'Aryanisation measures' were intensified. Over the following two years, some 60 per cent of small and medium-sized Jewish businesses such as department stores, law firms, and doctors' practices were expropriated, along with a host of small family-run retail outlets. This was an insidious process. The 'Jewish corner shop' simply vanished overnight. Non-Jewish private enterprise was delighted with this move, as it received the lion's share of additional state funding to stimulate the country's planned rearmament by 1940.

The basic German feeling of being a force to be reckoned with once more in Europe and the world left little room in the heads of the average man or woman in the street for racial policy. They were more interested in the news that the Duke of Windsor, who had abdicated as King Edward VIII earlier that year, paid a visit to the Führer at his Berghof retreat in October 1937 – especially since Hitler's British guest was accompanied by Wallis Simpson, the woman for whom he had renounced the throne. In the preceding month, the public imagination had also been captured by the state visit of Mussolini, who arrived in Germany in the company of his dashing foreign minister, Count Galeazzo Ciano. The Nazi propaganda machine stage-managed the visit as a grand pageant, with a huge rally in the Olympic Stadium, where fifty searchlights created an imposing 'tent of light'. This spectacle was designed to hint not only at the two leaders' quasi-divinity but also at the importance of the 'Rome–Berlin Axis', an alliance resulting from Mussolini's war of conquest in Abyssinia and military cooperation between German and Italian forces in Spain – an importance which it did not actually possess.

In this Germany, not least as a result of Goebbels' propaganda, the way politics was presented was now pure smoke and mirrors, deceiving people into believing in an illusory reality. However, in February 1938, this illusion appeared to have been seriously compromised by the Blomberg–Fritsch Affair. Yet even here the nation failed to recognise the truth of the matter. At a meeting with the Führer, minister of war Werner von Blomberg and the army's commander-in-chief Werner von Fritsch made known their misgivings about Hitler's plan to annex Austria and crush Czechoslovakia, citing the danger that the British and French might intervene. At this meeting, which was minuted by Colonel Friedrich Hossbach,[33] Hitler recognised that his ambitious military plans could not be realised with these traditionally minded officers at the helm. As a result, what turned out to be a deeply unsavoury affair provided him with the ideal opportunity to sweep these men aside.

As details of the affair were made known, they elicited sympathy from the German public for their Führer for having to work alongside an aristocratic minister of war married to a former prostitute who had posed for pornographic photos, and an army supreme commander who was rumoured to be a homosexual. The mores of the time condemned both as sheer abominations. Popular opinion saw it as only logical that Hitler should put himself in command of the army and personally appoint a staff of underlings in the form of the Armed Forces High Command (Oberkommando der Wehrmacht, or OKW). The change of leadership at the foreign ministry that Hitler implemented at the same time also met with general approval. Konstantin von Neurath, the outgoing foreign secretary, was widely viewed as 'yesterday's man', unlike his successor, the suave England expert and sparkling-wine manufacturer Joachim von Ribbentrop.

The new leadership structure of the army, which was entirely tailored to Hitler's requirements, was soon put to the test when German troops marched into Austria in March 1938. Public delight at this development knew no bounds, for Hitler had achieved what had been denied to Germans and German Austrians by the St Germain Treaty. It was an 'annexation' (*Anschluss*), even though this term is frowned upon in present-day Austria. Hundreds of thousands lined the streets to witness the Führer cross the River Inn at his birthplace of Braunau am Inn, the border between Austria and Germany, and make his way via Linz to Vienna. On 15 March, he delivered a pathos-laden speech to a huge crowd of rapturous supporters assembled on the capital's Heldenplatz, in which he announced 'before history the entry of my homeland into the German Empire'.

The day before, at the end of a speech he gave in Linz, where decades previously he had been an unremarkable schoolboy, it was evident that Hitler had his true agenda constantly in mind. Once again, he referred frequently to 'providence' and said: 'I do not know when you will be called upon to profess your faith. But I hope that day will not be long in coming. And when it does, I feel certain I will be able to stand before the whole German nation and point proudly to my homeland.' The listening crowd surely cannot have understood that he was alluding here to his war against 'Jewish Bolshevism'. Nor would they have realised that there was a direct link between the scenes of great rejoicing taking place in the 'Ostmark' province – as Austria was known after the *Anschluss* – and the violence and other outrages being perpetrated elsewhere, primarily against the Jews. Such outrages represented the ignored and suppressed collateral damage arising from a nation's unprecedented triumphal march, led by a Führer whose mindset had by this stage shifted completely onto an ecstatic, almost religious plane. People now began to speak of him as the 'greatest German of all time', while the 'German Christians', that section of Protestantism that was fiercely loyal to the Nazi regime, had already begun to treat him as a Christ-like figure.

Then again, Hitler appeared to warrant these superlatives when, six months after the annexation of Austria, he 'restored' the culturally German Sudetenland region of Czechoslovakia to the 'Greater German Empire'. The German occupation took place amid the peal of church bells and seemingly endless jubilation, and with the tacit blessing of the European powers. After the Austrian *Anschluss*, appeals for a similar intervention by Sudeten Germans, who were oppressed by the regime in Prague and had invested all their hopes in Hitler, had grown ever louder. They saw themselves as victims of the post-war order established at Versailles that had assigned their homeland of Bohemia and Moravia, which had once been outlying provinces of the former Austro-Hungarian Empire, to the newly created state of Czechoslovakia.

Hitler's real concern was not the Sudeten Germans, however. They were merely a pretext for him to crush Czechoslovakia, which he saw as the 'most dangerous forward post of Red Soviet power in Europe'.[34] Germans did not appreciate that Hitler's destruction of Czechoslovakia was a kind of preamble to his eastward expansion. Of course, they were fearful that all this might lead to a war, something that Hitler's diatribe against Prague at the 1938 Nuremberg Rally had hinted at. The looming disaster now stirred into action a handful of senior military officers such as Ludwig Beck, who had recently stepped down as chief of the Army General Staff or Erwin von Witzleben, who had called for a public enquiry immediately after Schleicher's murder in 1934. Having recognised Hitler for who he really was, they and a very small group of others began to line up in opposition to him. They made contact with foreign powers in the West and considered staging a coup. Yet the course of events was to cut the ground from under the feet of the so-called Oster Conspiracy (named after another of the plotters, Major General Hans Oster).

Instead of war breaking out, at the end of September 1938 the leaders of Germany, Great Britain, France, and Italy reached a negotiated settlement in Munich, after new British prime minister Neville Chamberlain had taken the extraordinary step of flying to meet 'Herr Hitler' three times within the space of a fortnight. The result was that the Sudetenland was annexed by Germany, and Chamberlain was hailed as a hero in Great Britain when he returned from Munich and announced that he had secured 'peace for our time'.[35] What he and the rest of the world did not know was that the piece of paper with Hitler's signature on it, which he proudly brandished in front of the press at London's Heston Aerodrome, was worthless.

Hitler, who had hoped for war, now earned the gratitude of the German people for having saved the peace in Munich with the other statesmen while at the same time asserting his will. In his diary, Goebbels noted: 'The word "peace" is on everybody's lips. The whole world is going mad with joy. Germany's prestige has risen enormously. Now we are once again a world power.'[36] This was also true of the Führer's prestige. From the standpoint of the 'national community', he seemed to have once more demonstrated that everything he touched eventually turned to gold. What thoughts must have been going through the heads of the officers who had been planning a coup d'état?

Even so, the Munich Crisis of September 1938 marked the end of Germany's salad days under Hitler. For he saw Munich as a setback, delaying his major war plans, and in response his policies turned even more aggressive, especially towards the Jews. In the autumn of 1938, by which time around 205,000 Jews had left the country, a sizable portion of those who remained were quite literally thrown out of Germany, as 17,000 Jews of Polish extraction were rounded up and transported by train to the German–Polish border, where they were driven into no man's land. Among them were the parents of one Herschel Grynszpan, a Jewish émigré living in France, who a few days after the deportations shot dead the German diplomat Ernst vom Rath at the Paris embassy. Hitler took this act as an excuse to stage the outrage that became known as *Kristallnacht*. On the night of

9–10 November 1938, 1,400 synagogues and other Jewish places of worship were set alight. Jewish businesses and homes were attacked and cemeteries desecrated. Eight hundred Jews were killed and 30,000 carted off to concentration camps.

This act of state-sponsored anti-Semitic terror, which was unprecedented in Germany, was followed by a comprehensive expropriation of German Jews. As punishment for the diplomat's assassination, a collective 'Jewish wealth tax' of one billion Reichsmarks was levied. This was followed by the 'Order for the Removal of Jews from German Economic Life' in November 1938, which saw all businesses that still belonged to Jewish proprietors forcibly closed and Jews banned from practising almost any profession. Other measures included excluding Jewish children from state schools and a ban on Jews attending any place of entertainment or recreation. These were intended to force Jews to disappear entirely from public life.

In particular, the nationwide pogrom on *Kristallnacht*, which everyone could witness, unsettled most Germans, who wanted to believe in their Führer. Many chose once more to delude themselves into believing that, for all his repudiation of the Jews, this outrage could not have been his doing. After all, at the Reich Party Congress, hadn't he appealed to the outside world to take in German Jews? And the world had refused to open its borders to them. Consequently, instead of Hitler, others often had to serve as scapegoats and be held responsible for what had happened. The paladins who surrounded him, especially the SS and its leader Heinrich Himmler, usually took the blame. Since June 1936 Himmler had been in control of the entire state apparatus of policing and oppression, which consisted of the regular uniformed police, the state secret police (Gestapo), the central state criminal investigation department, and the security service (SD) of the SS. He was also responsible for running the concentration camps.

*Kristallnacht* also acted as an enduring affront to devout Roman Catholics, who for years had been torn between their love of the Fatherland and resentment at the German 'alternative saviour' and his regime. In March 1937, Pope Pius XI had signalled his alarm to the Catholic faithful and the wider world in the encyclical *Mit brennender Sorge* ('With burning concern'), which had been written by the cardinal and archbishop of Munich and Freising, Michael von Faulhaber. In his missive, the pope made a special point of denouncing Hitler's racial legislation and his policy of enforced sterilisation. 'Whoever exalts race, or the people, or the state ... above their standard value and divinises them to an idolatrous level,' ran the encyclical, which was read aloud in Catholic churches throughout Germany, 'distorts and perverts an order of the world planned and created by God.'[37]

This attitude of the Catholic Church and its congregations was a major factor that helped usher in something of a new process of disillusionment among Germans at large after years of ecstatic triumphalism, and was lent further impetus when Hitler let his mask slip completely in late January 1939. Speaking in the Reichstag on the sixth anniversary of his seizure of power, he openly declared: 'If international finance Jewry inside and outside Europe should succeed in plunging the nations once more into a world war, the result will not be the Bolshevisation of the Earth and hence the victory of Jewry but the annihilation of the Jewish race in Europe.'[38]

Then, in March 1939, Hitler completed something that he had been intending to do the previous September when he ordered his troops to occupy the so-called 'rump' Czech lands and march into the capital Prague. This time, no cheering crowds lined the routes along which German forces advanced. Nor was it any different when Hitler appeared on the balcony of Prague Castle. This lightning operation had nothing to do any more with revising the Versailles Treaty, the excuse Hitler had used to justify all his previous incursions. Dark forebodings took hold throughout the continent, particularly since the next catastrophe was looming large.

The ongoing antagonism between Germans and Poles started to intensify. At the heart of the conflict was the city of Danzig, which had been administered by the League of Nations since Versailles. The city's German Gauleiter, Albert Forster, fanned the flames of nationalism and the Polish side followed suit. Hitler knew that he could count on the support of most Germans in this dispute, as the newly created Polish state had been awarded sizable former parts of Germany – namely West Prussia and Pomerania – in the Versailles settlement. The forcible expulsion of their German inhabitants, as well as the clashes over Upper Silesia, were still fresh in people's memories. Between 1919 and 1921 Poland had tried to gain control of the industrial region of Silesia. The end result was a partition that was greatly to Germany's disadvantage. Goebbels' propaganda inflamed the situation further by painting a dramatic picture of the plight of the German-speaking minority in Poland.

A report prepared by the Sopade – the exile organisation of the SPD, now resident in Paris after the fall of Prague – claimed that 'a military operation by Germany against Poland would be welcomed by the overwhelming majority of Germans'.[39] Admittedly, in saying this, the SPD was thinking in terms of only a limited conflict, but when Great Britain gave its assurance at the end of March 1939 that it would intervene to safeguard Polish sovereignty, a new European war seemed the more likely outcome, especially when Hitler responded by rescinding the Anglo-German Naval Agreement and the German–Polish Non-Aggression Pact. Just as in 1938, however, no one in Europe, not even Hitler, wanted a repeat of the First World War.

As before, the German people continued to place their faith in their Führer. They had no inkling that, for Hitler, the elimination of Poland would be the final piece in the jigsaw in preparation for his planned invasion of the Soviet Union. They still preferred to see him as truly embodying the role he was so fond of playing: the resolute champion of the nation. They were confident that things would go well on this occasion, too, as they always had done in the past. The myth-making around the Führer had done its part. As Mussolini once said, myth was a faith, a passion: 'It is not necessary for it to be a reality. It is a reality in the sense that it is a stimulus, and is hope, faith, and courage.'[40]

7

# The Hitler–Stalin Pact

*Why did these sworn enemies sign such an agreement?*

The Nazi–Soviet Non-Aggression Pact of August 1939 has remained a political hot potato right up to the present day. Prior to the break-up of the Soviet Union, Moscow always denied the existence of a secret supplementary protocol to the pact, in which the two dictators carved up Eastern Central Europe between them. In 1992, however, President Boris Yeltsin authorised publication of the document. In 2020, on the occasion of the 'Seventy-Fifth Anniversary of the Great Victory over Fascism', his successor Vladimir Putin declared that the pact had been necessary to safeguard the security and political interests of the Soviet Union at the time. According to Putin, the real cause of the Second World War was the Munich Agreement, in which the Western powers permitted the disintegration of Czechoslovakia against the wishes of the Soviet Union, and in so doing paved the way for Hitler's boundless expansion. The beneficiaries back then had been, he claimed, not only Germany but also Poland. For Stalin had apparently pushed for a coalition against Hitler and had only formed an alliance with him after Poland announced that it was 'unwilling to enter into any obligations regarding the Soviet Union'.[1] Moreover, Putin continued, it was only after the outbreak of war, when it became clear that German troops were about to 'swiftly occupy the whole of Poland' that the Red Army also invaded the country.

Such a blatant rewriting of history is reason enough to revisit the question of how the pact between Hitler and Stalin came about and what role it played in the strategic calculations of both dictators.

What Putin, with his twisted logic, brazenly tried to present to the world as the defensive action of a 'peace-loving Soviet Union' against National Socialist aggression, cannot be justified as such even in the most superficial way. For thanks to their aspiration to global revolution, the Bolsheviks under their leader Lenin had Central Europe in their sights right from the outset. This was no different under Stalin, even though priority was given to strengthening socialism within the Soviet Union; and Germany was assigned a key role in these plans for world revolution. If revolution succeeded there, it was argued, then there was nothing to stop it taking root in other European countries. The West saw things in exactly the same way. Accordingly, these nations regarded the antagonism between Germany and Russia as fundamental to maintaining the balance of power in Europe. Even after the First World War, therefore, British prime minister David Lloyd George noted: 'If Germany goes over to the spartacists, it is inevitable that she should throw in her lot with the Russian Bolshevists.'[2]

When, on 21 August 1939, the official German news agency issued the following communiqué, it was clear to any politically-minded contemporary that Europe would never be the same again: 'The Reich government and the Soviet government have agreed to sign a mutual nonaggression pact. The Reich minister for foreign affairs von Ribbentrop will arrive in Moscow on Wednesday 23 August to bring negotiations to a close.'[3] This news, which was confirmed by the Soviet TASS news agency soon after, was a global sensation and sent a shiver of horror down the spines of people in the liberal democracies. In the countries of the pact's co-signatories, however, the prevailing mood was one of utter bafflement.

After all, up until then Hitler and Stalin had been thought of as deadly enemies, while for over twenty years National Socialism and Bolshevism had been considered polar opposites.

Hitler's aspirations were focused entirely on the destruction of the Soviet Union. This formed the core of his 'global struggle' against 'International Jewry', whose most potent weapon was Bolshevism, as set out in the twenty-five-point programme of the NSDAP. Hitler's opinion of the Soviet Union was in a similar vein; he regarded it as the anteroom to Hell, for there 'the Jew', aided and abetted by the Bolshevik revolution, had wiped out the native Russian intelligentsia by means of 'inhuman torture and other cruelties' and had 'by means of random bastardisation succeeded in spawning an undifferentiated stew of inferior humanity'.[4]

If one divests Hitler's image of Stalin's empire – on whose territory he one day hoped to establish Germany's new *Lebensraum* – of its anti-Semitic, racist elements, then it is actually not so very wide of the mark. The civil war in Russia, which came hard on the heels of the October Revolution, had cost the lives of some eight million people. Then, in the late 1920s, Stalin ordered the systematic liquidation of the kulaks, the land-owning peasant class. Millions of peasants were deported or killed during the enforced collectivisation of Soviet agriculture. This act of mass murder was not aimed primarily at eradicating political opponents but at smashing the old systems of land management that had endured since the Tsarist period, with the goal of creating a classless industrialised society peopled by the 'new man'. (Hitler was also intent on forging just such a 'new man', albeit under very different auspices.) Lenin had prescribed such drastic measures on one occasion during the civil war when the Bolsheviks captured a region: 'Hang at least a hundred kulaks. String up hostages! And do it in such a way as to make people within a hundred-kilometre radius ... quake in their boots.'[5]

In the winter of 1932–3, Stalin's terror hit the Ukraine. The
Soviet Secret Service, the GPU – as the Cheka, founded by Felix
Dzerzhinsky, had been known since 1922 – had thus far been
unable to break the grip of local groups and gangs who had
thwarted the implementation of a functioning collective farm
system. Stalin wrote in September 1932 that the situation was
grim there. If the central state did not take firm measures, then
the Ukraine might be lost forever. The Politburo made a decisive
move. Its plan of action involved grain being transported out of
the Ukraine and sold abroad. In concert, GPU units confiscated
Ukrainian peasants' private stocks of provisions. The well-calcu-
lated result was an unprecedented famine in the 'breadbasket' of
the Soviet Union, to which seven million people fell victim.

Over the following years, the terror remained ever-present. For
the most part, indiscriminate killings of all children over twelve
years of age were carried out to meet fixed quotas among the
respective social groups – the aristocracy, the bourgeoisie, and
the peasantry. Such were the orders of the 'Leader', as Stalin
styled himself. Overzealous executioners were keen to show
off to Stalin by requesting that he raise the quotas. The mass
executions reached such proportions that disposal of the bodies
became a problem. The secret mass graves created by the Interior
Ministry (NKVD) soon spread throughout the Soviet Union. The
lucky ones among persecuted groups disappeared into one of
the numerous Gulags in the Arctic Circle or the Siberian steppe.
Nor did the crimes committed by the Bolsheviks against their
own people take place entirely in secret. Newspapers in the West
reported on the widespread deaths in the Ukraine and on the
purges that followed. Public-domain reports were supplemented
by unofficial sources of information. Thus, for example, the
United States had detailed intelligence about the Gulag system
of forced labour camps, as revealed by documents from the Stan-
ford University archives.[6]

As regards the foreign policy of the Soviet Union, it had by no means abandoned its aspiration to foment global revolution. On the other hand, it was guided by the dictum that it should at all costs avoid being encircled by the imperialist powers. As Japan, which had invaded and conquered Manchuria in the early 1930s, posed a dangerous threat in the East due to a low-level but ongoing conflict with the Red Army, Moscow deemed it imperative to exacerbate tensions between Germany and the imperialist nations to prevent the formation of any bloc against the Soviet Union. Already in 1931–2, at the cost of German–Soviet rapprochement as agreed at Rapallo in 1922 and renewed by the German–Soviet Friendship Treaty of 1926, Stalin had concluded non-aggression pacts with Poland and its 'protector' France. He also welcomed Hitler's chancellorship. What did a few thousand German communist comrades matter, who were left by the wayside by this manoeuvre, when set against the inviting prospect that now opened up to Soviet foreign policy? As a result of Hitler's aggressive rhetoric about revising the Versailles Treaty, Stalin now anticipated a conflict breaking out with Great Britain and France. In his estimation, a war would generate the right conditions for revolution in Germany and hence for the Soviet Union's sphere of influence to shift to the West.

From the very first day of his chancellorship, all of Hitler's policies were subordinated to his goal of eastward expansion. Initially, this meant that he needed to buy time to rearm the military, consolidate the territory of the Reich, and engage in diplomacy that was geared towards creating the optimal foreign-policy circumstances for his 'global struggle'. To begin with, the despised state of Poland, which Hitler scarcely ever mentioned in his programmatic writings, was at the heart of this policy. In early 1933, the latent tensions between Poland and Germany had increased still further. The main bone of contention was Danzig (Gdańsk). Even a military intervention by Polish forces no longer seemed out of the question. Conscious of the Reichswehr's military weakness at this stage, Hitler performed a volte-face in German policy towards Poland by declaring that he was prepared to recognise the eastern frontiers of the Reich. No politician of the Weimar Republic had ever dared to grasp this nettle, since it would have been tantamount to 'betraying the German cause'. Hitler's objective was to secure a treaty that he then fully intended to violate, which was why he was prepared to make concessions willy-nilly. The end result was that in January 1934, to great disbelief and astonishment both within Germany and abroad, a non-aggression pact was signed between the German Reich and the Poles, whom Hitler regarded as racially inferior. This agreement, which undermined the French–Polish mutual assistance pact (which had in any case been compromised by France's recent policy of rapprochement towards Moscow), was a purely tactical move prompted by Hitler's need to first eliminate Poland before embarking on his envisaged war against the Soviet Union.

In Hitler's eyes, however, the crucial prerequisite for such a move was an accord with 'racially kindred' Great Britain. He saw this major sea power as the natural partner of land-based Germany. He felt very strongly that Europe's autonomy could only be guaranteed if the two countries came to an arrangement. 'If Germany ... can fundamentally realign its political outlook so that it no longer runs counter to England's maritime and commercial interests, but focuses instead on continental objectives, then one perfectly logical reason for English hostility ... would be removed,' wrote Hitler, deferring his wider colonial ambitions for the distant future.[7] In his view, it had been the misguided naval policy of Germany's Second Empire that had challenged Great Britain and so made war between the two countries unavoidable.

As a further argument for joining forces with England,

where in his view the conflict between the races still hung in the balance, Hitler claimed that Great Britain's natural rival was the 'American Union', as he called the United States of America, rather than continental, eastward-looking Germany. Yet what he failed to take into account was that London essentially still clung to its traditional policy of maintaining a balance of power on the continent. The British government under prime minister Stanley Baldwin remained convinced that such a policy was vital for upholding the British Empire. A German continental super-power of the kind Hitler had in mind therefore represented a startling threat in London's estimation, whereas rivalry on the part of the United States, whatever form this might take, did not.

London observed the ongoing rearmament of National Socialist Germany with great disquiet. Equally alarming had been Germany's exit from the League of Nations and the World Disarmament Conference in Geneva in order to pursue this end. In an attempt to counter the aggressive line taken by Hitler, who had ridden roughshod over the provisions of the Versailles Treaty, in April 1935 the leaders of Great Britain, France, and Italy met at the town of Stresa on Lake Maggiore and signed an agreement reaffirming the treaties of Locarno, which Hitler was busy flouting. However, the strongly worded declaration that they formulated against his policies went unheeded. The British government was therefore all the more happy to secure the Anglo-German Naval Agreement, which was signed in June of that year. Germany accepted British pre-eminence on the world's oceans by agreeing to peg the relative strengths of the two fleets at 3:1 in favour of the British.

What Hitler saw as a first step in achieving a reconciliation of interests with Great Britain was viewed by the administration in London as a prelude to further disarmament agreements that it hoped to conclude with Germany. For Great Britain was desperate to hold its creaking Empire together and avoid a war in Central Europe at all costs. All the more so since the United States, after its intervention in the Old World and in the wake of the Great Depression and President Franklin D. Roosevelt's 'New Deal', had by now retreated into isolationism. France, meanwhile, was riven by internal political turmoil and had turned its gaze inward. Furthermore, where their arch-rival Germany was concerned, the French believed their security was guaranteed in some measure both by the country's military alliances with Poland and Czechoslovakia and by the construction of the supposedly impregnable Maginot Line along its eastern and northern borders.

The great majority of the political class in Britain saw Hitler as a vulgar continuation of Prussian militarism, a man who was staking everything on revising Versailles. London assumed that he would calm down once he had been tossed a few scraps. It was for this reason that Baldwin accepted the Naval Agreement's breach of the Versailles Treaty and took France's ensuing protest in his stride. He subsequently adopted the same attitude to Hitler's introduction of general conscription and his occupation of the Rhineland. The British were even prepared to grant concessions to Germany's policy of revision – as long as these could be seen as defensible in terms of self-determination and did not annul the 'balance of power' doctrine.

London's policy towards Germany must have made it clear to Stalin that his idea of provoking war between the capitalist powers, among which he counted Hitler's Germany, was not working. A change in Soviet foreign policy was called for. He now pinned all his hopes on his 'fifth column' within capitalist countries to stir up conflict between the nations of the 'class enemy'. In the summer of 1935, the Seventh World Congress of the Comintern supplied the ideological basis for this strategy. Fascism was now defined as a form of state in which bourgeois democracy had been supplanted by 'open terrorist dictatorship

of the most reactionary, most chauvinistic and most imperialist elements of finance capital'.[8] Whereas bourgeois society and
fascism had hitherto been regarded equally as enemies, the communists now declared themselves allies of all those forces that
preached a policy of confrontation towards fascism, and above
all against fascism in Germany. This opened up a wide spectrum
of activity that concentrated primarily on the realm of culture.
As a result, in no time an anti-fascist network of intellectuals
sprang up throughout Europe.

With the outbreak of the Spanish Civil War, Stalin's calculation appeared to have paid off. While the Soviet dictator sent
instructors, tanks, and aircraft with Russian crews to aid the
Popular Front government, the Comintern organised worldwide
resistance against the Spanish fascists. The KPD was particularly
active in the underground. It called upon all German anti-fascists
living abroad to take up arms. Appeals to aid the Popular Front
bore the names of politicians and writers like Wilhelm Pieck,
Walter Ulbricht, Ernst Toller, Herbert Wehner, Heinrich Mann,
and Arnold Zweig. In the capital of France, which had been governed since the beginning of June 1936 by a Popular Front under
the leadership of Léon Blum, the influential KPD supporter and
publisher Willi Münzenberg founded a 'War Committee for
Republican Spain'. Many thousands of volunteers from around
the world were recruited there and at offices all over Europe.
Anti-fascist fighters also came from across the Atlantic. Assembled into the so-called International Brigades, they were soon
fighting in Spain against Franco's Falangists, and saw themselves
as spearheading the liberation of Europe from fascism. Many
saw Stalin as the great hope for the world.

Now Stalin was even able to entertain the possibility of France
being drawn into a European war. Certainly, Léon Blum did not
shy away from the prospect. Giving evidence to a parliamentary
committee after the Second World War, he conceded that 'on

two occasions in the period from 1936 to 1937, the danger of war was extremely acute as a result of proposals I put forward'. For upon the outbreak of hostilities in Spain, Blum had been determined 'to supply war materials – primarily warplanes – to the Republican government regardless of the danger that this might provoke a war with Germany or Italy'.[9] Firm proposals for such deliveries had already been drawn up by Blum's defence minister Édouard Daladier, but in the face of opposition from London, which wanted anything other than a communist Spain, Blum was ultimately forced to shelve his plans for intervention – much to the annoyance of the Soviet dictator, who had been banking on a wider conflict.

Meanwhile, Hitler had been following Soviet foreign policy with all the intentness of the proverbial rabbit transfixed by the snake. He had reacted extremely aggressively to the Seventh World Congress of the Comintern. The Nuremberg Rally of September 1935 was a direct propagandistic response to it, with hawkish speeches amounting to a general call to arms to oppose 'Jewish Bolshevism'. When the Spanish Civil War broke out the following year, Hitler was profoundly unsettled, as he feared that Germany might be encircled by his Jewish-Bolshevik sworn enemy. Hitler wrote in July 1936:

If a communist Spain really does come about, then given the current situation in France, the Bolshevisation of that country, too, is only a matter of time and then it's goodbye to the Germany we know. Hemmed in between a powerful Soviet Bloc in the East and a communist French and Spanish bloc in the West, we could do very little if Moscow chose to move against Germany.[10]

Alongside the 'emergency measures' requested by Franco – namely, the dispatch of the Condor Legion – Hitler now also pushed through decisions that would ensure that the Reich was ready for what he saw as an inevitable major upcoming war against the Soviet Union. These measures included raising the length of conscription in all three branches of the German armed forces to two years. In a memorandum, he insisted that the German army should be ready to go to war within four years. He feared that he would not have any more time to play with.

Hitler's fears of encirclement increased almost to panic level when news came from Spain that the Soviet military was actively involved in the Civil War. Russian tanks under the command of General Dmitri Pavlov had wiped out a number of National-ist cavalry units south of Madrid. There were also reports of Soviet warplanes being sighted over Cartagena. A speeding-up of the military aid that Hitler had promised Franco was clearly required. Just a few days later, the Condor Legion stood ready for action in Seville. While Germany contributed mainly air force units, by January 1937 Italy, whose 'Duce' had meanwhile proclaimed the 'Rome–Berlin Axis', had dispatched a force of 50,000 ground troops to the Iberian Peninsula.

A settlement with Great Britain now became even more imperative for Hitler. Yet what had begun so promisingly with the Anglo-German Naval Agreement had by this time run aground. In the light of events in Spain and the danger they posed to Britain's key strategic positions at the western end of the Medi-terranean, Hitler speculated that it might still be possible to bring Britain on board. The major flaw in this reasoning was that by forming a united military front with Germany against 'Red' Spain, fascist Italy had, so to speak, automatically become Hitler's partner – the same Italy which, through its invasion of Abyssinia, was preparing to challenge Great Britain's dominance in the Mediterranean region.

No less fraught with problems for Hitler were the German–Japanese negotiations on forming an Anti-Comintern Pact, given that London's policies and those of Tokyo in the Far East were very hard to reconcile. Hitler gave a graphic account of the situation as he saw it to Hiroshi Ōshima, the military attaché at the Imperial Japanese embassy in Berlin, in September 1936:

> Europe is like a mountain valley with a massive boulder looming over it that threatens to break free at any moment, plunge down and bury every living thing beneath it. I believe that the only way of confronting this danger is if we break up the huge boulder that is Soviet Russia into its original histori-cal constituent parts again. I am therefore determined to do all I can to promote and hasten this development.[11]

It was something of a success for Hitler, at least psychologically, when the Anti-Comintern Pact was finally signed in November 1936. In it, the governments of the German Reich and Imperial Japan pledged to work together to counter this threat 'in the full knowledge that it is the aim of the Communist International, or Comintern, to undermine and despoil existing nation states'.[12] A secret agreement signed at the same time stipulated that in the event of an 'unprovoked attack or unprovoked threat of attack' by the Soviet Union against one of the co-signatory powers, the other party to the treaty undertook 'to take no steps whose ulti-mate effect would be to provide relief in any form to the Union of Soviet Socialist Republics'.[13] In addition, in undertaking to conclude no political treaties that ran counter to the spirit of the pact, the two countries effectively agreed to coordinate their foreign policy positions on Russia. Even so, this article of the treaty was watered down by a series of exemption clauses.

German efforts to reach an accommodation with Great Britain over the Spanish problem had meanwhile stalled. Neville Cham-berlain, who became prime minister of the United Kingdom in May 1937, was, like his predecessor, only prepared to make concessions as long as they did not upset the balance of power in Europe. In this regard, the Spanish Civil War presented a considerable challenge to London, for in the event of a victory for Franco and the forces supporting him, this balance would indeed be jeopardised, along with the British position in the Mediterranean. From a British perspective, a victory for the Popular Front, backed by the increasing involvement of the Soviet Union (the Spanish state's gold reserves had already been relocated to Moscow) was no less dangerous. Like Hitler, the British government feared that such an eventuality might soon see France fall prey to communism too, and this would likewise seriously disturb the balance of power on the continent. In light of these considerations, Chamberlain pursued an even stricter policy of neutrality towards Spain than Baldwin.

Accordingly, Hitler's endeavours to create the ideal conditions for his great war against the Soviet Union got no further. By the start of 1937 another problem was troubling him, and moreover one that chipped away at his set-in-stone worldview. In Russia, a new wave of terror had begun, in the course of which some eleven million people were affected in some way by the state's repressive measures, according to estimates by the Russian historian Natalya Lebedeva.[14] The state bureaucracy and the military were the principal targets of this round of purges, but Hitler, who saw Stalin as the tool of the Jews, was now perplexed to find that many Jews were among Stalin's victims.

So it was that figures like Grigory Zinoviev, Lev Kamenev, Georgy Piatokov, and other notable Jewish leaders of the Bolshevik revolution were condemned in humiliating show trials in Moscow and ultimately shot. Those who were liquidated also included Karl Radek and Béla Kun. Goebbels noted Hitler's bafflement in January 1937: 'More show trials in Moscow. Once again, exclusively against Jews. Radek etc. Führer still undecided whether this signals a covert anti-Semitic trend there. Maybe

Stalin does want to frighten away the Jews after all.'[13] As far back as the 1920s, Hitler had thought such a development not entirely out of the question when he wrote in his 'Second Book' that a change might come about within Russia, in other words the Bolshevik world, where 'the Jewish element could conceivably be replaced by a more or less Russian, nationalistic one'.[14]

Even so, Hitler found it impossible to countenance the idea that his arch-enemy Stalin of all people might be the person to shape the Soviet Union into something resembling a National Socialist state. Having said that, as another diary entry by Goebbels indicates, Hitler was initially at a loss what to think: 'No one can make any sense of what's going on in Moscow.'[15] Eventually Hitler found an explanation for himself, to the effect that Stalin and 'his eunuchs' must be 'sick'.[16] The chaotic situation that Hitler diagnosed was then entirely consonant with his image of 'the Jew', who, according to his way of thinking – to quote Goebbels – was 'the ferment of decomposition' and of 'disintegration'. He used this analysis to justify the decision he had arrived at a long time ago when he concluded: 'The Jew must be exterminated.'[17]

Hitler, then, was still lacking a settlement with Britain that would enable him to begin his war against the Soviet Union. Believing himself to be increasingly pressed for time, his policies grew even more aggressive. He was convinced that the vast Soviet empire with its inexhaustible supplies of raw materials was in a position to rearm far more quickly than Germany. This was why he gradually persuaded himself that he would have to launch an attack on the Soviet Union even without Britain on his side. London would just have to accept it as a fait accompli. After all, he told himself, the only response to the annexation of Austria had been a few diplomatic notes of protest. Crushing Czechoslovakia would be the real acid test. At the very last moment – the German invasion having already been set for 28 September 1938

– war was averted by the aforementioned shuttle diplomacy of British prime minister Neville Chamberlain.

Hitler regarded Munich as a defeat and a dangerous delay in implementing his master plan. Notwithstanding his disappointment, however, he concluded from Chamberlain's readiness to go over the heads of the Prague government and cede the Sudetenland to Germany that the aristocratic British PM was fundamentally weak. Hitler was also emboldened to pursue the course he had embarked upon as fascist Italy had in the meantime joined the Anti-Comintern Pact, thus aligning itself with Germany. Positive developments in the Spanish Civil War also worked in Hitler's favour. After the Nationalist army scored yet another victory at the Battle of the Ebro in the summer of 1938, the final defeat of the 'Reds' was clearly in sight. Since the autumn, Franco's forces had been advancing on Barcelona and by the year's end occupied the whole of Catalonia.

Irrational factors also increasingly came to play a role in Hitler's growing conviction that he could act 'without England' though not 'against England'. After all the successes he had enjoyed so far, he talked himself into believing that he was the infallible instrument of destiny, and that this destiny would allow him to complete his mission. Around this time, he declared:

> However weak the individual may be ... when compared with the omnipotence and will of Providence, yet at the moment when he acts as Providence would have him act he becomes immeasurably strong. Then there streams down upon him that force which has marked all greatness in the world's history.[18]

Hitler was counting on the aid of that same force when, in the winter of 1938, he prepared to crush what he disparagingly termed the 'rump Czech lands', or the 'Soviet Republic on the Vltava'.

When German troops marched into Prague in mid-March 1939, the initial response of the Western powers was to issue the customary notes of protest, although London's tone was noticeably harsher than before. His Majesty's government still did not fully recognise Hitler's ultimate aim. Just as the ambivalent image of the NSDAP during the so-called period of struggle had enabled it to occupy a highly fluid position between monarchism and socialism, so the enduring foreign-policy traditions of Imperial Germany provided a smokescreen for Hitler's real intentions. To an outside observer, the governance of the Third Reich appeared to consist of a juxtaposition or even a jumble of policies geared towards continental expansion on the one hand and a traditional Wilhelminian approach on the other, as manifested especially in the colonial political ambitions of the foreign ministry and the German navy's high command but also in the country's commercial outlook. In the same way that it had, at the time, been a fatal error on the part of Hitler's erstwhile conservative and aristocratic partners to assume that he was simply after a seat at the top table – a miscalculation that had enabled him to seize power – now the different faces presented by German foreign policy misled London into thinking that Hitler's urge for continental expansion could be held in check with the odd concession.

Yet by pursuing such a policy, Chamberlain came under growing political pressure at home. As a consequence, he decided to send an unequivocal signal to Berlin in case policymakers there were planning an assault on Poland. This signal was based not least on the miscalculation that the Polish armed forces were fully capable of withstanding an attack by the Wehrmacht. It was not only in London that their fighting strength was wrongly thought superior to that of the Red Army. This view had its origins in the Polish–Soviet War of 1919–21. While Lenin's forces were endeavouring to spread the global Bolshevik revolution westward, the

Poles were trying to restore their country to its borders of 1772, which entailed pushing the Polish frontier with Russia eastward. After a spell of fighting when the advantage shifted this way and that, at the Battle of Warsaw the Polish army under Marshal Józef Piłsudski inflicted a crushing defeat on the Soviet forces and pushed them back deep into the Ukraine. Such memories were still fresh in the mind of the British prime minister when he now publicly pledged to defend Poland's independence, and shortly afterwards that of Romania and Greece as well.

London's guarantees, which marked the end of the British policy of appeasement, represented the most serious setback that Hitler had faced since 1933. He reacted like a cornered wild animal by immediately issuing the 'Case White' directive for the invasion of Poland that still spoke in terms of 'England holding back'.[19] Then, in a speech to the Reichstag on 28 April 1939, he simultaneously terminated the Naval Agreement with the British and the Non-Aggression Pact of 1934 with the Poles. He also flatly rejected US President Franklin D. Roosevelt's attempts to lecture him about the criminality and futility of war (earlier that same month, after the Italians invaded Albania, Roosevelt demanded that Mussolini and Hitler promise not to attack thirty specific countries). He concluded by reminding Roosevelt, whose country had meanwhile positioned itself squarely alongside Great Britain, that the German people had laid down their arms once before in reliance upon the promises of a US president, only to find themselves treated by their enemies 'like the Sioux Indians in days gone by' in the ensuing peace negotiations.[20]

It was in these circumstances, with a hate-filled Hitler believing himself to be in a political cul-de-sac, that Stalin entered the scene. Back in September 1938, he had tried in vain to put pressure on the French government in the hope that he might coerce it into open military intervention to assist the Popular

Front government of Spain, which by then was in its death throes. Moscow had then proceeded, right to the bitter end, to urge London and Paris to stand firm in the Sudetenland crisis, but if it had not been apparent before, the Munich treaty finally demonstrated to the Soviet Union the clear danger of becoming isolated. Worse still, the notoriously mistrustful Stalin feared that the imperialist powers might even reach a new accommodation with Hitler, thereby creating the conditions for the German dictator to begin his eastward expansion. Against the backdrop of the ongoing conflict in Manchuria, where repeated clashes had taken place between the Red Army and Imperial Japanese forces, such an idea called for urgent action in Moscow's eyes.

Stalin believed that he could now, at a stroke, turn the situation to the Soviet Union's advantage if he gave Hitler carte blanche for the war he was planning against Poland. This would – he hoped – lead to the Western powers declaring war on Germany and make the objectives regarding the West, which the Soviet Union had been pursuing since Hitler's seizure of power, realisable at last. Edvard Beneš, the president of Czechoslovakia and an ally of the Moscow dictator, wrote in his memoirs that the Soviet Union wanted a non-aggression pact with Germany 'in order to win time so that later, when the other combatant nations were exhausted and weakened, it could enter the fray and continue to spread global revolution.'[21]

Yet Stalin would not have been Stalin if he had not taken a two-pronged approach. While the Soviet ambassador in Berlin made the first tentative moves towards establishing a Soviet–German pact on 17 April 1939, the dictator ordered foreign minister Maxim Litvinov to float the suggestion in London of a tripartite alliance between Great Britain, France, and the Soviet Union, and to back this up with a military accord. However, in line with the dictum that he had already adopted in Munich of keeping the pariah Soviet Union as far as possible from the mainstream of European politics, Chamberlain was disinclined to take up Litvinov's suggestion. Under pressure from the pro-Soviet wing of his party led by Winston Churchill, at the end of May he eventually instructed the British chargé d'affaires in Moscow to present some alternative ideas from London and Paris – a move that prompted the start of negotiations, albeit not at the highest level.

When Stalin dismissed Litvinov, who was of Jewish descent, in early May 1939 and named Vyacheslav Molotov as his new minister of foreign affairs, he was sending out a clear signal to Berlin about the Kremlin's future policy direction. This message was not lost on Hitler, who was persuaded by Ribbentrop to conclude an accord between Germany and the Soviet Union. In Germany, anti-Bolshevik propaganda was suspended for the time being. When the Condor Legion returned from Spain – the Civil War there having ended when Franco's Falange took Madrid – and was honoured with a grand military parade in Berlin at the beginning of June, in his address Hitler refrained from castigating the 'global Bolshevik peril', a phrase he had so often used in connection with events on the Iberian Peninsula. Instead, he confined himself to making oblique references to 'international forces' and 'isolationist politicians' who were allegedly to blame for the outbreak of the Spanish Civil War.[22]

By now Hitler had decided to respond positively to the Soviet overtures and enter into an agreement with Stalin. As with the German–Polish Non-Aggression Pact, he saw an accord with the Soviet Union as an interim solution that would eventually present him with an opportunity to eliminate the other party to the agreement. Through a strictly time-limited alliance with Stalin's Soviet Union, Hitler hoped not only to be able to thwart a feared alliance between the British, the French, and the Russians and so avert the danger of Germany being encircled. Above all, he expected it to have a psychological impact on London. For a close alliance between Germany and the Soviet Union would – or so he assumed – dispel any inclination on Great Britain's part to get involved militarily on the continent. In a show of bravado, he revealed to Carl Jacob Burckhardt, the League of Nations high commissioner for the Free City of Danzig, what he planned to do if things did not run according to his expectations:

> Everything I do is directed against Russia; if the West is too stupid and blind to grasp that, then I will be forced to make common cause with Russia and crush the West, and once it has been defeated I'll turn all my assembled military might on the Soviet Union.[23]

Hitler, fearing that the British might thwart his campaign against Poland by making concessions, urged his diplomats to make haste. This also seemed advisable in the light of the negotiations that were taking place between Britain and the Soviet Union. Stalin was generous in agreeing to the terms proposed by the German dictator, and Hitler, sensing his imminent triumph, was keen to let the outside world know all about his diplomatic coup. Finally, on 23 August 1939, Ribbentrop and Molotov signed a non-aggression pact in the presence of Stalin, in which each side assured the other that it would not intervene in any armed conflict in which its co-signatory became involved. In addition, a secret additional protocol, which Stalin had insisted upon, defined the two powers' respective spheres of influence in Eastern Central Europe. Latvia, Estonia, and Finland, and parts of Romania and Bessarabia, were deemed to belong to the Soviet sphere. The same was true of the east of Poland (which would cease to exist as a country). The dividing line was set along the rivers Pilica, Narew, Vistula, and San, roughly corresponding to the Curzon Line – the eastern border of the reconstituted state of Poland established at the Paris Peace Conference. As a consequence of the Polish–Russian War and the Peace of Riga in March 1921, this border had in the meantime been pushed some 200 kilometres further to the east.

It was clear to the Germans that Hitler's pact with Stalin would create the conditions for an isolated war against Poland. Some even regarded it as a sign of 'destiny'. Most people, however, continued to ask themselves the same anxious question: would Britain take its guarantees at face value and forbear to intervene? They had no inkling that the stakes were much higher than this for their Führer. He assured the handful of insiders within his close circle of confederates, who knew that his entire focus was on the Soviet Union and who feared that the NSDAP would be damaged by the pact, that party members knew him and would trust him: 'they know that I will never abandon my principles and they will recognise that the ultimate objective of this risky game is to eliminate the danger from the East'.[24]

Among his allies, the pact with the Soviet Union cost Hitler his credibility, having only recently initiated an anti-Comintern pact against it, including in Japan, since the entire thrust of Tokyo's foreign policy of backing the Third Reich was left in tatters by the German–Soviet arrangement. Tendering his resignation, prime minister Hiranuma Kiichirō noted in disbelief that the European world was 'complex and strange'.[25] The new administration under Abe Nobuyuki and foreign minister Kichisaburō Nomura, while maintaining a position of strict neutrality towards events in Europe, bent its efforts towards improving relations with the Western powers and reaching a settlement with the United States.

Hitler's other partner in the Anti-Comintern Pact, Mussolini, whose country had concluded the 'Pact of Steel' with Germany in May 1939, was no less appalled. He would presently accuse the German dictator of betraying his own anti-Bolshevik objectives. Hitler's pact with Stalin was troublesome to Mussolini not least because he feared Germany would, through its planned attack on Poland, drag Italy into a major European war. For this reason, the 'Duce' made Italy's role in this enterprise contingent upon Great Britain's reaction. Only in the event that 'the conflict remains localised will Italy extend to Germany all forms of political and economic assistance that are requested'. Otherwise, Mussolini informed Hitler, Italy would have to stay out of the conflict, as it was not yet ready for war.[26]

Like a man possessed, Hitler was now resolved to launch an immediate attack on Poland. On 22 August 1939, he told the Wehrmacht's High Command: 'We have nothing to lose and everything to gain ... There is still a high probability that the West won't intervene. With steely resolve, we must take the risk ... We are faced with the stark alternative of either striking now ourselves or surely being annihilated sooner or later.' He told them that there would be a 'propagandistic excuse for starting the war, no matter whether it is credible or not. Nobody will later ask the victor whether he told the truth or not', for might was right, he claimed.[27] The only response of the Army High Command to this was a deafening silence and worried faces. On 26 August, Hitler set a firm date for the invasion in order to finally begin the prelude to his real war.

Poland was also set on a course for war. In no way cowed by the German and Soviet encirclement and Hitler's threats that he would no longer tolerate assaults on ethnic Germans among the Polish population, Warsaw got carried away with jingoistic tub-thumping and the belief that, in the event of war, the Polish army would soon be at the gates of Berlin. In doing so, the Polish government was relying on London's guarantees and on military assistance from Great Britain and France. Yet since the 'Grande Nation' had little desire to die for Danzig, the head of the French government tried instead to act as a moderating influence on all those involved. Like Chamberlain, and also Mussolini, who hosted a peace conference, prime minister Daladier was still banking on Hitler acting sensibly.

What followed was a war of nerves. Chamberlain, whose foreign secretary signed a British–Polish military assistance treaty on 25 August 1939, was determined to take an uncompromising stance and force Hitler to relent. For his part, Hitler offered all manner of concessions to London if it would only agree not to stand in the way of a 'settlement' of the 'Polish question' – by which he meant if Great Britain simply accepted the elimination of Poland. In this event, he promised British ambassador Nevile Henderson that he would sign agreements guaranteeing the continuance of the British Empire. He even held out the prospect of German assistance in this. In addition, he put a 'sensible limitation' of armaments on the table and pledged to recognise Germany's western frontier as definitive.[28] However, the British government, which knew it had the backing of Roosevelt, turned down Hitler's offer, although he continued to doubt that they were in earnest. Instead he hoped that, on this occasion too, he would achieve his aims without Britain and France declaring war.

Stalin was counting on the opposite – namely, a war in Europe – which now seemed within touching distance. He was under no illusions that Hitler would break the Nazi–Soviet Pact if he emerged victorious from such a conflict. In that eventuality, he would have gained enough time to fully arm his Red Army for the great fight against National Socialist Germany. This contingency planning encapsulated the difference between the two dictators. Hitler – whose thinking was entirely governed by his racially based ideological worldview and who thought he had his back to the wall and that time was against him, hemming in his room for manoeuvre – staked everything on a single roll of the dice. He told Goering, who advised him against such a risky undertaking: 'In my life I've always gone for broke.'[29] Stalin was quite the opposite. With a constant focus on maximum security, he consistently acted in a rational and calculating manner; he knew that there could only be one loser from the pact.

# 8

# Hitler's Other War

*What were its distinct features?*

An exhaustive secondary literature has been written on the Second World War in general, and on Hitler's role as a military commander in particular. Commentators have highlighted the most diverse aspects of this latter topic, but they have largely omitted discussing how the criteria he employed in waging war were fundamentally different from those of his adversaries. Whereas even his direct counterpart Stalin's thinking – for all communism's claims of bringing salvation to the world – remained firmly rooted in realpolitik, Hitler's strategy was determined by irrational factors based on racial ideology. As a result, many of his decisions were met with incomprehension – or to put it more accurately, their sheer irrationality put them beyond the bounds of the comprehensible. As this remained the case even where his orders had to be translated into action, in other words within the high commands of the Wehrmacht, Kriegsmarine, and Luftwaffe, his policy had further serious ramifications for German military decision-making.

This situation, which sounds implausible at face value, sprang from various different causes. The most important of these was Hitler's self-image, for he saw himself as one of very few people who had determined that world history was driven by an eternal struggle between the races. He believed that he had been chosen by 'providence' to lead Germany, as the principal Aryan power, into this struggle. All in all, he regarded his generals and admirals as military one-track specialists, assuming from the outset that they would not know how to deal with his 'superior perception and insights'. As a result, he did not even attempt to share his knowledge with them. Conversely, from the very beginning, the general staff officers had a problem with the idea that Hitler the autodidact could possibly perform the role of commander-in-chief of an army of millions. Leaving aside the question of his aptitude as a strategist, he had, they reasoned, been merely a private during the First World War and had never attended a military academy or any similar institution.

While several individuals who were not general staff officers had risen to the highest echelons of the German military during the rapid rearmament programme of the 1930s, the elitist caste mentality of the imperial period still continued to exert a strong influence. These men had been entirely shaped by the Great War, in which they had taken part in more or less senior rankings. It was this experience, alongside the humiliations to which they were subjected by the Western powers at Versailles, that coloured their mental and emotional outlook – including their conceptions of which powers Germany should and should not collaborate with.

Accordingly, the army top brass, who still had the secret collaboration between the Reichswehr and the Red Army during the Weimar period fresh in their minds, welcomed the Hitler–Stalin Pact. From their standpoint, a war against the Russians, which was the lynchpin of Hitler's whole strategy, made no sense at all. For them, the enemy was to the west – apart, that is, from the despised Poland which, in collaboration with the Allied powers, had snatched large tracts of German territory. To the German naval hierarchy, which felt completely wedded to the tradition established by Tirpitz, Great Britain was the enemy – the same Britain that Hitler had, as early as the 1920s, identified as Germany's future partner in the great race war against the Jewish-dominated powers. As he was now in charge, the generals and admirals were sometimes required to carry out orders that ran counter not only to their own instincts but also to all military logic.

This situation was already the case when Germany launched its invasion of Poland on 1 September 1939. Inasmuch as Hitler had assembled almost all the country's military assets for this operation, the defence of the Reich in the west was, recklessly, left totally exposed. The chief of the high command of the Wehrmacht, Wilhelm Keitel – who earned the unflattering nickname 'Lakeitel' (a portmanteau word blending the German term for 'lackey' with his surname) for his shameless opportunism and obsequious attitude to Hitler – told the Nuremberg war crimes trials that an attack by the French and English at that stage 'would have met with no resistance'.[1] All the while, no one in the German command structure could predict how the campaign against Poland would play out or, most importantly, how long it would last. In spite of the recently signed British–Polish Mutual Assistance Treaty, Hitler had pinned all his hopes on Britain (and hence also France) ultimately acquiescing in the annihilation of Poland. This expectation was groundless wishful thinking driven by his unrealistic worldview.

The ultimatum issued by the British the next day, making war in Europe inevitable, was a worst-case scenario for Hitler. 'What now?' he is alleged to have asked Ribbentrop.[2] For any peaceful solutions were now closed off to him. In his view, the time pressure he felt – again born of his delusion about a creeping global Jewish conspiracy – required that he get to grips as soon as possible with the real conflict he sought with the Soviet Union, and that meant taking Poland out of the game with all haste. It was not only the military leadership who remained totally unaware of Hitler's thoughts on this score.

Great Britain now duly went to war against Germany, swiftly followed by the most important Commonwealth countries, but this was not because of Poland. Rather, the British government, which had counted on Hitler displaying a political pragmatism that he simply did not possess, took this step because it could not accept German hegemony in continental Europe. These had been the same grounds for declaring war on the German Second Empire in 1914, exacerbated on that occasion by Germany's aggressive naval policy. Despite taking account of that latter factor, therefore, Hitler was bound to fail in his attempt to make an ally of Britain. Yet he was proved right in his supposition that the United States would inherit Britain's mantle as the leading world power. For the USA was to emerge from the Second World War as the foremost maritime superpower. Great Britain became the junior partner of the Americans and lost its empire piece by piece.

However, in September 1939 London's attention was not focused that far into the future but on the 'here and now'. Although Great Britain was prepared for war, it did not – leaving aside its provision of ongoing consignments of aid to Poland – have the capacity to launch a major relief offensive in the west. France's procrastinating attitude had also played a part. This lack of action in the west confirmed Hitler's assumption that the topic of potential British collaboration was still on the table. Otherwise, he reasoned, why wouldn't they have taken this opportunity to attack his unguarded rear? Moreover, the course of the Polish campaign gave him cause for optimism. No one had envisaged that the German tank and infantry divisions, with close air support from dive bombers, would totally overwhelm Poland's forces, some of which still comprised mounted cavalry units. By 8 September, German armoured spearheads had already reached the outskirts of Warsaw. A few days later, the entire Polish army was encircled west of the River Bug. On

27 September Warsaw surrendered after coming under sustained aerial bombardment, and on 6 October the last Polish units capitulated at Kock and Lublin in the east of the country, bringing the Polish campaign to a victorious conclusion in less than six weeks. The regions that had been lost to Germany at Versailles – West Prussia, Poznan, and Upper Silesia, together with all the western Polish voivodeships (which would subsequently become the Nazi *Gau* of Wartheland) – were rapidly absorbed into the Greater German Empire.

While Stalin was alarmed by the Wehrmacht's overwhelming superiority, generally speaking he was pleased with the outcome. Georgi Dimitroff, general secretary of the Comintern, recorded the Great Leader's view of the imminent war he expected to break out between the capitalist powers:

> We have no objection to them tearing into one another and depleting their forces. It would be no bad thing if Germany were to undermine the position of the richest capitalist countries (England above all) ... We can manoeuvre, and play one side off against the other so that they really get in each other's hair.[3]

Moscow had the capacity to do this, since it not only guaranteed strategic support for Hitler's war but would also supply a substantial part of the necessary raw materials.

On 17 September 1939, Stalin, who had signed a nonaggression pact with Poland, ordered his Red Army to invade the country. The defenders had little to counter the sheer weight of this onslaught. After just five days, the Soviet operation, which had barely been noticed by the outside world, was wound up after Soviet forces reached the demarcation line agreed in the Hitler–Stalin Pact, along the former Curzon Line. In Brest-Litovsk, where Lenin's representatives had brought the war with

Imperial Germany to an end in 1918, the two dictators who had wiped Poland off the map held a joint victory parade. And on 28 September 1939 the signing of the German–Soviet Border and Friendship Treaty shifted the demarcation line a little further east to the River Bug. Step by step, eastern Poland and the Baltic states were Sovietised and incorporated into the Red Imperium. Stalin demanded concessions and a redrawing of the border on the Karelian Isthmus from neighbouring Finland, but the Finns resisted, prompting Stalin to order his Red Army to commence hostilities along the whole of Finland's eastern frontier in November 1939 (the so-called Winter War).

As millions of people were ethnically cleansed and forcibly relocated around East Central Europe, and as the SS and the GPU set about systematically murdering thousands of Jews and members of the Polish governing elite, those responsible spoke in soothing tones about a swift restoration of peace. Molotov was at pains to stress the peace-loving nature of the Soviet Union, and lambasted Britain and France as aggressors. At the beginning of October, Hitler extended a peace offer to London. It was his lifelong ambition, he explained, to bring the two peoples together. The following month Rosenberg remarked on Hitler's attitude on this matter: 'The Führer stated on several occasions that he still regarded a German–British accord as the right course of action, particularly in the long term ... We would have moved heaven and earth to achieve this, but a rabid Jewish-led minority prevailed.'[4]

London and Paris, however, turned down Hitler's peace proposal. As there was still a profound reluctance to launch a ground offensive from France against Germany, at Churchill's urging, in December 1939 the Anglo-French Supreme War Council decided to send an expeditionary force to Scandinavia. Its primary objective was to secure the Norwegian ports of Narvik and Bergen. In British hands, they would not only make it easier to close off access to the Atlantic from the North Sea but would also enable the Allies to blockade shipments of iron ore, vital to the Reich's war effort, from neutral Sweden. Since the waters around the north of Sweden froze over in the winter months, the ore had to be transported by train to the warm-water port of Narvik, from where it was shipped along the Norwegian and Danish coasts to German ports.

The strategists of the German navy also had the coast of Norway in their sights. It had long since been an article of faith for the Maritime Warfare Command and its head, Grand Admiral Erich Raeder, who found themselves literally on the front line when war broke out, that the outcome of the conflict would be decided on the high seas, across which the supply lines of the combatant nations ran. They completely miscalculated in believing that Hitler would recognise this too, and that he would be convinced of the necessity to concentrate all Germany's military resources on the fleet once its sphere of influence on the continent had been secured through the rapid rearmament of the army and air force.

However, from the navy's point of view, the war against Great Britain began much too soon, with British dominance of the world's oceans still unrivalled. As Germany did not have the resources to mount a large-scale blockade operation, the only place where 'British sea power was to be challenged head-on' was the North Sea.[5] In addition, limited sorties by the fleet through the Denmark Strait out into the North Atlantic were also envisaged. In light of this, the Norwegian coast and its ports took on even greater significance for the German navy. German control of these would provide far wider operational possibilities. Yet the naval strategists overlooked that Hitler's sole concern was to secure Europe's northern flank and the supply of raw materials that were vital to Germany's survival. Likewise, they remained wholly unaware of the Führer's continental strategic objective in the East, to which everything else was subordinated, let alone the racial ideological impetus that underpinned it.

Operation Weserübung ('Exercise on the River Weser'), the code name for the German occupation of Denmark and Norway, began on 9 April 1940. It came within a whisker of failing, for the Germans pre-empted the landing of a British and French expeditionary force on the Norwegian coast by a mere few hours. The result was a naval and aerial battle in the North Sea that threatened the bridgehead that the Germans had established, especially since local forces also offered resistance. Only after several weeks of fighting at sea, in the air, and on land, and repeated instances of panic by Hitler – who time and again issued contradictory orders to the responsible generals at Armed Forces High Command – was the situation in Norway finally stabilised by the end of April, although far to the north, in Narvik, the fighting raged on for several weeks more.

Even after the costly Norway campaign, Hitler stubbornly and dogmatically clung to his strategic ideas of an agreement with Great Britain. He now started to believe that this would ensue once he had conquered France. He had originally intended to initiate the campaign against Germany's 'arch enemy' in 1939. However, this course of action was postponed on no fewer than twenty-nine occasions, mostly due to adverse weather. In truth it was primarily the experiences of the First World War, of getting bogged down in four years of trench warfare, that gave Hitler's generals pause for thought and caused them to advance all manner of arguments for perpetually postponing the invasion date. It was finally set for May 1940.

The invasion of France was to follow a revolutionary campaign plan. Rather than reprise the Schlieffen Plan, where the main advance had taken place in the northern part of the front, the idea now was to achieve a lightning victory by means of Erich von Manstein's 'scythe cut', a swift armoured thrust through the difficult terrain of Belgium's Ardennes Forest. Breaking through to the English Channel would split the enemy's forces and ultimately lead to their annihilation. This bold plan, which conventional strategy held to be impracticable, was actually a complete success. Only two days after the start of the campaign, on 12 May 1940, the Wehrmacht made the decisive breakthrough at Sedan. Soon after, the French front behind the River Meuse collapsed in the face of the German onslaught. On 19 May, German Army Group A reached the Channel near the mouth of the Somme before swinging north. Meanwhile, Army Group B had been advancing from that direction through Belgium. A 400,000-strong British and French army – including the whole of the British Expeditionary Force (BEF) – found itself trapped and, abandoning its heavy equipment, fell back in panic to the coastal strip around the port of Dunkirk.

At this decisive moment in the war, Hitler now took a remark-able decision. On 24 May 1940, he ordered the German advance on Dunkirk to come to a halt. At this point, a mere 18 kilo-metres separated the tank divisions of the Waffen-SS from the surrounded Allied forces. By means of this 'halt order', which contrary to normal practice was transmitted uncoded, Hitler quite consciously gave the British the opportunity of evacuat-ing their Expeditionary Force across the Channel. The military top brass were aghast. Franz Halder, the German chief of staff, was supposedly 'apoplectic with rage', in a way that no one ever saw him before or since. He said something to the effect that the General Staff could not be held responsible for the decision that had been taken at the very top.[6] Even in the Armed Forces High Command (OKW), which was home to Hitler's opportun-istic henchmen, officers were reportedly 'dumbfounded' by his decision.[7]

These reactions once again underline how little the German military, who were entirely focused on the business of waging war, were able to empathise with Hitler's world. Hitler later told Gerd von Rundstedt, commander-in-chief of Army Group A, who only obeyed the halt order under protest, that 'he had hoped to come to an agreement with the British earlier if he allowed the BEF to escape'.[8] Not long after Dunkirk, Hitler laid out the bigger picture as he saw it to his inner circle: 'The army is the backbone of Britain and her Empire. Because we neither wish nor are in a position to inherit that role, we must give Britain a chance. My generals failed to grasp that!'[9]

By allowing a total of 338,228 Allied troops, including 123,000 French, to escape from the beaches at Dunkirk, Hitler – in Halder's words – 'ruined' the victory in the west. However, this was forgotten over the ensuing weeks, for between 5 and 25 June 1940, the second part of the Western campaign saw the remainder of France's military power decisively crushed. The Marne, the Somme, Verdun, all names which for a whole generation had been synonymous with courageous sacrifice and mass slaughter, now presented no obstacle whatsoever to the new Wehrmacht, which marched into Paris on 14 June. The French government under Marshal Philippe Pétain, which had meanwhile decamped to Bordeaux, called for a ceasefire. Appeals by Churchill and Roosevelt to the French to hold firm had fallen on deaf ears.

Hitler was now at the height of his power and glory. Keitel pronounced him the 'greatest military commander of all time'.[10] The Army High Command, too, which had hitherto been more reticent in recognising his abilities as a commander, hailed the high-risk gambler and acknowledged his strategic genius. German public opinion on the home front was no less fulsome in its praise. The people on the streets of the capital, who greeted their Führer like a god on his return from campaign, were positively enraptured. Hitler's approval ratings were never so high as during these summer days of 1940.

The shame of Compiègne and Versailles had finally been

expunged. On 21 June 1940, the French delegation was forced to accept the terms of surrender in the very same railway carriage where Matthias Erzberger had once signed the armistice ending the First World War. These terms stipulated that France should remain a sovereign country together with her colonies. In view of the ongoing war against Great Britain, the entire French coast right down to the border with Spain was to come under German occupation. France – apart, that is, from Alsace-Lorraine, which was de facto annexed by Germany – now consisted of an occupied and an unoccupied zone. The latter had its provisional capital at Vichy. In a deliberate echo of the Versailles Treaty, a reduction of France's armed forces to just 100,000 men was required. On the other hand, the French navy remained unscathed; in any case, with its principal bases at the southern French port of Toulon and Mers-el-Kébir in Algeria, it was beyond the grasp of the Germans. The idea behind this concession was to prevent the French navy from defecting to the British.

The ceasefire was only due to enter into force once a parallel agreement had been signed between France and fascist Italy. For on 11 June, Italy had declared war on Great Britain and France, the latter having by then already been defeated. Mussolini was keen to take part in Hitler's victory parade. Calculating that Great Britain would soon be forced to give in, he believed he was on the brink of making swift gains, above all at the cost of France, in the Mediterranean, where he dreamt of building a new Roman Empire. Yet an Italian offensive against France across the Alps had stalled with heavy losses after just a few kilometres. Thus, when Mussolini concluded an armistice with France on 24 June 1940, the only slim pickings he reaped were negligible territorial gains on this front.

Henceforth, Hitler was the master of continental Europe. Civilian Reich commissars governed both Norway and the Netherlands. Belgium and the occupied zone of France were under German military administration. Of necessity, Vichy France also took its cue from Berlin. Nonetheless, most countries – including the United States and the Soviet Union – still recognised it as the legal government of France. Franco's Spain exercised a benevolent neutrality towards the Third Reich. Italy was now Nazi Germany's brother in arms – albeit a somewhat unreliable one, since the Mediterranean would presently prove to be the 'Achilles heel' of the Rome–Berlin Axis.

In Great Britain, meanwhile, Winston Churchill had become prime minister. The 'miracle of Dunkirk', as British propaganda now reinterpreted the BEF's headlong flight across the English Channel, had given him a good start in the role. Also, in his maiden speech as prime minister in the House of Commons, he had very skilfully promised his compatriots nothing more than 'Blood, toil, tears and sweat',[11] for Churchill was determined to see the war through to the total defeat of Germany. In a memorandum, Robert Vansittart, chief diplomatic adviser to his majesty's government, went to the heart of the matter when he wrote:

> the German *Reich* and the Reich idea have been the curse of the world for 75 years, and if we do not stop it this time, we never shall, and they will stop us. The enemy is the German Reich and not just Nazism ... All possibility of compromise has now gone by, and it has got to be a fight to the finish, and a *real* finish.[12]

Churchill knew that he had the backing of Roosevelt and the powerful United States in this fight. To that extent, Britain and the Commonwealth were not 'alone', as the prime minister claimed in the title of the volume of his war memoirs that relates to this period (volume 4 of the twelve-volume paperback edition). In mid-June 1940, Roosevelt put forward a bill in

Congress for a naval shipbuilding programme. His contention was that America's naval forces should be strong enough that they could operate in the Pacific and the Atlantic simultaneously. As an immediate measure to support Great Britain, with whom talks had begun at General Staff level to try and devise a common strategy, Roosevelt sanctioned the dispatch of fifty ex-US Navy destroyers. As a sign of its resolve, at the beginning of July the Royal Navy bombarded the French fleet at anchor in Mers-el-Kébir, after its commander had refused to surrender to the British or join forces, whereupon Vichy France broke off diplomatic relations with London.

Yet despite this hardening of war fronts, Hitler sent his desired partner nation another peace offer on 19 July 1940. In his so-called 'Appeal to Reason', he reiterated that he had no desire to harm the British Empire. At this moment he felt duty-bound to make one last appeal in all conscience to Britain, he claimed in the course of his speech, for he could see no compelling reason why hostilities should continue between the two countries.[13] He sincerely meant this – after all, he maintained, it had for many years been his heartfelt wish that the two Aryan nations should join together; but this overture also came to nothing. Everyone within his close circle now expected Hitler to 'punish' Great Britain for its obduracy. Everything pointed to an imminent showdown. As evidence of his determination, even prior to extending his peace offer, Hitler had issued a directive for 'Operation Sea Lion', the invasion of Great Britain. Yet he was actually not inclined to undertake such an operation, given that the conditions were not right for it anyway, as long as the British enjoyed not only naval superiority in the English Channel and the North Sea but also air superiority there as well.

For Hitler the situation appeared to get increasingly difficult. As ever, it was the time factor above all that worried him. While the United States continued to arm itself and Great Britain, the

danger in his eyes came increasingly from a rapidly rearming
Soviet Union. Stalin, who had been counting on a long, drawn-
out conflict between Germany and the West, was rattled by the
lightning-fast German victory over France. He found himself
fearing once more that the British aristocracy might reach an
accommodation with Hitler after all, leaving him free to turn
his powerful war machine against the Soviet Union. However, by
his reckoning the Red Army was still not in a position to emerge
victorious from a war with Germany.

To improve his starting position for the war against Nazi
Germany that he saw as unavoidable in the long term, while
the world's attention was focused elsewhere, Stalin had already
ordered the Red Army to occupy Latvia and Estonia along with
the demilitarised strip along the border with Lithuania, which
according to the terms of the German–Soviet treaty of 1939 actually lay within the German sphere of influence. Farther to the
south, Moscow had also annexed the eastern Romanian regions
of Bessarabia and Northern Bukovina, thereby advancing closer
to the Romanian oilfields that would be vital for the German war
effort. Nor did Stalin stop there; he presented Finland, whose
Winter War against the Soviet Union had ended in stalemate,
with a new set of demands and dispatched heavy concentrations
of troops to the western frontiers of his empire.

These moves put Hitler in a state of pathological dread. He
even began to entertain the possibility that the Soviet Union
might launch an attack on Germany. In addition to deploying
German troops to the east, he now tried a high-risk gambit
which, if it failed, would inevitably bring the destruction of the
Reich. Hitler did so all the same because he was obsessed with
the idea that Germany would undoubtedly perish if it fell into
the deadly embrace of 'international Jewry'. He himself had
once compared the country's situation with that of a cancer suf-
ferer.[14] An operation might just cure the patient, whereas not to

intervene would entail certain death. In late 1940, he presented his deliberations on this matter to his astonished generals:

> England's hope is Russia and America. If all hope in Russia is lost, then America will drop out of the picture too, because Russia's demise will see Japan's importance in East Asia increase massively ... Once Russia has been destroyed, that will spell the end of England's last hope. Germany will then be master of Europe and the Balkans. Conclusion: in the course of this struggle, we must finish off Russia.[15]

This occasion was the last opportunity for Germany's military leaders to have intervened, as fighting on two fronts ran counter to all rational methods of waging war. Instead, in the euphoria of the historic victory over France, they came to share Hitler's crazy view of the world. Nothing was too fantastic to persuade them to have withdrawn their allegiance from him. Accordingly, the Army High Command now began to draw up initial plans for the Russian campaign, codename 'Fritz'. Two principles were to be observed. As the wherewithal did not exist to fight a war of attrition in either the east or the west, the 'Jewish-Bolshevik' arch enemy needed to be crushed in another lightning war lasting just a few months. Moreover, the campaign should be over and done with as quickly as possible – in other words before the United States actively entered the war on the side of the British. Finally, the date for the attack to commence was set for May 1941.

Quite independently of the Russian campaign, until it began Hitler was still intent on leaving no stone unturned to avoid a looming war on two fronts if he possibly could. In mid-August 1940 Goering launched an air offensive against Great Britain; Hitler's hope was that this would bring the British to their senses. However, in its arsenal the Luftwaffe had neither strategic bombers nor long-range fighters to protect them. Added to this was the greater efficiency of British aircraft production. During the Battle of Britain, the defenders turned out twice as many planes from their factories as the Germans. Thus, the balance of power shifted with every day that passed during the air war over Britain and the English Channel. As a result the Germans had to break off their offensive in the face of the disastrous losses they were incurring.

As London now believed the danger of a German invasion to have been averted, Churchill's war cabinet decided to deliver on its promise of going on the offensive on the southern periphery of Europe. Attention was focused on the area under Italian fascist control. The Allied objective was to establish a front there and engage in a war of attrition that would sooner or later tie up large numbers of Wehrmacht troops and force the Germans to divert their forces. This approach, which was fully in the spirit of Great Britain's imperial and maritime tradition, would characterise Churchill's strategy in the years that followed.

Hitler's thoughts of waging an interim war against the British concentrated on the Mediterranean region. The Armed Forces High Command examined the possibility of undermining Britain's position in the Mediterranean by eliminating its bases at Gibraltar or Suez with the help of the Italians, the Vichy French, and perhaps even the neutral Spanish. The top echelons of the German navy viewed everything in a far larger strategic context. They calculated that war in the Mediterranean would tie up large sections of the British fleet and thereby improve the unfavourable conditions facing Germany in the Battle of the Atlantic; the Vichy naval bases at Dakar and Casablanca would also be used in this conflict. Yet this plan came to nothing, not only because of the limited resources of the German navy but also thanks to Mussolini, who made every effort to keep the Germans out of the Mediterranean. The 'Duce' still believed that an accommodation could be reached between Germany, Italy, and Great Britain.

Japanese imperial leaders in Tokyo now began to foster the same hopes of profiting from Hitler's war that Mussolini had once entertained. With Germany's victory over France and its ongoing struggle against Britain, Japan saw an opportunity to seize their colonial possessions. Admittedly, Hitler was horrified by the idea of Britain's empire in the Far East falling prey to the 'Yellow Peril'. Nonetheless, the Tripartite Pact concluded between Germany, Japan, and Italy in September 1940 was of the utmost importance to him. The Far Eastern imperial power would put Great Britain under pressure in East Asia and furthermore provide a counterweight to the United States. In Hitler's estimation, this plan would keep America's naval forces occupied and overstretched in two oceans, the Atlantic and the Pacific. While Raeder and other naval commanders considered this occasion a decisive turning point in the war against Britain, Hitler simply hoped that it would buy him time – time, that is, to conclude the Russian campaign in 1941, before the United States decided to intervene directly in the European theatre of war.

Just how little even his foreign minister Joachim von Ribbentrop knew about Hitler's real motives and intentions is reflected in the former's proposal that a coalition 'between all those continental powers that have ever come into conflict with Great Britain should be forged against the island'.[16] He hoped that a continental bloc would thereby come into being, stretching from Madrid to Yokohama and forming a global political counterbalance to the Anglo-Saxon maritime powers. As the nucleus of this continental bloc, Ribbentrop envisaged a four-power pact between Germany, Japan, Italy, and the Soviet Union. To this end, he tried to dispel Stalin's fears about encirclement, which had been reawakened by the Tripartite Pact, and to deflect Soviet expansion southwards instead, in the direction of India, as a way of easing tensions arising from the divergent interests of the Soviet Union and Japan in the Far East. Ribbentrop put himself forward as a mediator and invited Molotov to Berlin. On 2 October 1940, he had expressly reassured the Soviet minister of foreign affairs that nothing would change in German–Soviet relations.

Hitler gave his foreign minister free rein, since he identified a possible interim solution in the western cornerstone of the continental bloc at least. This proposition would require a reconciliation of interests between Italy, Vichy France, and Spain. In this context, the German dictator spoke in terms of a 'grand deception':[17] in other words, these countries bordering on the Mediterranean could only be forged into a united front against the British by making false promises to them and playing one off against the other. He attempted to do just that – meeting Mussolini, Pierre Laval, Franco, and Marshal Pétain in quick succession in October 1940 – but failed. The Spanish and the French wanted to wait and see how the war progressed, while the Italian dictator, unable to match the British militarily in the Mediterranean and still intent on keeping the Germans out of his sphere of influence, soon found himself in difficulties when he ventured to take on Greece in that same month.

When Stalin's foreign minister duly arrived in Berlin in November 1940, it once more became clear to Hitler that time was short for a solution to the Russian problem, for Molotov, who knew that the German side was under pressure, brazenly called for an expansion of the Soviet sphere of influence far into Central Europe. Stalin's territorial demands were no longer confined to Finland, Romania, Bulgaria, and the Dardanelles; he now laid claim to Hungary, Yugoslavia, the western part of Poland, and the straits exiting the Baltic Sea. Hitler spoke of the 'end of Central Europe' if the Soviets were granted entry to Europe in this way. On 18 December 1940, he signed 'Directive No. 21', or 'Operation Barbarossa', the codename that had already been in circulation for some weeks for the campaign against Russia.

The directive ordered that the Wehrmacht – even before hostilities against Britain had drawn to a close – should hold itself in a state of readiness 'to crush Soviet Russia in a swift campaign'.[18]

In the Army High Command, where exuberance and a belief that anything was possible had reigned after the victory over France, a more sober outlook had now returned in light of the worrisome overall strategic situation. The conflict was now splintering off in all directions. It would defy all reason to embark upon a campaign against Russia as well. Walther von Brauchitsch, the army's commander-in-chief, thought Hitler's objectives so absurd that he instructed his liaison officer in the Armed Forces High Command 'to find out whether the F[ührer] really wants a military engagement [with the Soviet Union] or is just bluffing'. Brauchitsch was duly informed that Hitler reserved the right to take any decision he chose, having never taken the pact with the Soviet Union completely seriously anyway, 'since its worldview was so unfathomable to me'.[19]

The generals themselves now tried to fathom what Hitler wanted to achieve with the Russian campaign. 'Barbarossa: Point unclear. We won't hurt the English with it. Our economic situation won't improve appreciably. The danger from the West [!] cannot be underestimated,' wrote Franz Halder, Hitler's chief strategist and planner.[20] Yet no one raised open objections to the operation; the generals had learned to be ultra-cautious and did not want to entirely rule out another stroke of genius on Hitler's part like the one against France. Moreover, they were cowardly and feared falling out of favour with Hitler or being replaced. They therefore continued planning an operation that every expert military strategist would surely have condemned as an irresponsibly risky roll of the dice.

Even so, in December 1940 Halder tried to make the Russian campaign irrelevant by suggesting that the bulk of German military activity be shifted to the southern periphery – a proposal clearly demonstrating that he did not have the faintest idea of what motivated his commander-in-chief. He was harshly rebuked by Hitler, despite the fact that his intervention would have been eminently sensible from an overall strategic point of view, for Italy's war against Greece was threatening to turn into a complete fiasco. Rome's forces suffered one defeat after another in the borderlands between Albania and Greece. Mussolini now urgently needed help. Why not straightaway combine support for the 'Duce' with a renewed campaign against England? This struck Halder as all the more pressing because, in the interim, the numerically inferior British Mediterranean fleet had begun to operate with complete freedom of action on the 'Mare Nostrum' against Italian naval forces that were in many cases obsolescent.

According to Hitler's way of thinking, however, the Russian campaign was the only factor determining the scale and nature of the German intervention in the Mediterranean. In his view, the central issue there would be to secure the south-eastern flank for the major thrust eastwards, so he decided to send Luftwaffe units to the eastern Mediterranean. His idea was that this would constitute a limited German action to relieve the Italian campaign against Greece and add to the steady build-up of air power in Romania in order to prevent any attempted British landing on the coast of Thrace. Hitler was worried primarily about the Romanian oilfields. For, as he once stated, 'without ... at least four or five million tonnes of Romanian petroleum, we would not be able to wage war'.[21]

German assistance for Italy again brought all those into the arena who, contrary to Hitler's ideas, advocated shifting Germany's military focus to the Mediterranean region. The question of a reconciliation of interests between Spain, Vichy France, and Italy thus came to the fore once more. With Hitler's approval, another attempt was made to win Madrid round to mounting a joint operation against the British territory of Gibraltar in return for all kinds of promises of German aid. In addition, German planners studied the feasibility of air strikes to block the Suez Canal. These were pipe dreams rather than realistic proposals, devised by Hitler in order to keep Mussolini, who had latterly grown more subdued, in the alliance. He told his Axis partner, who had no inkling of his real objectives, that the closure of both approaches to the Mediterranean would 'turn it into the British fleet's grave within three to four months' (in other words, just in time for the Russian campaign to begin).[22]

Of course, the plan came to nothing. Instead, Italian military adventurism experienced another debacle: the British launched a ground offensive in North Africa in December 1940, driving Italian units not just out of the eastern region of Libya bordering Egypt where they had advanced in September of that year. In no time, the loss of the whole of Tripolitania and hence the entire Italian position in North Africa seemed on the cards. Hitler feared that this would seriously jeopardise the survival of the Axis, and in turn would place in doubt his own war in the east planned for 1941. In January, this drastic prospect prompted him not only to dispatch Luftwaffe units south but also to send an anti-tank division to Tripolitania. This detachment was the embryo of the 'German Afrika Korps' under Erwin Rommel.

By the time the first German advance parties arrived in Tripoli in mid-February 1941, the British had already halted their offensive in order to send troop detachments to Greece. Churchill wanted to establish a line of defence there against the anticipated German offensive to relieve the beleaguered Italian forces. However, this operation failed miserably because the Wehrmacht had advanced with astonishing speed across Yugoslavia into Greece. Belgrade fell to German forces on 13 April 1941, and by 27 April the swastika was flying over the Acropolis in Athens. Greece surrendered, and the British were forced once more to retreat in disarray from the European mainland, initially

to Crete and then, after the island was taken by Goering's para-
troopers, to Egypt. In the process, many thousands of British
Empire soldiers were captured by the Germans. Despite this
setback for the British, Churchill's war in the Mediterranean
fulfilled its purpose: German forces were fragmented and Hitler
was forced to postpone the start of his Russian campaign from
May to June 1941.

Briefing within the Wehrmacht about this major impending
operation was on a strictly need-to-know basis. Rommel was
not informed. He believed that he was fighting on the war's decisive front against the British, and on his own initiative pushed
forward to Tobruk and the Egyptian border. He saw his advance
in the context of the German campaign in the Balkans and
thought that he would be bound to receive reinforcements –
which never arrived. Accordingly, he found himself in a difficult
position, from which he was only just able to extricate himself.
From an outsider's point of view, his advance looked as though
it was part of a grand coordinated operation by the Axis to bring
about the downfall of the British military presence in the eastern
Mediterranean. The German public, too, thought that this was
the case. A report on the public mood prepared by the *Sicherheitsdienst* (SD), the intelligence agency of the SS, in early June
1941 found that 'the overwhelming majority of the populace ...
anticipates an attack on Cyprus and the Suez Canal'.[23] This was
also the assumption in Great Britain.

The psychological effect on the entire Arab world was immense,
causing a universal atmosphere of seething unrest. Resistance
to British governance in Egypt began to crystallise around King
Farouk. In Iraq, Arab nationalists led by Rashid Ali al-Gailani
tried to seize power in April 1941 and drive the British out of the
country. Violent clashes broke out in May. Many people were
convinced that British rule in the Near East was drawing to a
close. However, this proved to be a mirage. These developments

once more raised Hitler's hopes that Britain would finally give in. He did not want to contemplate another outcome. If as a result of this war the long-established European powers were to lose their colonial empires, then this would be to no one's advantage, he claimed at this time, since this would see 'the rise of an American imperialism'.[24] In his speech to the Reichstag in May 1941, he reiterated that he had not wanted to go to war against Britain, and attacked the 'small clique' (around Churchill) who, motivated by 'hatred and greed', had spurned his efforts to reach an accommodation.[25] This being said, he wasn't about to make a peace offer to London, since he believed this would be interpreted as a sign of weakness on his part.

Instead, this fell to his deputy Rudolf Hess, who – unlike most people – was perfectly au fait with the crude racially ideological worldview of his leader and the strategy he derived from it. In a move that was as audacious as it was foolhardy, on 10 May 1941 he flew to Scotland to try and make contact with those groups in Britain that were amenable to Hitler's way of thinking. Of course, this 'madman's errand',[26] as one commentator has appositely dubbed Hess's peace mission, came to nothing. The precise details of what happened will most likely never be known, as many of the confidential British government papers on the subject remain closed to researchers. This has certainly provided ample fuel for all kinds of conspiracy theories. Even Hess's death – more than forty-five years later at Spandau Gaol in Berlin – has been linked to this abortive peace mission. A former German chancellor confided in this author that it was not suicide but an assassination on the orders of the then British prime minister and ardent Churchill-admirer Margaret Thatcher; the reason given was that if Hess had been released by Soviet leader Mikhail Gorbachev – a distinct possibility mooted at the time – he would have been able to reveal the 'real' story behind his flight to Scotland.[27]

What is indisputable is that Hess's flight was brilliantly exploited by Churchill to exert pressure on the American president to intensify the cooperation between Britain and the United States. The British and American general staffs had already agreed that the primary common objective of future joint war planning would be first to overcome Germany and only thereafter deal with the situation in the Pacific and East Asia, where it was assumed there would be a war with Japan – which Washington positively provoked through trade embargoes and a rigid policy of containment. As the sea lanes across the North Atlantic were seen as essential to Britain's survival, the US navy undertook to protect convoys destined for its partner nation, while the British fleet would continue to conduct most of its operations in the Mediterranean. Churchill had thereby achieved his aims. It was easy to find a reason for the United States to enter the war and only a matter of time, since clashes between the German navy and the American fleet would be unavoidable; and all the more so as German naval commanders were intent on disrupting Atlantic convoys through the use of U-boats, which had taken on even greater importance after the sinking of the battleship *Bismarck* on 27 May 1941.

The Soviet Union did not as yet figure in British and American plans for the war against Germany. Yet, with the Allies fully aware of German preparations to invade Stalin's empire – which they monitored with growing incredulity – it was already regarded as a partner. Intelligence service reports, including Hitler's directive and the date set for the invasion, 22 June 1941, were passed to Moscow by London and Washington. Stalin regarded this as nothing more than a blatant attempt to get the Soviet Union on side against Germany. The Soviet dictator was even more certain after being briefed about the failure of Rudolf Hess's mission by his top spy in London, Kim Philby. Stalin continued to categorically rule out any possibility that Hitler might embark on a war on two fronts: that is, by attacking his country before ceasing hostilities with Great Britain.

The Soviet dictator thought that he was safe and looked confidently towards the future. By now, the rearmament of the Red Army for war against Germany was well advanced. Defence Minister Semyon Timoshenko and Chief of the General Staff Georgy Zhukov were already working on an operational plan to forestall a German surprise attack. By 1942, the Soviet Union would be in a position to put it into action. Stalin was convinced that he had sufficient time at his disposal. Indeed, he even made an effort to revive relations with Germany, which had flagged somewhat since Molotov's visit to Berlin. In line with this, the second German–Soviet trade pact, which was signed in January 1941, was fulfilled to the letter. A week before the invasion of Russia began, Stalin instructed the news agency TASS to broadcast the message that reports about a German attack on the Soviet Union had no basis in reality.[28]

Although Stalin took note of information provided by his security services warning of the major build-up of German forces on the border, he did not assign much importance to it. Likewise, he dismissed rumours of an impending attack, which had meanwhile begun to circulate throughout Europe, as simple disinformation. He even ignored an intervention by Churchill, who made a personal appeal to him for the first time. Nor did his apparatchiks behave any differently. When British foreign secretary Anthony Eden again told Moscow's ambassador in London, Ivan Maisky, about Hitler's plans, he replied: 'An attack? ... I don't believe it! It'd be crazy.'[29] How firmly everyone in the Kremlin was convinced that Hitler would never dare to wage a war on two fronts is also evident from the first reaction to news of the German invasion. Stalin's former foreign minister Litvinov recalled that 'everyone there was certain that the Royal Navy would steam across the North Sea and launch an attack

on Leningrad and Kronstadt that had been prearranged with
Hitler'. It was with almost total disbelief, Litvinov continued,
that people registered that this was not in fact the case[30] – and all
simply because the Russian leadership assumed that Hitler was a
rational, coldly calculating and power-hungry politician, failing
to recognise his true nature.

As far as Hitler was concerned, just as in the First World War,
the Jewish-directed global conspiracy had continued to develop
over the past months, forming a united front against Germany.
However, as he proclaimed in his address to the German people
on the occasion of the invasion of Russia, the victory of the
'Axis powers' in the Balkans 'for the time being thwarted the
plan to keep Germany bogged down in months of fighting in
southeastern Europe and while that was happening to complete
the deployment of Soviet Russian armies'. Now, he declared, 'the
time has come to counter this plot by the Jewish Anglo-Saxon
warmongers and the equally Jewish string-pullers in the Bolshevik Central Committee in Moscow'.[31]

The Russian campaign was to be the realisation of the idea
that had germinated in Hitler's mind during the chaos of the
revolutionary period, when 'Jewish Bolshevism' had sought to
engulf Germany while it was at its lowest ebb. Ever since then,
all his actions had been in the service of this one great goal.
Now, through his war of extermination, he would wipe out
the 'Jewish-Bolshevik' leadership and decimate the Slavic 'subhumans', with the aim of exploiting them later as a great pool
of slave labour when Germanic settlers came to occupy the lands
to the east. This massive new *Lebensraum* with its rich deposits
of raw materials – Hitler's India – was also intended to make the
German continental empire self-sufficient, thereby creating the
necessary conditions for Germany's fight against the remaining
'Jewish global enemy'.

A gigantic military assault mechanism was set in motion at

0315 hours on 22 June 1941. In addition to 690,000 troops from other Axis countries, more than three million German soldiers alongside 3,500 tanks and artillery pieces – organised into three army groups, and with close air support from almost 2,000 aircraft – advanced across a broad front of 1,500 kilometres with the objective of crushing the Soviet Union. Yet the Soviets' war machine was even larger and was numerically far superior to that of the attacking force, as the Red Army had at its disposal three times as many tanks and double the aircraft. But although their weapons' technology was a match for that of the Germans – or, in the case of their tanks, even superior – the Red Army was deficient in training and operational leadership. This factor alone presented the attackers with a chance of success. They would need to out-manoeuvre their adversary in a new lightning campaign, which, moreover, had to happen across vast spaces. The intention was to successfully wrap up the insane operation before winter set in, by which time the German advance would have reached a line running from the Caucasus along the River Volga and up to Arkhangelsk.[32] There was no plan B, since German resources could not stretch to a long war of attrition in either the East or the West.

The German people had been prepared for anything except a war against the Soviet Union. However, they realised that something was afoot. The strangest rumours had started to circulate. These were picked up by the SD: 'The word is that Stalin is coming to Berlin and that the Ukraine will be leased out to Germany for 99 years.' Eight German divisions had already occupied the region, it was said. The troop movements of recent days along the eastern border were being seen in this context, the SD reported on 12 June.[32] Then, when the astonished German populace was finally told about the attack on the Soviet Union, they questioned the purpose of this campaign, since fighting on two fronts had been the principal problem for Germany in the First World War.

To begin with, hardly anyone realised that the campaign that had just begun was a war of extermination. Even top officials in the Nazi regime like Alfred Rosenberg were not kept informed about the true nature of the operation. In a speech on 20 June, Hitler's chief ideologue outlined the political requirements for the impending war against the Soviet Union, stating that the key thing would be to revive the aspirations for freedom felt by all the peoples of the East 'in a shrewd and purposeful manner and to make them a reality in a very particular form of state'. According to Rosenberg, individual states should be organically carved out of the vast territory of the Soviet Union and built up in opposition to Moscow 'in order to liberate the German Empire for centuries to come from the Eastern nightmare'.[33]

This is how everyone expected the Germans to proceed. In London and Washington, where there was general incomprehension at Hitler's invasion of the Soviet Union, it was naturally assumed that the German dictator would utilise the liberation movements in the East and pursue a policy of divide and rule that might ultimately bring about the collapse of the Soviet regime. Indeed, this is what the subject peoples of the Soviets also thought. In the Baltic states, the soldiers of the invading Wehrmacht were therefore greeted as liberators. It was no different in the Ukraine. Counting on Hitler's support, Ukrainian nationalist groups led by Jaroslav Stezko and Stepan Bandera immediately proclaimed an independent state, but in Hitler's war, these 'Slavic subhumans' were not envisaged as partners of the 'master race'.

Instead of bringing freedom from Moscow's tyranny, which would have mobilised millions against the Soviet regime, Hitler's armies brought terror and death. The Army High Command, which even in the lead-up to the Russian campaign had acquiesced in Hitler's criminal directives such as the 'Commissar Order' of 6 June 1941, went along with his war of extermination.

It was also complicit in the slaughter of civilians carried out behind the advancing front by Heinrich Himmler's four mobile 'task forces' made up of security police and SD men, with their eighteen 'special units' ('Sonder-und Einsatzkommandos'). The Wehrmacht even provided logistical support to the SS and SD for their programme of genocide against Jews, Soviet commissars, Roma people, and 'sundry other subhumans'.

The military leadership did this out of a sense of overweening arrogance, all the more so since it appeared that the struggle against the Russians, which was conducted with unyielding ferocity, would be decided west of the Daugava and Dnieper rivers. Red Army forces, caught unawares and unprepared, and whose air support had largely been destroyed in the first hours of the invasion, were overrun. Poor morale also played a part, with Soviet soldiers defecting en masse to the Germans. The first weeks of the campaign saw more than a million taken prisoner or killed. Halder noted with satisfaction on 3 July 1941 that in his view it would 'not be an exaggeration to say that the campaign against Russia was won within the space of a fortnight'.[34] Hitler himself, who was no less confident of victory, indulged in apocalyptic fantasies, claiming that he wanted to raze Leningrad and Moscow to the ground. Nor did he stop there. While the head of the SS, Heinrich Himmler, drafted a 'General Plan for the East' covering the organisation and exploitation of the vast conquered territories, Hitler was already making plans for the period after 'Barbarossa'. In mid-July he presented Hiroshi Ōshima, who had been promoted to the post of Japanese ambassador to Berlin, with the idea of an offensive alliance directed against the United States.

Once again, however, things turned out very differently: in mid-July 1941 the situation on the Eastern Front evolved in a way that was anything but positive for the Wehrmacht. The Red Army began to mount counteroffensives in the Greater Smolensk area. Its fighting morale had significantly improved and the large number of deserters had declined sharply, as Hitler's war of extermination left the Russians with no alternative but to fight to the bitter end, unleashing some extraordinary forces on the Soviet side. Increasing numbers of people heeded Stalin's call to fight as partisans. Thus, for many Red Army soldiers who in truth wanted nothing to do with the communists, the desperate defensive action undertaken by a hated regime really did over time develop into a 'Patriotic War', a slogan newly coined by Stalin's propagandists.

By the end of July Hitler was forced to order the Army Group Centre to go over to the defensive. Since the campaign had to be completed before the onset of winter at all costs because the attacking armies were not equipped for a drawn-out conflict let alone a winter war, everything now became a hopeless race against time. On 25 July 1941, Keitel recorded that the Führer, beset by worry, had been asking himself: 'How much time have I got to finish off Russia, and how much more do I still need?'[35] Hitler's mounting panic over the imminent failure of his lightning war triggered fierce disagreements over how to proceed on the Eastern Front. Against the advice of the Army High Command, which favoured advancing on Moscow, Hitler eventually ordered the main weight of the German attack to focus in the north on taking the city of Leningrad, and in the south on the Donbas region and the Crimea, with an eye to pushing forward and seizing the oilfields of the Caucasus.

At the beginning of August, Army Group Centre brought the battle of encirclement at Smolensk to a successful conclusion. In the north, the Wehrmacht continued to advance on Leningrad. In the south, the Germans reached Kiev. Yet despite a string of German victories, the fighting was immeasurably more arduous than anticipated, making progress far too slow. The cause was the catastrophic underestimate of the number of troops available to the Red Army, which was growing in strength all the time. It seemed to be able to call upon an inexhaustible supply of reservists. Another major factor was the huge distances involved that overstretched German supply lines. In August, when Goebbels visited the Führer at the 'Wolf's Lair', his forward headquarters in East Prussia, he encountered a Hitler whose physical strength was visibly impaired. He spoke about his desire to bring the campaign in the East 'to a ... satisfactory conclusion' by the onset of winter, which would probably arrive in mid-October.[36]

An 'Armed Forces High Command Memorandum on the Strategic Situation in Late Summer 1941', sanctioned by Hitler, stated unequivocally that there was no prospect of bringing the campaign against the Soviet Union to a victorious conclusion by the end of the year.[37] This outcome could only mean that Hitler's plan of campaign, which was predicated on a lightning war, had failed. His response was to escape from reality, in raising once more the question of an agreement with Great Britain, which he had intended to reach by defeating the Soviet Union. Now all that remained for Hitler was a bottomless well of hatred for his adversaries. After a meeting with Hitler, Goebbels recorded his leader's thoughts in his diary: 'Right now Stalin ... Churchill, and Roosevelt are the three principal ... enemies of the National Socialist revolution.' Among these 'leaders of the great global conspiracy against Germany, Roosevelt is undoubtedly the most cynical'.[38]

Not long before, in the full glare of publicity on board US and British warships anchored off Newfoundland, Roosevelt had proclaimed his close alliance with Churchill. The Atlantic Charter that resulted from that meeting on 14 August 1941 enshrined the principles of global free trade, the freedom of the seas, and the right of all people to self-determination. Even in the negotiations leading up to this accord, it was clear that Great Britain would be assigned the role of junior partner. Roosevelt and Churchill announced their intention, 'after the final destruction of Nazi tyranny', of working towards the establishment of a system of collective security.[39] The Soviet Union was not mentioned once in these Anglo-American deliberations about the future shape of the world that were clearly informed by the spirit of Woodrow Wilson's Fourteen Points. When the Atlantic Charter was drafted, the assumption was that Stalin's Russia would be unable to withstand the onslaught of the German armies.

Over those summer months of 1941, the Soviet Union under Stalin was engaged in a life-and-death struggle. As early as mid-July, the Georgian dictator had turned to the Western powers for help; after it transpired that the Red Army, against all expectations, was holding its own against the Germans, the communist empire became an important factor in Allied war planning. Stalin pressed Churchill to open up a second front against Hitler in northern Norway or France, and asked Roosevelt to supply large quantities of arms and munitions. The Anglo-Saxon powers showed themselves more than willing to accede to these requests. All knowledge about Stalin's reign of terror, which had cost the lives of millions of Russians before the war, was put to one side. The threat to the Western world was now perceived as coming from Germany rather than the Soviet Union. In the same way that Stalin, after signing the pact with Hitler, had calculated on the Western powers becoming embroiled in a war against Germany and on the benefits he might reap from this, so Churchill and Roosevelt now speculated that the Soviet Union's war with Germany would spare them more bloodshed. To this end, they were prepared to send their new ally huge quantities of war material and to glorify Stalin's war in pathos-laden speeches, as for instance when the British prime minister waxed lyrical in a radio broadcast: 'the cause of any Russian fighting for his hearth and home is the cause of free men and free peoples in every quarter of the globe'.[40]

In 1941, the Soviet Union was still completely on its own, since it took some time for the American aid programme to start. The orders Stalin issued to the Red Army were correspondingly brutal: surrendering was regarded as an act of treachery towards the Soviet Union. To reinforce this edict, he decreed that the families of Red Army soldiers who had been taken prisoner would be deported. The measures he put in place ruined the lives of millions of innocent people. The Soviet dictator, who at the beginning of August appointed himself as commander-in-chief of the armed forces, introduced a strict penal regime that saw almost a million soldiers court-martialled and more than 157,000 put before firing squads.

In consequence, the battle across the vast expanses of Russia reached heights of brutality hitherto unseen. On both sides, for the most part, no prisoners were taken. For the Wehrmacht, this was standard procedure in the case of communist partisans. An order issued by Walter von Reichenau, in which soldiers in his army were instructed to summarily execute captured partisans, stated that every member of his unit 'should fully understand the need for harsh but just retribution to be meted out to Jewish subhumans'.[41] This order was held up as a model example by Hitler and was adopted by other commanders. While isolated members of the Wehrmacht might still have had some scruples about such conduct, the slaughter perpetrated by the SS and SD behind the lines turned into a regular bloodbath.

Faced with the looming failure of his Russian campaign, Hitler abandoned any last vestiges of protection for Jews within his sphere of power and took steps to bring about their extermination. Then, in September, an apparent opportunity to topple the Soviet colossus after all seemed to open up for him. A string of victories by his forces appeared to put within touching distance a successful end to Operation Barbarossa before winter descended. In the encirclement battle at Kiev at the end of

September, five Soviet armies comprising a million men suffered a crushing defeat. At the start of that same month, German forces had managed to overrun Estonia and to cut off Leningrad. The outcome of the war would now be decided by a major offensive against Moscow, as Halder had advocated many weeks before. Two million men and 2,000 tanks were assembled by the Army Group Centre for 'Operation Typhoon'. The assault began on 2 October 1941. Shortly afterwards, the Red Army was routed in the battle of Vyazma and Bryansk. A mere 150 kilometres now stood between the German armoured spearheads and Moscow, where the embalmed corpse of Lenin was hastily removed from the mausoleum on Red Square.

Hitler's self-belief had returned. Certain of victory, he announced that the enemy was broken. He thought that he had achieved his greatest goal. Revelling in fantasies of triumph, he told his closest confidantes that he had no intention of accepting Moscow's surrender. In conversation with his secretary Martin Bormann, he maintained that by eradicating 'Jewish Bolshevism' they were doing 'mankind a great service ... whose momentous significance our men in the field cannot grasp as yet'.[42] As he anticipated putting his National Socialist empire in the vanguard of the final showdown against the last great bastion of 'international Jewry', he told another interlocutor: 'Once we are masters of Europe, then we'll occupy the most dominant position in the world.' In his elation, the accommodation with Britain that he so hankered after even paled into insignificance, although he assumed that the British would be shrewd enough to 'come over to us'. Clearly alluding to the Jews of America, Hitler declared: 'England doesn't interest me anymore; only those who are behind it.'[43]

At first, any further advance towards Moscow was hampered by the mud of the Russian autumn. In no time, the roads running east were transformed into bottomless quagmires. For Hitler, these were all just interruptions on the path to final victory, which – as Halder claimed – 'no power on earth can now deny us in this conflict'.[44] German forces waited for the winter frost to set in, which they believed would enable them to deliver the coup de grâce to the 'Bolshevik monster'. No one on the German side imagined that it would be capable of mounting any appreciable resistance after the devastating defeats it had suffered. Even so, these were weeks of high tension leading up to 19 November 1941, when the end of the muddy season ushered in the second phase of the Battle of Moscow. The Germans did not have sufficient manpower to surround and besiege the city. As a result, it was decided they would mount a full-frontal assault on the Soviet capital.

German hopes evaporated within just a few days, however. Unexpectedly, the Red Army put up fierce resistance. The onset of winter became their ally, as the German Eastern Front army attempted to fight in summer equipment. On 1 December 1941, Fedor von Bock reported that the time was fast approaching 'when our troops' ability to fight will have been utterly exhausted'.[45] Four days later, after consultation with the Führer's headquarters, he ordered a halt to the advance. Then, on 6 December, the German army found itself facing total catastrophe. Under the supreme command of Marshal Georgy Zhukov, the commander who would go on to take Berlin, the Soviets staged a counterattack. It was spearheaded by divisions from Siberia that were ideally kitted out for winter warfare. Stalin was in a position to deploy them in this battle because he had received reliable reports from Tokyo that Japanese expansion would focus on the Pacific region.

And so it was that Germany's Russian campaign came to grief outside the gates of Moscow, with the golden cupolas of the Kremlin already in sight. 'General Winter', with its −42 °C temperatures, was not primarily to blame for this failure, although National Socialist propaganda was quick to make this claim. It was simply that the distances involved were insurmountable, as was the material superiority of an adversary whose capacity to resist had been fatally underestimated. Yet the decisive factor was Hitler's configuring of the campaign as an ideological war of racial extermination. From the outset, this prevented any anti-Bolshevik alliances from being formed with the oppressed peoples of Russia. Moreover, it was the prime mover in unleashing the resistance of the Red Army and in forging Stalin's Soviet Union, a multi-ethnic prison based on repression and terror, into a nation. This consequence remains one of the great ironies of history.

However, it was not just the fate of the Russian campaign but the outcome of the Second World War that was decided outside Moscow. Stung by his failure, Hitler now leapt ahead by embarking on a 'decisive world war' against the great 'Jewish' financial powerhouse of the 'American Union' that he had originally imagined future generations of Germans would have to wage in alliance with the British. Japan's war against the United States, which began with the attack by aircraft of the Imperial Japanese Navy on the US naval base at Pearl Harbor in Hawaii, provided him with this opportunity. Yet it also allowed him to convey the impression that he still had a firm grip on matters. In actual fact, his declaration of war on the USA on 11 December 1941 was the act of a man who had already plunged into the abyss and would proceed to drag many down after him.

# 9

# The Genocide of the Jews

*How could it have happened?*

The origins of the genocide of the Jews of Europe lie in the chaotic period following the First World War, when Hitler's racially driven ideological mindset began to take shape. From 1919–20 onwards, all his hate-fuelled aspirations were informed by the notion that 'International Jewry' had a stranglehold on Germany. Over and above this, the conflict with the supposed Jewish world conspiracy was for him a life or death 'global struggle',[1] whose outcome would leave 'Germany either as a world power or completely non-existent.'[2] Nothing changed by a single iota when he then took to the major political stage and subsequently became chancellor. However, by that time he had learned to exercise some degree of restraint in public. That is to say, he took into account tactical considerations, initially with regard to the sensitivities of the German public, then to those of his conservative alliance partners, and finally to the image of the Third Reich in the outside world – not remotely meaning, however, that he had recanted his racial ideology or resiled from his intention of eliminating the Jews. But did that automatically imply their physical extermination, a topic he had often written and spoken about as leader of the insignificant political splinter group called the NSDAP?

When Hitler attained absolute power after Hindenburg's death, he gradually let his mask slip. The time for tactical considerations was now at an end. In the ensuing period, a remarkable reciprocal effect becomes apparent, once more underlining how obsessively and manically his whole personality was permeated by the ideology of race. For whenever Hitler – who in any case was tormented by the thought that time was against him – saw the supposed threat posed by 'international Jewry' increasing, or whenever he suffered a setback by having to curtail the political and strategic measures he had implemented to contain that threat, his consistent response was to radicalise and accelerate his sanctions against the Jews. The former was evidently the case in July 1935, when Stalin, through the World Congress of the Comintern, began to mobilise against fascism and hence against Hitler's National Socialism. There is a clear connection between this event and the enactment of the Nuremberg Laws on race just a few weeks later that Hitler announced at the Party Congress.

Alongside the systematic marginalisation and isolation of German Jews, the idea of 'removing' – that is, expelling – the 394,000 Jews still resident in Germany at the end of 1936 gradually came to the fore in Hitler's thinking as a consequence of Stalin's involvement in the Spanish Civil War and the paranoid fears of encirclement to which this gave rise. After a conversation with Hitler in November 1937, Goebbels noted in his diary: 'The Jews need to be removed from Germany, indeed from the whole of Europe. This will take some time, but it will and must happen. The Führer is firmly resolved to do this.'[3]

The annexation of Austria, which added 200,000 more Jews to the population of the Reich, brought with it a massive speeding-up of the emigration plan. Hitler instructed Rosenberg to 'continue to promote Jewish emigration from Germany by all possible means', with the stream of emigrants being channelled in the first instance to Palestine,[4] where Zionist organisations were preparing to establish a Jewish state. Before long, this process fell within the purview of the 'Jewish Department' of the SD's main office (the Gestapo), which used all means at its disposal – including the use of violence and blackmail – to hasten this enforced expatriation, after first dispossessing those involved. In order to speed up the process, in August 1938 the head of the Jewish Department, Adolf Eichmann, set up a 'Central Agency for Jewish Emigration' in Vienna that worked closely with Jewish organisations in the Gau Ostmark (as Austria was known after the *Anschluss*). At the same time, the security police and the Gestapo, who increasingly took on responsibility for the 'Jewish Question', cooperated with Zionist representatives from Palestine.

Yet Hitler's calculation that this would be the way for him to be rid of Germany's Jews turned out to be wrong, as the Zionists soon encountered fierce resistance from the Arabs to their resettlement of Jews in Palestine. This plan in turn prompted intervention by the British mandate forces, who curtailed Jewish emigration and intercepted at-sea attempts by illegal migrants to reach Palestine by boat. One by one, other countries now closed their borders to fleeing German Jews or at least reduced their admission quotas. The July 1938 conference on Jewish refugees convened at the instigation of Washington at Évian on the shores of Lake Geneva, attended by delegates from thirty-two countries, did virtually nothing to ameliorate this situation. Even the United States, which after Palestine had taken in the largest numbers of Jewish migrants, was loath to relax its strict immigration rules at Évian. Any German Jewish refugee who wanted to emigrate there required an impeccable certificate of good conduct from the police, which in the interim had become unobtainable from the Reich authorities. Even those Jews who were willing to try settling abroad illegally could no longer do so via official border crossings, since the red 'J' in their passports, which was now stamped on the documents following diplomatic representations by the Swiss, marked them out as refugees. Refugees were deemed undesirables, not least because foreign governments did not wish to be seen as indirectly supporting the expulsion measures.

Golda Meir, who later became president of Israel, attended the Évian Conference as a delegate of a Zionist organisation and reported:

> sitting there ... and listening to the delegates of thirty-two countries rise, each in turn, to explain how much they would have liked to take in substantial numbers of refugees and how unfortunate it was that they were not able to do so, was a terrible experience. I don't think that anyone who didn't live through it can understand what I felt at Évian – a mixture of sorrow, rage, frustration, and horror.[5]

However, knowledge with hindsight about events and a contemporary perspective are two different things. The conference delegates would surely have been unable to imagine what Hitler was still capable of in his racial fanaticism. What's more, racism was rife throughout the world at that time, most especially in the country that instigated the Évian Conference.

Hitler remarked upon the outcome of the conference in mid-September 1938:

> Now, though, when the nation is no longer willing to let itself be sucked dry by these parasites, everyone is up in arms about it. Not that they're prepared in these democratic countries to abandon their hypocritical querying in favour of finally doing something to help. Quite the contrary, in fact – all they do is frostily assert that there's no room for them there, of course![6]

As the expulsion of the Jews from Germany – by the autumn

of 1938, some 205,000 had left – became even more difficult as a result of foreign countries' increasing unwillingness to take them in, Hitler was prompted to take more radical steps. Indeed, it may also have played a part in his decision to eradicate the hated state of Czechoslovakia. However, the latter was stymied by the Munich Conference and the resolution of the Sudetenland question. For Hitler, who felt pressed for time, these considerations represented a serious setback, and became another factor behind his adoption of even more drastic measures against the Jews within his sphere of control. Both the cloak-and-dagger operation in late October 1938 to expel 17,000 Polish Jews who were living in the Reich and also *Kristallnacht* (9–10 November) should be seen in this context. Such actions were the 'start of a new German approach to the Jewish Question', as the Nazi newspaper *Völkischer Beobachter* proclaimed.[7] Where Hitler was concerned, this 'new approach' was intended to bring some urgency to bear on the matter. His aim was to intimidate the Jews and force them to leave the country – a country that was to be made 'Jew-free' as quickly as possible.

For this eventuality, however, Hitler needed the cooperation of foreign countries, which continued to make little effort to take in German Jews. In this regard, the pogrom that took place on *Kristallnacht* was primarily meant to force potential host countries to sit up and take notice – as a threat by Hitler, so to speak, that he would stop at nothing if they refused to change their minds. After speaking with Hitler, Hermann Goering summarised what the Führer was aiming for: 'This is the only possible way now. The message he wants to send to other countries is this: Why do you keep going on about the Jews? – Just take them in!'[8] In November 1938, Hitler's old comrade-in-arms, who was tasked with 'solving the Jewish Question', not only set about intensifying domestic political terror against German Jews but also became a driving force behind their enforced expatriation.

After a variety of potential countries for them to be deported to, such as Colombia, Ecuador, and Venezuela, had been discussed within the SS, Madagascar was decided upon as the most favoured location. Even in the run-up to the Évian Conference, Rosenberg had suggested that this island in the Indian Ocean be earmarked as a place for the Jews to emigrate to. Madagascar, he argued, was large enough, had a subtropical climate and belonged to France, the country where Jewish emancipation had begun. A plan was duly drawn up with the participation of the president of the Reichsbank, Hjalmar Schacht. The idea was to finance the emigration with an international loan secured by Jewish assets within Germany, and for all Jews who were fit for work and their dependants to be relocated to Madagascar within the space of three to five years.

On Hitler's orders, in late December 1938, Schacht entered into negotiations in London about the plan to finance Jewish emigration. These talks began very promisingly, and the Reichsbank president was appointed by Hitler as the 'Special Envoy for the Promotion of Jewish Emigration'. On 20 January 1939, however, the negotiations encountered a serious setback. On that day, a dispute arose between Schacht and Hitler over economic policy, which led to Schacht being dismissed from his post as Reichsbank president. In his anger, Hitler now also refused to release Jewish assets as security for the loans raised abroad that were meant to finance the emigration of the Jews. Responsibility for the 'implementation of Jewish emigration from all regions of the Reich' now devolved to the Gestapo and its head Reinhard Heydrich. In February a 'Central Reich Agency for Jewish Emigration' was established in Berlin. From here on in, Heydrich became the key figure in directing National Socialist racial policy.

The problems with the emigration plan, but also the knowledge that any expansion eastwards would immediately bring millions more Jews under the Reich's control, caused Hitler to escalate his policies regarding the Jews to a new level. Henceforth, he became fixated on solving the question of what to do with Germany's Jews within the wider context of the eastern territories, the focus of his planned expansion. He revealed what shape such a solution would take in a speech on 30 January 1939, in which he spoke openly about 'exterminating the Jewish race' if it ended up dragging the world into another war.

These monstrous statements by Hitler when he was in crisis mode were quite evidently not taken particularly seriously by outside observers; he was, after all, known for his intemperate tirades. Besides, the threat to exterminate the Jewish race appeared to be beyond all imagining. As a result, the West continued to view the tragic plight of the Jews with indifference. The situation became even more perilous for them when London cut emigration to Palestine still further in February 1939 and, with an eye to the Arab support it needed for protection of the strategically important Suez Canal, proceeded to water down its support for the establishment of a Jewish state. As a consequence, the only route left open to Jews was to emigrate illegally to Palestine. Even so, from the autumn of 1938 to the autumn of 1939, over 80,000 more left their German or Austrian homelands.

Following the destruction of Poland, the Jews who lived there were corralled into urban ghettos, principally in Warsaw, Cracow, Lublin, Radom, and Łodz (now renamed Litzmannstadt). Meanwhile, Adolf Eichmann, who organised the systematic expulsion of Jews from the 'Protectorate of Bohemia and Moravia' – as the rump Czech lands were now known – was working on a plan to resettle them in an 'agricultural reserve' near the small Polish town of Nisko, south of Lublin. Hitler fleetingly toyed with the idea of deporting some 300,000 Jews 'of slender means' from the 'old Reich' and Austria (the 'Ostmark') to the Nisko region. However, he shelved the plan for military and strategic reasons. Nevertheless, he had still not wholly abandoned the idea of a

'Jewish Reserve' within the 'Government General' (the territory of former Poland under German rule), where from the end of October 1939 Jews had been required to do forced labour and wear the yellow Star of David on their clothes.

The close connection between Hitler's policies towards the Jews and his prosecution of the war is evident from his receptiveness to the revised Madagascar resettlement plan put forward by Heinrich Himmler in the spring of 1940. At the end of May, the head of the SS presented this proposal to Hitler as the best and most humane way of dealing with the problem. According to Himmler, the German public shunned 'the Bolshevik method of physically exterminating an entire people out of an innate conviction that it was both un-Germanic and impractical'.[9] Hitler was buoyed up at the time by the triumphant progress of the campaign in the West, and so readily agreed to the SS and the foreign ministry continuing to pursue this plan, which dominated official thinking about the future of Germany's Jews throughout the summer of 1940. In mid-August Goebbels noted after a meeting with Hitler: 'We're planning to ship the Jews off to Madagascar at some future date. There, they too can develop their own state.'[10] And yet the enterprise came to nothing, premissed as it was on the expectation that Great Britain, which controlled the sea routes to the island, would eventually give in to Germany.

As long as Hitler kept hoping to reach an accommodation of whatever kind with Great Britain, he was clearly wedded to the idea of potentially being able to use the Jews under his control as 'bargaining chips'. This only changed when, at the end of July 1941, it became apparent that his attempted lightning campaign of extermination against the Soviet Union, and hence his entire war strategy, had failed. He promptly set about intensifying his war on the race front. Hitler the racial ideologue now focused all his attention on the last feasible element in his vision of reshaping the world – the systematic murder of the Jews. It was therefore surely no coincidence that Heydrich, the head of the Reich Security Main Office (*Reichsicherheitshauptamt*, or RSHA), was tasked on 31 July 1941, the day after Hitler had been forced to order the Army Group Centre to temporarily switch to the defensive, with 'making all necessary organisational, functional, and material preparations for a comprehensive solution of the Jewish Question within the German sphere of influence in Europe'. In addition, the head of the RSHA was instructed to 'submit ... in the near future a general plan ... for carrying out the desired final solution of the Jewish Question'.[11]

In parallel with preparations for the 'final solution', behind the lines on the Russian front the systematic killing of Jewish women and children by the mobile death squads, which had started the moment the campaign began, was expanded. On 14 August Himmler declared: 'We don't want to repeat the mistake we made in Poland of herding the Jews into ghettos. They are nothing but breeding grounds for diseases and illnesses.'[12] Thereafter the slaughter of Jews reached unprecedented levels, in Kamenez-Podolski, Zhitomir, and Kiev, where over the course of three days in September 1941 35,000 Jews were shot dead in the ravine at Babi Yar. After the war, one of the men who took part in this massacre reported:

> The Jews had to strip and great piles of clothes built up. After that they were made to walk to the edge of the pit and lie down. Then they were shot ... They all went to their deaths quite calmly. There was no screaming or crying ... We were given schnapps in great quantities to help us get through the sickening acts we were perpetrating.[13]

According to a report by Operational Unit A, up to 15 October 1941 it alone liquidated 118,430 Jews and 3,387 'communists'.

By the end of the year, the number of people murdered by these units would grow to half a million.

One of the primary measures envisaged in the Final Solution was for the 'original Reich region and the Protectorate from West to East to be cleared and kept free of Jews as quickly as possible'.[14] Some 750,000 Poles, Jews, and non-Jews alike had already been deported from those parts of Poland annexed by the German Reich to the Government General, and now in addition around 60,000 Jews were to be relocated by the end of 1941 to the Wartheland region, more precisely the large ghetto that had been created in Litzmannstadt. From there, they would soon be transported further east. The first deportation order from the Reich capital, which was still home to some 70,000 Jews – with around another 300,000 in the original Reich lands and the Ostmark – was issued on 14 October 1941. The deportation lists were drawn up in Berlin – as they were throughout the country – by the Gestapo, together with leaders of Jewish communities, who were ordered to cooperate.

Between 16 October and 13 November, more than 20,000 Jews arrived in Litzmannstadt from the Reich and the Protectorate, principally from Berlin, Cologne, Vienna, and Prague. As one ghetto resident recalled:

> It was incredible. They arrived, very smartly dressed, looking well and clean but with very few belongings. Over time, we'd got used to deprivation. But they were totally unprepared for what faced them – the hunger, the overcrowding, the dirty water. They were accustomed to a different standard of living, and as a result they perished in larger numbers than people who'd been here a long time.[15]

Hundreds of thousands of people lived in this large, walled ghetto – or to be more precise, they were forced to vegetate there, penned up like animals. Not just malnutrition but also epidemics led to high rates of mortality, an outcome that the Germans had factored in. However, the plan to concentrate Jews from throughout the Reich in Litzmannstadt was only partially successful, as legal provisions and interventions by industrial concerns – especially armaments factories vital to the war effort that declared skilled Jewish workers to be indispensable – but also some 'sentimental objections' as Goebbels put it, conspired to frustrate this aim.

Around the same time as trains filled with Jews from the 'old Reich' were heading in the direction of the Litzmannstadt Ghetto, Heydrich imposed a travel ban not only on German Jews but on all Jews living in areas occupied by Germany. The authorities wanted to be able to get hold of them in order to commit them to the Final Solution, meaning that the order to carry out the second phase of the Final Solution – i.e. the phase relating to the systematic 'cleansing' of Central and Western Europe – must have already been issued at this stage. This sup-position tallies with Adolf Eichmann's assertion during his 1961 trial in Jerusalem that he was summoned by Heydrich 'two or three months' after the start of the Russian campaign. According to Eichmann the head of the RSHA told him: 'The Führer has given orders for the physical destruction of the Jews.'[16] Likewise, Bruno Streckenbach, a high-ranking colleague of Heinrich Himmler, testified after the war that the head of the SS and his second in command (Heydrich) had spoken about Hitler issuing such an order, although they did not specify whether this had been by word of mouth or in writing.[17]

Accordingly, the preparations for the genocide of the Jews commenced at around the end of August or the beginning of September 1941 – in other words, at a time when Hitler had realised that the Russian campaign could not be completed by the year's end and hence that his entire war plan was threatened with failure. Moreover, his adversaries' closing of ranks – in August Churchill and Roosevelt had signed the Atlantic Charter – enabled the dictator to identify clear battle lines in the war: with Germany on one side and the 'global Jewish conspiracy' on the other. In September 1941, the US president had authorised US naval vessels to open fire on any warships of the Axis powers that ventured close to the North Atlantic convoy routes. Furthermore, their new ally Stalin had just ordered the deportation of ethnic Germans from the Volga region, thousands of whom were liquidated. Hitler now believed that he had to respond by wiping out the Jewish population of Europe, so as to weaken his sworn enemy by depriving it of its main gene pool. From his crude Social Darwinist viewpoint, there could only be one winner in this struggle. 'We are under no illusions that the war can only end either with the Aryan peoples of the world being eradicated or with Jews disappearing from Europe,' he reportedly stated around this time.[18]

By mid-November 1941, when the battle for Moscow began and the war thus entered what a newly hopeful Hitler regarded as its decisive phase, Hitler had positively spurred on his principal agent of the Jewish genocide and his leading ideologue to expedite matters. A few days after Hitler's meeting with Himmler and Rosenberg at the Wolf's Lair on 16 November, Himmler spoke to Heydrich about 'eliminating the Jews' in the Government General in Poland.[19] The day after, Rosenberg told selected representatives of the Nazi propaganda machine that the German-occupied Soviet regions were 'destined to resolve a question facing all the peoples of Europe: namely, the Jewish Question'. Rosenberg maintained that this could 'only be resolved through a biological eradication of European Jewry in its entirety'.[20]

It is unsettling to note that the National Socialist bureaucrats who now set about implementing this crime against humanity still thought that they needed to establish a legal framework for the deportation of Jews from Reich territory. The 'Eleventh Decree to the Law on Citizenship of the Reich' summarily made Jews into 'enemies of the people and the state' and allowed them to be automatically stripped of their German citizenship as soon as they crossed the border. This decree was promulgated on 25 November 1941, in other words just after the first trains carrying Jews from the 'old Reich and the Ostmark had set off, bound this time not for the Litzmannstadt Ghetto but directly for Riga, Kaunas, and Minsk, where the new arrivals – numbering in the tens of thousands – were systematically murdered by SS death squads. In total, some 230,000 adherents of the Mosaic faith who had been living in the Reich were killed.

In order to expedite the deportation and extermination of millions of European Jews, in mid-November Eichmann, at the behest of the head of the Reich Security Main Office, was busy organising an inter-ministerial conference that was scheduled for 9 December 1941. However, the catastrophic outcome of the Battle of Moscow, the Japanese attack on Pearl Harbor, and the ensuing German declaration of war against the United States occupied the full attention of the Nazi state, and the conference was postponed.

Although the moment for Hitler that triggered genocide was the failure of his 'global struggle', the widening of the conflict into a world war now had to serve as a propagandistic justification for the mass slaughter. Goebbels noted:

With regard to the Jewish Question, the Führer is determined to put his foot down. He prophesied to the Jews that if they precipitated another world war it would bring about their destruction. That was no empty threat. And now the world war is upon us, and so the annihilation of the Jews must be the necessary consequence.[21]

Eleven million European Jews, five and a quarter million of them in Eastern Europe, were to come within the purview of the Nazis' Final Solution. These figures were noted by Eichmann, who made a transcript of the meeting that Heydrich scheduled for 20 January 1942 in a villa on the shores of the Wannsee in Berlin. At the start of the conference, Heydrich provided an overview 'of the fight against this enemy thus far'. He said that the primary objective had been 'to cleanse German living space of Jews by legal means'. Despite all the difficulties, such as 'increasing restriction of entry permits or the cancelling of such', Heydrich reported that by 31 October 1941 the authorities had still managed to force 537,000 Jews from the original Reich territory, the Ostmark, and the Protectorate of Bohemia and Moravia to emigrate.[22] Then, he went on, this emigration had been supplanted by the 'evacuation' of Jews from the East. Those who had been exempted from this measure, and would continue to be so, were Jews over the age of sixty-five, severely disabled Jewish war veterans, and decorated war heroes. These individuals would instead be transported to the so-called 'ghetto for the elderly' at Theresienstadt (Terezin) in Bohemia.

In the course of the Final Solution, Jews were to be hunted down throughout the continent and, to quote Eichmann's minutes of the meeting:

> allocated for suitable labour in the East. Able-bodied Jews, segregated according to sex, will be taken in large work columns to these areas to mend the roads, in the course of which action doubtless a large number will be eliminated by natural causes. The possible final remnant will, since it will undoubtedly consist of the most resilient portion, have to be treated accordingly, because it is the product of natural selection and would, if freed, become the nucleus of a new Jewish revival.

Eichmann's transcript deliberately toned down the actual language used;[23] he later testified that the real talk had been 'of killing and eliminating and exterminating'.[24]

The process of genocide, the basics of which were agreed at the so-called Wannsee Conference, was set in motion that spring. Hitler's mouthpiece Goebbels noted at the end of March 1942:

> The prophecy which the Führer made about them for having brought about a new world war is starting to come true in a most terrible way. There is no room for sentiment in these matters. If we did not resist the Jews, they would destroy us. It's a life-and-death struggle between the Aryan race and the Jewish bacillus. No other government and no other regime could muster the strength for such a root-and-branch solution as this. Here, once more, the Führer is the unwavering champion and advocate of a radical solution, which is necessitated by prevailing conditions and is therefore inevitable. Fortunately, the war presents us with a whole range of possibilities that would not be open to us in peacetime.[25]

By these 'possibilities', Goebbels meant that, under the cover of the war and outside Reich territory, or at least on its easternmost borders as well as in the Government General of the Polish territory and further east, it would be easier to implement the extermination of Europe's Jews. Not least, the experiences gleaned from the systematic eradication of 'lives unworthy of life' (i.e. the severely mentally ill and physically disabled people) had shown that it would be hard to put such measures into practice on the territory of the 'old Reich'. Some 70,000 psychiatric patients, including many thousands of disabled children, fell victim to this large-scale killing operation, which began at the outbreak of war 'for the purposes of racial replenishment'. They were put to death using exhaust gases at several

euthanasia centres. However, the so-called 'T4' euthanasia programme, which could not be kept secret, had to be abandoned
in August 1941. Resistance from the Roman Catholic Church
forced Hitler to take this step. Among other protests, the Bishop
of Münster, Clemens August Graf von Galen, spoke out bravely
from the pulpit against the practice of euthanasia, denouncing it
as murder and lodging a legal objection to end it. As the termi-
nation of 'worthless existences' became more widely known, it
prompted a growing disquiet among the German people that put
a stop to the programme, especially in view of the bitter struggle
the Wehrmacht was then enduring on the Eastern Front.

In the eyes of the perpetrators, the East was an ideal place to
carry out these crimes against humanity, since during the first
four decades of the twentieth century death and violence had
been the order of the day in these former westernmost regions
of the Tsarist empire like nowhere else in Europe. In the light of
this policy, historian Felix Schnell has spoken of 'realms of fear'
and a 'new quality of violence', which began with the pogrom
of the Jews of Kishinev in 1903 and climaxed in the pogroms
carried out there during the Russian Revolution.[26] These events
were followed by the Stalinist terror, which claimed millions of
lives, particularly during the time of the Holodomor (the Great
Famine) in the early 1930s, when the population of the Ukraine
was systematically starved and millions more perished. As the
Bolshevik perpetrators were often identified with Jews, anti-
Semitism was rife in the 'realms of fear', although there were
also a number of other root causes.

When the Wehrmacht invaded the Baltic states, Byelorussia,
and the Ukraine at the start of the Russian campaign, it had the
effect of unleashing the indigenous population's anti-Semitism.
More than fifty pogroms took place. After the Soviets withdrew
in the face of the German onslaught, killing the inmates of all
the gaols before they retreated, thousands of Jewish people were

murdered. This took place, for example, in the Galician city of Lvov, under the sympathetic gaze of the mobile death squads of the security police and SD, whose commanders had been ordered by Heydrich 'not to place any obstacles in the way of efforts by anti-communist and anti-Jewish groups in the newly conquered territories to clean up their own communities. On the contrary, such actions are – albeit covertly – to be fomented and if necessary intensified and channelled in the right direction.'[27] Presently, many thousands of individuals from these home-grown anti-communist and anti-Semitic groups would be recruited to help put the National Socialist genocide plan into operation.

Likewise, farther to the west, anti-Semitism was also omnipresent in the Government General. It stemmed from the Tsarist period, when this area had been the site of the 'Pale of Settlement' – a region where the authorities allowed permanent settlement by Jews, who were often regarded as being in league with Bolshevism. The Catholic Church of Poland took a confrontational attitude towards the Jews; in a pastoral letter before the war, its primate Cardinal August Hlond accused them of being 'the advance guard of godlessness, the Bolshevik government and revolutionary subversion'.[28] An abhorrence of Judaism was also evident in Polish politics. The central government in Warsaw, for instance, mooted the idea of settling Polish Jews on Madagascar, the very same island that had been the focus of National Socialist interest. In 1937, with the consent of Paris, a Polish government commission had travelled to the Indian Ocean island to investigate potential settlement sites. The following year Poland's foreign minister opened negotiations with his French counterpart on leasing land on Madagascar where 30,000 Jewish families could be resettled annually. Poland was looking to relocate a total of around half a million people.

The industrial extermination of millions of Jews was to take place in the 'Bloodlands', as Timothy Snyder has called the vast area stretching from Poland through Byelorussia to the Ukraine, far from the blacked-out living rooms of ordinary German citizens in the Reich.[29] How many people on the home front would even know where places like Belzec or Sobibór were? Trains from Germany and the Protectorate started heading to these sites and others in the spring of 1942. At the extermination camps, new arrivals died an agonising death, killed in sealed rooms by the exhaust gases from petrol and diesel engines. Thousands upon thousands of Jews from the Government General, where the authorities had begun to clear the ghettos, were also murdered in the same way in Belzec and Sobibór and later that same year in Treblinka too. Preparations for the German summer offensive on the Eastern Front meant that these activities focused initially on the area around Lublin. On 19 July Himmler ordered that the 'relocation' – by which he meant the murder – of the entire Jewish population of the Government General should be completed by the end of 1942. Among other things, the reason given for this operation, which was to be kept secret and in which T4 euthanasia specialists were to be involved, was to safeguard 'the security and cleanliness of the German empire and its spheres of interest'.[30] This act of mass murder in the region with the highest density of Jewish population in Europe was given the innocuous-sounding codename 'Operation Reinhard' – the Christian name of Himmler's principal agent of the Final Solution, Heydrich.

In June 1942, the model Aryan Heydrich – whom Hitler had, in the autumn of the previous year, appointed as deputy Reich protector of Bohemia and Moravia alongside his role as head of the RSHA, and who was meant to 'clean up' the Czech lands – succumbed to the severe injuries he sustained in an attempt on his life. His death saw the passing of an ice-cold, intellectual man of action, who was completely committed to the ideology of race war and the organisational role he had been assigned in it. Goering is reputed to have once remarked that Himmler's 'brain was called Heydrich'.[31] The head of the SS announced that they had a solemn duty to avenge his assassination by setting about 'properly exterminating the enemies of our people with no mercy or weakness'.[32] As Himmler told the officers in his organisation, this slaughter was to happen within a year.

Even before Operation Reinhard began with mass deportations to the death camps from the districts of Radom and Warsaw, an order had been issued for the first deportation of 100,000 Jews from the occupied countries of Western Europe: namely, Belgium, the Netherlands, and France. In Occupied France, the bloodhounds of the SS were aided in their raids on Jewish communities by the French police. The prime minister of the collaborationist Vichy government, Pierre Laval, had agreed to make all stateless Jews in the occupied and unoccupied zones – for the most part emigrants and their families from Germany and Austria – available for 'transportation', in return for a German pledge to spare anyone holding French citizenship from being deported. In doing so, Laval also consented to the deportation of Jewish children. Only in the small part of France that was occupied by the Italians did Mussolini's authorities prevent the French police from arresting Jews, since the government in Rome, which at Hitler's urging had introduced some anti-Jewish laws, wanted no truck with deportations.

Up to September 1942, when the Wehrmacht's demands on the railway network meant that the operation had to be temporarily suspended, a total of 40,000 Jews from France, the Netherlands, and Belgium (a number that would rise to 200,000 by the war's end) were transported to Sobibór, Maidanek, and above all Auschwitz, which would become a byword for the Nazi genocide. Under Himmler's direction this former camp, which was originally built to house Soviet prisoners of war, became the main site of mass extermination. His reason for choosing this location, as he once revealed, was 'because of its good transport

links, and secondly the ... site is easy to cordon off and camou-
flage'. The latter precaution was necessary because Auschwitz,
which was situated in the part of Poland annexed by the Reich,
was home to a large facility set up by the SS and the IG Farben
chemical concern manufacturing synthetic fuel urgently required
for the war effort.[33]

In the sub-camp of Birkenau, where the railway sidings were
located, Jews were herded out of the cattle trucks they had been
transported in and 'selected' by SS doctors. Some were assigned
to work duties, while others, the overwhelming majority, were led
away to the gas chambers under the pretext of being disinfected.
There, in buildings that had been disguised as farmhouses, they
were gassed with a hydrogen cyanide insecticide called Zyklon B.
The commandant of Auschwitz, Rudolf Höss, who the previous
year had undertaken experiments with the gas on Soviet POWs,
wrote in captivity in 1947:

> Having arrived at the 'farmhouse' they were ordered to strip.
> To begin with they went into the chambers perfectly calmly ...
> Until, that is, some began to grow suspicious and talk about
> suffocation and extermination. And then a kind of panic
> would immediately ensue. But those who were still standing
> outside were quickly shooed into the chambers and the doors
> clamped shut. When the next transports arrived, we made
> sure to search out any troublemakers beforehand and keep a
> close eye on them. If any unrest arose, those responsible were
> discreetly taken behind the building and dispatched with a
> small-calibre pistol; the sound of the shot wasn't audible to
> the others.[34]

Höss was the prototype of a camp commandant, an unpre-
tentious individual who questioned nothing and who prided
himself on doing his duty with the utmost obedience. With such

an attitude, Höss, whose life hitherto had been hallmarked by failure, was one of those people whom the SS leadership deemed eminently well-suited to putting industrial mass murder into practice. Accordingly, he rose to become commandant of the Reich's largest extermination camp. This position came with a number of perks, such as his own horse and a family home. It did not appear to bother Höss that the villa, with a large garden where his children played, was only a stone's throw away from the camp crematorium, and that children the same age as his were routinely gassed, along with women and old people, in nearby Birkenau. He was completely acclimatised to the world of the death camp.

One of the most incomprehensible elements of the Nazi genocide was that the SS men who staffed the extermination and concentration camps and their superiors led completely normal lives. They celebrated and cultivated the community of the 'Order of the Death's Head', a fellowship of 'racially pure' Nordic people and a close-knit group that never doubted the rectitude of its activities, despite all the horror surrounding it. This was only possible because, here in the east, life was primarily about just one thing: ensuring one's own survival. The chances of this happening were infinitely better for those who worked as sentries or clerks in the death camps. A Waffen-SS frontline soldier's chance of surviving the Russian campaign was slender. Moral scruples no longer had any place in such a world. In addition, the executioners, especially those of higher rank, were inculcated with an unquestioning belief in a simple 'truth' – that the Jews were a corrosive and destructive influence that was inimical to everything German.

No one needed to din this message into the SS Reichsführer Heinrich Himmler, whose background was in the educated middle class. He was one of very few people in the Nazi 'master race' elite who understood Hitler's insane ideology. Furthermore, he even styled himself as the reincarnation of the first German king, Henry the Fowler, holding nighttime dialogues with the dead monarch at Henry's catafalque in the cathedral at Quedlinburg every year on the anniversary of his death, and lost himself in fantasies about the eastward march of the ancient Germanic tribes. Yet in reality Himmler, who was present even at the Beer Hall Putsch of 1923, was seen as a pedantic pen-pusher and mocked by the crude butchers within his own organisation. After the war, his chief of staff SS General Karl Wolff reported that at a shooting of around a hundred people that had – not without ulterior motive – been specially 'laid on' for him in mid-August 1941, Himmler suffered a fainting fit and almost collapsed when bits of brain spattered onto the lapel of his uniform jacket. In the event, however, he managed to 'pull himself together' and speak briefly to members of the firing squad beside the mass grave about their difficult but 'necessary task'.[35]

For all his oft-proclaimed certainty that the extermination of the Jews was the correct course of action, Himmler was not entirely devoid of scruples. When he visited Auschwitz-Birkenau in July 1942 and observed the 'entire process of extermination' right through to the disposal of the bodies, he deplored the fact that they were thrown into mass graves. He immediately ordered that the mortal remains of all those killed in Birkenau should be exhumed and cremated. Himmler also issued instructions for an efficient crematorium to be built at Birkenau. The SS Reichsführer's main concern was to leave no trace behind for posterity to find. Evidently he still had vestiges of a bourgeois mindset, which made him aware that a different truth existed alongside his construction on reality.

In Himmler too, albeit later than Hitler, we can observe some form of internal radicalisation that went hand-in-hand with setbacks for Germany in the war. So it was that, at the very height of the Stalingrad crisis in January 1943, Himmler pointedly signalled a resumption of the final phase of Operation Reinhard, which had been delayed the previous year, by organising mass deportations from the Warsaw Ghetto. After these encountered fierce resistance from the Jews living there, in mid-February he ordered its complete destruction 'since we will surely never be able to pacify Warsaw or eradicate its criminal elements if we allow the ghetto to remain'.[36] The unequal battle between the SS and the Jewish defenders of the ghetto, who put up a desperate resistance, lasted a month. By the time it was all over, the number of Jews either killed or deported amounted to more than 56,060. Following the demise of the Warsaw Ghetto, all the other ghettos in the Government General, which were still home to some 250,000 Jews, were dismantled and their inhabitants transported to the extermination camps. In all, around three million Polish Jews perished in the Holocaust.

In south-eastern Europe, despite every assistance from Ribbentrop's foreign ministry, Himmler found it difficult fulfilling Hitler's requirements. Apart from Serbia, which early on declared itself 'Jew-free', the Romanian and Bulgarian governments initially complied with German demands in view of the early successes of the Russian campaign and the anticipated hegemony of the Third Reich over continental Europe. Thus, Bucharest deported Jews from the regions of Bukovina and Bessarabia, which had been recaptured from the Soviet Union, to Transnistria, which was under the control of Romanian forces, where they were forced to languish in ghettos. However, some Jews were also driven into the Ukraine, where they fell victim to the German mobile death squads. Some 287,000 Romanian Jews lost their lives.

Although the government in Sofia did deport around 12,000 Jews from the newly conquered territories of Thrace and Macedonia, it did not send any from the Bulgarian heartland to the death camps. Likewise, despite Hitler's personal appeal to the

Hungarian head of state Miklós Horthy, Budapest only handed over a few thousand 'alien Jews' to the German death squads operating in the Soviet Union. As the war began to turn against Germany, however, the administrations of these countries showed less and less inclination to cede to the growing pressure put on them by the Reich government to deport their entire Jewish populations. They feared that this would compromise their ability to strike their own peace deals with the Western allies. The situation was very different in Greece; of the 70,000 or so Jews who had been living there, only 8,500 survived the genocide.

Whereas the fascist regime under Mussolini in Italy had prevented a wholesale deportation of Jews, after his fall from power in the autumn of 1943, the SS had a free hand in the dwindling area controlled by Germany on the Apennine peninsula. Himmler could now make a start on the 'de-Jewing' process there too. As early as October, a series of raids in the Italian capital saw a thousand Jews rounded up by the SD and transported to Auschwitz. Yet the operations ordered in Italy by the SS Reichsführer did not bring the expected results, since here too the Germans were reliant upon the support of the local authorities. Consequently, a law was dictated to the Italian puppet regime under Mussolini in Salò that ordered all the country's Jews to be placed in concentration camps. Even so, the great majority of Italian Jews were able to evade the clutches of the Nazis and the domestic police. Up to October 1944, a total of around 7,500 Jews from Italy were deported, mostly to Auschwitz.

The general public in the West had long since become aware of the genocide thanks to newspaper and radio reports in the media. This was no different at the Holy See. Cardinal Eugenio Pacelli, formerly papal nuncio in Munich during the period of the Soviet Republic, who was elected pope in 1939 and took the pontifical name Pius XII, was informed in May 1943 about the scale of the genocide of Jews on the former territory of Poland.

In his sermons and public speeches he condemned genocide without explicitly addressing the question of German culpability. Evidently, one major reason why the pope shrank from issuing a searing condemnation of the Third Reich was because he thought it would be tantamount to expressing support for Bolshevism. His attitude was reflected in a communiqué that one of his closest aides, Domenico Tardini, handed to the United Kingdom's envoy at the Holy See to pass on to his government. The text of this message ran as follows: 'European and Christian civilisation is threatened by two dangers: Nazism and communism. Both are materialistic, anti-religious, totalitarian, tyrannical, cruel, and militaristic ... Only if the current war removes both dangers, Nazism and communism, can Europe find peace in the union and co-operation of all nations.'[37] In 1944, neither the White House nor 10 Downing Street shared the pope's view in this matter.

Washington and London seemed curiously disinterested in the fate of millions of European Jews. According to recent research, ever since the Wannsee Conference it had been clear to the Roosevelt administration what would happen to the Jews. Yet this had no ramifications whatsoever. Washington had only reluctantly followed the lead of British foreign secretary Anthony Eden. At the urging of the World Jewish Congress and the Polish government-in-exile in London, Eden had drafted a United Nations' declaration, which was ultimately signed by the United States, Great Britain, the Soviet Union, and eight governments-in-exile of countries occupied by Germany, as well as the French National Committee headed by General Charles de Gaulle. This document, which was read out on BBC radio in December 1942, spoke about conditions in the concentration camps, where those who were able-bodied 'are slowly worked to death ... The infirm are left to die of exposure and starvation or are deliberately massacred in mass executions.' The authors of

the declaration reckoned the number of victims of these atrocities in 'many hundreds of thousands'.[38]

There was a certain reticence among the Western powers
regarding such initiatives. One can only speculate what the
reasons for this might have been. Was the actual scale of the
crimes being committed beyond their comprehension? Did their
own racism play a part? Or was it the knowledge that they were
in league with a mass murderer who was every bit as bad as
Hitler? Certainly in Roosevelt's case, another factor was that he
was wary of laying himself open to the charge by his Republican
opponents that he was putting Jewish interests before those of
Americans. Therefore, whenever he was asked what he planned
to do about the Nazi concentration camps, he repeatedly side-
stepped the question by replying that the best help for the Jews
would be as swift an Allied victory as possible.

Looming defeat only signalled to Hitler the urgent necessity
for him to put into practice one further major element of his race
war against Europe's Jews. This was the extermination of the
Hungarian Jews, which Horthy had thus far resisted. Hitler, the
fanatical Jew-hater, was completely in thrall to the experiences
he had undergone in 1919, at the time of the German soviet
republics. Just as in Bavaria, he claimed, in Hungary too at that
time 'the Jews had been fully instrumental in organising revolutionary subversion'.[39] After Horthy was deposed in 1944 and a
puppet regime installed in Budapest alongside a German pleni-
potentiary, Hitler lost no time in putting his plan into action. The
operation was spearheaded by a 'Special Hungarian Unit' under
the command of Adolf Eichmann. The Jews were corralled into
ghettos and from there transported by train to the extermination camps. Representations made to London and Washington
to slow or halt the deportations by bombing the Hungarian
railway network were rejected by the governments there. A terse
note of 23 June by a colleague of US assistant secretary of war

John McCloy recommended that the government 'stall' on the request. The official reason given for this failure to act was that the Americans lacked the operational capacity – even though the US Army Air Force (USAAF) was by that stage conducting regular missions against targets in the Upper Silesian industrial region.[40]

The deportations from Hungary came to a halt in July 1944. Interventions by the Vatican, Switzerland, Sweden, Spain, and Turkey proved decisive in bringing this about. Likewise, the International Committee of the Red Cross under its president Carl Burckhardt stepped in for the first time, having hitherto refrained from taking such a step for fear of losing access to prisoner-of-war camps in Germany. By the time Eichmann's 'Jewish operation' ceased, a total of 380,000 Hungarian Jews had been murdered. Of these, at least 250,000 died in Auschwitz. On occasion in this death factory, as many as 8,000 people were gassed in a single day; after first being 'utilised' (i.e. divested of all reusable resources such as their hair and gold fillings in their teeth), their corpses were reduced to ashes in the highly efficient incineration ovens supplied by the Erfurt firm of Topf & Sons.

Just before the killing of Hungarian Jews began at Auschwitz, at a meeting in Sonthofen Himmler told a group of SS generals:

You may well appreciate how hard it has been for me to carry out the military order I was given, which I have followed and executed with total obedience and conviction. If you were to say to me: 'We can see the necessity where the men are concerned, but not the children,' then I would only remind you that we cannot possibly allow a generation of hate-filled avengers to grow up, whom our children and grandchildren would then have to deal with because we, their fathers and grandfathers, were weak and cowardly enough to bequeath them this problem.[41]

Some months previously, in an infamous speech he delivered in Posen (Poznań) to Nazi Gauleiters and other leaders, the SS Reichsführer declared:

> Most of you will know what it's like to see a hundred corpses lying side by side, or five hundred or a thousand. And to have seen this through and – aside from some exceptional instances of human weakness – to have remained decent, has made us hard. This is an unwritten and never-to-be-written page of glory in our history.[42]

This is one of the most shocking testimonies to where ideological blindness and an obsession with duty can lead. It also testifies to self-delusion, for after Stalingrad even Himmler must finally have been in no doubt that the war was lost for Germany. As the end drew ever closer, in an attempt to save his own skin he tried to make contact with the Allies – in other words, with those whom he had decried throughout his political life as the puppets of 'international Jewry'.

In Hitler's eyes, these actions on the part of the SS Reichsführer were disgraceful, and one of the greatest disappointments of his entire life. Hitler himself cleaved to his compulsive, delusional belief in the 'global Jewish conspiracy'. Thus, in the 'political testament' that he composed in his bunker beneath the wasteland of ruins that was Berlin in April 1945, he 'exhorted' the nation to continue to observe 'the racial laws' after his death. In this document Hitler sought to justify himself and to apportion blame. He claimed he had left no doubt as to 'who carry the real guilt for the murderous struggle: the Jews!' He went on:

> I have further left no one in doubt that this time it will not be only millions of children of Europeans of the Aryan peoples who will starve to death, not only millions of grown men

who will suffer death, and not only hundreds of thousands of women and children who will be burned and bombed to death in the cities, without those who are really responsible also having to atone for their crime.[43]

Eight days after Hitler dictated this text – which he did just before committing suicide – the Second World War ended. Without him, the genocide of Europe's Jews would not have occurred. In peacetime, he had contented himself with brutally expelling Jews from the Reich, a process he hoped to expedite by stripping them of their rights and property. When the war began, he planned to deport them to the East. It appears like the delaying moment in the downfall of a tragic actor when, after his victory over France, Hitler revived plans he had in the interim shelved to create a homeland for the Jews on Madagascar. It was only after his war of extermination against the Soviet Union failed that he cast aside the last civilised norms of behaviour and ordered the physical extermination of the Jews of Europe. As a consequence of Hitler's mania, more than six million Jews were murdered during the Second World War, some four million of whom perished in the extermination and concentration camps. To be sure, Stalin had an immeasurably larger number of people killed in the name of liberating the workers of the world, but never before had a mechanism of mass extermination been set in motion so calculatedly and methodically. This was what made the Holocaust so specifically German.

# 10

# Defeat

## *Why did Germany fight on to the bitter end?*

Hitler's war plan came unstuck outside the gates of Moscow in December 1941. On sober reflection, the outcome of the conflict was already decided at this juncture, even before it truly became the Second World War with the Japanese attack on Pearl Harbor and Germany's subsequent declaration of war on the United States. Up to this point, some five million people had lost their lives. By the time Germany was thoroughly defeated (and the capitulation of Japan) three and a half years later, more than fifty-five million had died, with some estimates even placing the figure at seventy million. Of the seven million Germans who perished in the Second World War, two-thirds were killed in the final year of the conflict. The devastation of their country also took place to a large extent during this same period. Accounts of this period generally explain why the Germans kept up a futile fight to the proverbial last bullet by pointing to the mindset of German society at the time and its slavish obedience to Hitler.[1] One factor less frequently taken into account is that a dictatorship, and especially a wartime dictatorship, has its own very particular set of laws and rules. These include not only a lack of transparency where political decision-making processes are concerned but also systematic disinformation through propaganda. Finally, the apparatus of oppression must also be factored in. In such circumstances, only a handful of people tend to resist, since doing so is a matter of life and death.

The ever-worsening situation facing the Wehrmacht on the Eastern Front was no secret to the German public in December 1941. However, the propaganda machine was adept at concealing the responsibility borne by the high-risk gambler Hitler and his loyal military commanders for pushing German forces to the brink of the abyss. In the reports it regularly compiled on the public mood on the home front, the security service of the SS pointed to widespread disquiet among 'national comrades' in light of both the 'enduring fierce resistance being shown by the Soviets on all sectors of the Eastern Front' and of rapidly mounting losses among German troops. No one believed in a swift end to the Russian campaign any more. As the SD reported immediately before Hitler declared war on the United States:

> People are fearful that even in the spring of next year, the ensuing thaw will prevent a German advance and that a new offensive will only be possible in the summer, by which time the Soviets will have had ample time and opportunity to throw newly equipped troops into the fight and make good the heavy material losses they have suffered with the shipments of supplies they have been receiving in the meantime from England and America.[2]

Even though the populace lacked much hard-and-fast information about the situation, their assessment of the ongoing progress of the campaign in the East was not entirely unrealistic.

Nonetheless, for the present only a vanishingly small number of people believed that Germany could possibly be defeated in the war. Just a glance at the map of Europe appeared to refute any such idea. The swastika was flying over the whole of the continent. In its bulletins, the weekly *Wochenschau* newsreel laboured this point to allay people's concerns about developments on the Eastern Front. Many Germans persuaded themselves that, even if the enemy were to launch counteroffensives, say in North Africa or Russia, nothing about this extensive hold on power would change any time soon. Besides, in the East, there were the rigours of winter to contend with; Nazi propaganda was keen to present temperatures as severe as 42 degrees below zero as the real reason for why the campaign there had run into difficulties. Moreover, many still believed in the Führer, who in their view had generally in the past been able to extricate the nation from precarious situations. They evidently suppressed any realisation that it was he who was to blame for these predicaments in the first place.

When Hitler decided that attack was the best form of defence by declaring war on the United States on 11 December 1941, nobody in Germany was particularly surprised, unlike at the start of the Russian campaign, which had caught them totally unawares. According to a report by the SD, the widespread opinion often heard was that this was 'merely official confirmation of a state of affairs that already existed in reality'.[3] The public now had to come to terms with the realisation that the war would be a long drawn-out affair with no prospect of outright victory. The one hope that remained to Germans was that it would end with a peace settlement between the combatant nations, but to get to this negotiated peace would require further military successes for the Axis powers.

These victories were duly forthcoming in the Far Eastern theatre of war. The armed forces of Imperial Japan, which had struck a spectacular first blow with the attack on Pearl Harbor on 7 December 1941, now invaded the north of British-controlled Malaya, Hong Kong, the Philippines, and the islands of Guam and Wake, while from Thailand they advanced towards the southern tip of Burma. Japanese forces also made a bid to overrun the Dutch East Indies by occupying parts of Borneo. These advances were nothing short of a triumphal procession by Germany's new ally, whom no one seemed capable of halting. Many Germans were convinced that this would surely have a major impact on the way London conducted the war in Europe – all the more so when, in February 1942, the military bastion of Singapore, Britain's key strategic position in Southeast Asia, fell to the Japanese.

Hitler continued to cling to the unrealistic notion that Britain might give in, fantasising about Churchill stepping down and the coalition between Britain and America collapsing. Although the British prime minister had not been toppled after the fall of Singapore, Hitler told himself that if India too were now to come under threat, the British would mutiny and oust Churchill. In both the armed forces and Army High Commands, which made a point of shunning the political realm and where minds were focused on the dramatic situation on the Eastern Front, officers obsequiously went along with Hitler's wishful thinking. Meanwhile in the Naval High Command, which saw Britain as the principal enemy, Japan's entry into the war was invested with all manner of fanciful strategic possibilities, regardless of any practical considerations. The German navy's top brass began to think in grand, global terms without realising that their commander-in-chief had no intention of budging one iota from his eastern objective, or from his race war against 'Jewish Bolshevism'.

Hitler's rigid, dogmatic, and ultimately forlorn insistence on waging the war as he originally envisaged it had led him, in the great Eastern Front crisis of December 1941 to January 1942, to dismiss from the outset any thought of a strategic withdrawal as the only rational military solution to the unfolding military debacle. In accordance with his dictum of 'victory or ruin' – with everything ultimately culminating in destruction – he had instead, to the horror of his military commanders, called for 'fanatical resistance'. Not an inch of territory was to be abandoned. In this assertion he was blessed with enormous good fortune. For the Eastern Front held, thus sparing German forces from suffering the same fate that had befallen Napoleon and his Grande Armée in 1812. Granted, this success had less to do with Hitler, who took over supreme command of the army from von Brauchitsch and replaced thirty-five generals, but more with a cardinal error on the part of the Soviet High Command, which failed to consolidate its offensive, leaving Red Army forces too thinly dispersed along the 1,500-kilometre front that ran from Leningrad through Moscow right down to the Sea of Azov. As a result, at no single point were the Russians strong enough to make the decisive breakthrough. The upshot was that the German generals were lulled once more into believing in Hitler's 'genius'.

Hitler, let alone his generals, did not have the faintest idea of how the Wehrmacht, already hopelessly overstretched in the East, might begin to face up to the United States. From a military point of view, Germany's strategic capabilities had long since been exhausted, even when one took into account that the United States and Britain, as a result of having to commit forces to both the Atlantic and Pacific theatres, would not be in a position to intervene in Europe until at least 1943. It must have been clear to anyone in the German high commands that the war could no longer be won and that the catastrophe could only assume greater proportions. Any of the generals who might have cared to take a closer look would surely have noticed that Hitler's belief that the British would come to an accommodation with him after all and leave control of continental Europe to him had no basis in reality – but then, as we have noted, the generals studiedly shunned the political realm.

Consequently, a mixture of misplaced loyalty, opportunism, careerism, and simply a hopeful reliance on Hitler's 'genius' saw the great majority of general staffers carry on regardless. The supreme commander of the Wehrmacht prescribed the way forward and the military commanders were required to put it into operation. Hitler's intention was now to make a 'second attempt' to crush the Soviet Union. This grandiose scheme saw huge distances bridged with the stroke of a pencil and forces brought into play that only existed on paper. The focus this time was on the Caucasus region in the far south of Stalin's vast empire. Hitler, and presently his compliant generals too, believed that seizing the oilfields there would deal a fatal blow to the Soviet war effort while at the same time solving a key problem for German forces – a shortage of fuel. 'It's obvious that operations in the year 1942 must see us take possession of the oilfields. If this doesn't come off, we won't be able to conduct operations the following year,' announced Keitel naïvely,[4] as if the Soviets would not, in the event of being forced to withdraw, immediately set about destroying the oil-producing facilities.

Faced with such a momentous task, the general staff officers paid no attention to the indescribable crimes being committed against the Jews that had begun to coalesce into a systematic act of genocide. They considered that this area too was not within their remit; this was especially true of the army commanders on the Eastern Front. The barbaric war being waged by both them and the Red Army made this very easy. There was no place for humanity in these circumstances. This cruelty even went so far that the executions of partisans by the special task forces were viewed as a welcome distraction by soldiers on the Eastern Front, with the hangings being captured on cine film so that those who were lucky enough to make it to their next furlough could show them to their families when they went home on leave.

Meanwhile, the 'home front' stood firm; Germans believed that they owed the men suffering on far-flung battlefields that much, and the dictatorship's bureaucratic apparatus continued to run like clockwork. The same was true of the implementation of the Final Solution, in which a whole series of ministries was involved. It was no secret to them what would happen to the Jews, since they had access to Eichmann's minutes of the Wannsee Conference, thirty copies of which were in circulation. The sixteenth copy, for example, was assigned to the foreign ministry and bore the initials of Ribbentrop's undersecretary, Ernst von Weizsäcker. Admittedly, this was a topic that was treated with great discretion, with only a very limited number of Nazi functionaries at first being aware of the full horror of the operation.

Ordinary German citizens who witnessed the expulsion of Jews at first hand turned a blind eye. Worries about their own husbands and sons at the front eclipsed any concern about the fate of those who were being deported. In wartime the dictatorship's reach into every aspect of people's lives had become all-pervasive. Protest was severely punished, and resistance equated with sabotage and made punishable by death. When the Jews of Berlin were driven through the streets of the city to the railway embarkation point at Grunewald station, Nazi Party members distributed leaflets claiming that the Jews were to blame for everything, and stating that anyone who showed them compassion was committing 'treason against the nation'. Acts of resistance like the sermon preached by the Catholic Provost Bernhard Lichtenberg from Berlin's St Hedwig's Cathedral, in which he said that he was prepared to share the fate of those deported to the East so that he could pray alongside them, were the exception. In May 1942, Lichtenberg was sentenced to two years in gaol for 'abuse of the pulpit', and later taken to the Dachau concentration camp, where he fell gravely ill. In November 1943 the churchman died. A large crowd accompanied the funeral cortège to his own parish cemetery, where he was laid to rest.

In the spring of 1942, Germans once again had cause to look to the future somewhat more optimistically. Although Britain still refused to yield, it appeared – even before the great summer offensive commenced on the Eastern Front – that fortune was turning in the Axis powers' favour. Reports came through in March of new victories on the Eastern Front. In North Africa, meanwhile, British Empire forces were on the retreat. In June 1942 Erwin Rommel, Germany's favourite general, finally captured the port of Tobruk, the scene of fierce fighting the previous year, and proceeded to advance on the Egyptian border. In the War of the Atlantic, German U-boats scored considerable successes, sinking a tonnage of merchant shipping that American shipbuilding could not keep pace with. All this – loudly trumpeted by the Nazi propaganda machine – combined to form one great, seemingly coordinated scenario that was, against the backdrop of Japan's anticipated imminent thrust towards India, destined to destabilise the British Empire. In actual fact, in the Pacific theatre of war, the great sea and air battle at Midway Island in June 1942 had already seen the tables turn decisively in favour of the Allies.

The mood of optimism in Germany did not last long. Although Operation Braunschweig, the summer offensive in the southern sector of the Eastern Front that began in June 1942, scored some notable early successes, a crushing victory against the Red Army failed to materialise. The bulk of Stalin's forces had pulled back to the River Volga, where they established their main defensive line, enabling the Wehrmacht and its allies to make considerable territorial gains. The northern attack group approached Stalingrad, while the southern group advanced even further east to reach the oil-producing region around Maykop and the Caucasus. Images of German mountain infantry hoisting the swastika flag on the summit of Mount Elbrus were designed to demonstrate Germany's expanding power to a domestic audience, but glossed over the fact that even where supply lines existed they had proved wholly inadequate in provisioning German forces over such huge distances. It was therefore almost inevitable that the German summer offensive would turn into an unparalleled debacle. The same situation arose as in the preceding year, with military commanders urging a withdrawal. In late 1942, the chief of staff of the Army High Command, Fritz Halder, declared that this was 'the only possible decision'.[5] However, in September 1942 Hitler relieved his chief military planner of his post. The watchword for the Wehrmacht continued to be: no retreat, whatever the cost.

The same thinking applied in North Africa, where Rommel's advance had ground to a halt at the British defensive position of El-Alamein. In November, the British, with an overwhelmingly superior force, went on the offensive. Hitler's order to the Afrika Korps to hold firm – he telegraphed Rommel to instruct him: 'You must show your troops no other path than that leading to victory or death'[6] – was disregarded by the 'Desert Fox'. By ordering a retreat, something that had no repercussions for him by dint of his enormous popularity, he delayed the loss of the Axis powers' position in North Africa to the Allies. When American and British forces landed in Algeria and Morocco on 8 November 1942, in other words to Rommel's rear, it was clear that this defeat would be only a matter of time.

In the wake of these landings, a now largely forgotten chapter in the history of the Second World War was played out. For now it was Vichy French forces who engaged the Americans and British in Algeria and Morocco. Vichy France under Marshal Philippe Pétain, which had been recognised by most countries in the world, broke off diplomatic relations with the United States. Yet that same Pétain allowed François Darlan, his governor in North Africa, to conclude a secret truce with the Allies. Sensing that Pétain was attempting to double-cross him, Hitler ordered German troops to occupy the remainder of France, a move that once more demonstrated to the German public that the tables were turning in favour of the anti-Hitler coalition.

It was the city on the Volga bearing the name of the Soviet dictator that in the eyes both of the world and of German 'national comrades' marked the real turning point of the Second World War. At the end of November 1942, an Axis force of over a quarter of a million men – Germans, Romanians, Italians, and Croatians – found itself encircled by the Red Army in the greater Stalingrad region. A request by the commander-in-chief of the German Sixth Army, Friedrich Paulus, that he be allowed to attempt a breakout from the Stalingrad 'cauldron', was denied by Hitler, who ordered him to await the arrival of a relief force. Until then, he told Paulus, Goering's Luftwaffe would supply the Sixth Army by air. Both these plans failed. The result was death on a vast scale, culminating in the surrender of what remained of the Sixth Army. More than 100,000 German soldiers went into Soviet captivity; of these, only some 6,000 would eventually return home.

Hitler's reaction to the capitulation at Stalingrad was deep contempt for Paulus, whom he had made a Field Marshal not long before the end of the battle for the city. His expectation was that Paulus, who knew that no officer of that rank in German history had ever been taken prisoner, would fight on to the death. Accordingly, Paulus's actions were also concealed from a shocked German public for a time after the disaster, and even the radio bulletin of 3 February 1943, which began and ended with excerpts from Wagner's opera *Rienzi*, made no mention of the actual circumstances, when it reported that the Sixth Army had 'under the exemplary leadership of General Field Marshal Paulus and true to its oath of loyalty to the last breath, succumbed to the superiority of the enemy and to unfavourable circumstances … Generals, officers, NCOs and other ranks fought shoulder to shoulder to the last bullet. They died in order that Germany might live.'[7]

In addition to serving up risible empty rhetoric such as this, the regime now began mobilising the German people in a way that had never been done before, through the medium of propaganda. The idea was to turn Stalingrad into a kind of rallying call. The people were to be presented unsparingly with the clear alternatives of victory or utter destruction, so as to prepare them for the concept of 'total war'. In his notorious speech of 18 February 1943 at Berlin's Sportpalast, propaganda minister Joseph Goebbels invoked Stalingrad as 'fate's great alarm call'.[8] He went on to present the catastrophe as a fortunate act of providence and a profound catharsis for the German people. It was only the 'heroic sacrifice' of Stalingrad that – according to Goebbels' propaganda – had brought the salutary recognition that nothing but an unshakable will could lead to total war and hence to 'final victory'.

Goebbels ended his speech by posing the rhetorical question: 'Do you want total war?' and bellowing at his audience of hand-picked zealots the time-honoured phrase: 'Now, people rise up and let the storm break loose!'* This address, which was broadcast in its entirety on state radio, including the full half-hour of thunderous applause that ensued, left the listening German public under no illusions. Indeed, this was its intended effect. A security services report on how it had been received concluded: 'It appears to have had ... an enormous impact, and in general a very favourable one.' The German people, whose spirits had been at a very low ebb, had, according to the SD report, been 'positively yearning for a clear explanation of how things stood. Notwithstanding its very frank presentation of the gravity of the situation, the speech by Reich minister Dr Goebbels had a very calming effect and reinvigorated people's confidence and trust in the war effort.'[10]

While this may well have been a case of the report's authors

---

* Translator's note: Goebbels' words 'Nun Volk, steh' auf, und Sturm, brich los!' are an allusion to a line from the work *Männer und Buben* ('Men and boys') by the nationalist poet Theodor Körner (1791–1813), who was killed during the German uprising against Napoleon.

putting a rhetorical gloss on things, there is no denying that the minister of propaganda's speech really did have something of a galvanising effect, in that it confronted the nation with the stark reality of war. The shocking images he invoked of the rampaging 'Jewish-Bolshevik' enemy left no room for illusions. The catastrophe of Stalingrad and the rapid seizure thereafter by the Red Army of Kursk, Belgorod, Demiansk, Kharkov, and Rostov represented an enormous challenge to the Germans – a challenge which would in the first instance be a psychological one. As Goebbels envisaged it, it would still take almost a year and a half to reach a state of total war.

'But where is the Führer?' many Germans wondered. The fact that he appeared to have positively gone to ground meant that his aura, already tarnished since Moscow, faded still further. In addition, very little now remained of the persuasive power his oratory once exuded, as evidenced by people's reaction to his first public utterance after months of silence on 21 March 1943. A report by the SD in the Bavarian city of Würzburg stated: 'People found the unemotional language and the monotonous delivery strange ... in some cases, the tone of voice even had a depressing effect.'[11] Even so, Germans did not find Hitler primarily to blame for the dramatic developments. Instead, quite remarkably, they continued to exonerate him of responsibility for all the mistakes and atrocities they heard about from men returning from the Eastern Front. They pinned the blame for this on others – incompetent generals, bureaucratic Nazi Party bigwigs, and above all Himmler's SS. Thus, even a much-diminished Hitler remained a towering presence, and Germans kept on hoping that he would find a way out of the crisis. After all, who else would?

The German people, who in view of the high death toll and the steadily worsening living conditions longed more than ever for an end to this unwinnable war, still had no idea of the world of delusion their Führer was trapped in. Hitler did not intend to budge one inch from his doctrine of 'victory or destruction'. He was more firmly convinced than ever before that 'international Jewry' would stop at nothing to wipe him and his National Socialist Germany – indeed, Germany as a nation – off the political map. When he learnt about the Casablanca Conference in mid-1943, at which Churchill and Roosevelt agreed that the war should be prosecuted until Germany surrendered unconditionally, he saw this wholly new departure in international law as final confirmation of his racially conditioned ideological worldview and hence of the absolute necessity of his 'global struggle'.

Consequently, he regarded the peace feelers that Stalin put out, first at the very height of the Battle of Stalingrad in December 1942 and then on two further occasions via the neutral Swedish government in Stockholm, as nothing other than Jewish skulduggery. Hitler saw what the Soviet dictator, who ostensibly supported the 'unconditional surrender' formula reached at Casablanca, was playing at in making these offers. Stalin was using them to put pressure on his Western allies, whom he deeply mistrusted and still thought capable of joining forces with Hitler against the Soviet Union. He was encouraged in this belief by their ongoing delay in opening the 'second front' on the continent that he had called for, and by the Soviet Union still having to bear the brunt of the fighting against Nazi Germany, despite the Allied landings in North Africa. Up to this point, over ten million people had been killed on the Soviet side, and Stalin knew that millions more would follow and that it would take a monumental effort in resources before victory was achieved.

Stalin therefore feared that the Soviet Union might ultimately be so weakened that the capitalist powers would be able to deprive it of the fruits of its hard struggle – those very same powers that had set their face against every post-war territorial claim staked by Moscow at the negotiations on a treaty of alliance between Great Britain, the USA, and the Soviet Union. By contrast, a unilateral armistice with Germany at this juncture would have enabled Stalin to push his forces far to the west, up to an agreed line of demarcation. Then, after Germany had been so worn down by a long war of attrition against the Western Allies that it was unable to offer resistance, Soviet forces could advance from that line to occupy much of Central Europe.

Hitler suspected that this was Stalin's plan and was doggedly determined to maintain his fight against 'international Jewry' to the very last bullet. After the failure of his lightning war against the Soviet Union, he was intent on seeing through to its conclusion the programme that he had begun of exterminating Europe's Jews; in the light of his impeding defeat, this task assumed an even greater importance for him. Likewise, where the war of extermination in the East was concerned, he clung unswervingly to his racially motivated dogmatism in turning down flat any political overtures or initiatives, of which there was no shortage after Stalingrad. Foremost among these was the demand voiced in various quarters that greater concessions be made to the different peoples of Russia in order to mobilise them against Bolshevism.

This attitude, which even some of his loyal followers found themselves shaking their heads at in disbelief, was seen by certain members of the officer corps who had always kept Hitler at arm's length, as yet further proof that their supreme commander was not in fact a great military strategist but a fanatic who was leading Germany to disaster. Accordingly, a small group of junior officers – foremost among them Henning von Tresckow, chief of staff of the Second Army and an early opponent of Hitler – began to plot against their supreme commander. Von Tresckow, who was imbued with both Christian values and soldierly ethics, regarded Hitler's war of extermination as an 'insanity' and the genocide of the Jews as a catastrophe and left no stone unturned in trying to mobilise the generals and field marshals in his circle against the dictator. However, his efforts came to nothing. While many abhorred the crimes that had been committed, neither Erich von Manstein or Günther von Kluge – to name just two of the most notable commanders on the Eastern Front – wanted to move against Hitler. On being approached, Manstein retorted: 'Prussian field marshals do not mutiny.'

After the Second World War, those high-ranking officers who survived took refuge in their self-image as career soldiers. They did unquestionably come from a tradition where great store was set by oaths, loyalty, and obedience, and in which a rigid separation of politics and military matters had become almost an article of faith. Yet this did not absolve them of their moral and patriotic duty to do away with Hitler. They alone would have been able to do so. Instead, they cravenly and pusillanimously waited to see how things unfolded, so as to ensure that they were ultimately on the 'right side'. This policy remains an indelible stain on the reputation of the German officer class, who thereby condemned hundreds of thousands to a futile struggle and sent them to their deaths, while at the same time facilitating the murder of millions of Jews.

One of the bitterest truths is that it took the catastrophe of Stalingrad for opposition to Hitler within the military to really take off. Its initial focal point was the private apartment of the former chief of the army general staff, Ludwig Beck, who along with several other like-minded individuals had wanted to rise up against Hitler as early as 1938. To begin with, Beck, the former mayor of Leipzig Carl Friedrich Goerdeler, the officers Hans Oster and Erwin von Witzleben, and a handful of others were on their own, since Hitler's early military triumphs had succeeded in dazzling the vast majority of Germans and making most of them, including even the later would-be assassin Count Claus Schenk von Stauffenberg, blind to the atrocities carried out in Poland. Even after the tide of war had turned against Germany outside the gates of Moscow in the winter of 1941, and when Hitler assumed personal command of the armed forces, Stauffenberg applauded this decision and thought it would pay off. 'It's in the nature of such a formidable and strong-willed individual,' he wrote. After recuperating to some extent from being seriously wounded in Tunisia in 1943,[12] Stauffenberg was assigned the new role of staff officer at the headquarters of the *Ersatzheer*, the 'Replacement Army', a unit that trained soldiers to reinforce first-line divisions at the front. This unit was housed in a building called the 'Bendlerblock' in Berlin.

If the German officer class only rose up against Hitler late in the day, then this was because they were the children of November 1918. Like their fellow Germans, they too were absorbed into the new nation, and their thoughts also turned to the great injustice the country had suffered. In Hitler, they did not see the racist fanatic but rather the great revisionist who wiped away the shame of Versailles and restored to the military its pre-eminent position within the state. They also regarded the Nazi state as the old empire reborn – only more modern and imbued with the spirit of 'Prussian socialism' as described by Oswald Spengler. For instance, in the 1930s Lieutenant Colonel Caesar von Hofacker of the Luftwaffe, who became a staff officer working for the German military commander of occupied Paris, saw 'the person of the Führer as nobly epitomizing ... that socialism of bearing which manifests itself through sobriety and austerity'.[13]

These conservatives had also wholeheartedly endorsed Hitler's suppression of the Jews. Even after the outbreak of war, Goerdeler advocated the creation of a Jewish state overseas and urged his compatriots not to forget 'the large measure of blame borne by the Jews ... who irrupted into our public life in a manner that lacked all the required restraint'.[14] Tresckow, meanwhile, stated that 'despite being motivated by the best of intentions, the Anglo-American, a.k.a. Jewish, concept of democratic capitalism ... ends up as the handmaiden of communism and Marxism'.[15] Count Berthold Schenk von Stauffenberg, the brother of the Hitler plotter, admitted: 'In the realm of domestic politics, we largely subscribed to the basic ideology of National Socialism. Its racial theories struck us as quite sound and promising for the future.' However, the plotters considered the way these were implemented as 'heavy-handed and excessive', he claimed.[16] Like most of the Wehrmacht's officer corps, he could not remotely have imagined the severity of the racial, ideological delusion to which their supreme commander had fallen prey.

It was only when the realisation dawned that the war against the Soviet Union was unwinnable, along with increasing awareness of the genocide being perpetrated against the Jews, that some officers decided to act. After talking to Beck and Goerdeler, who had long opposed the idea of killing Hitler, in mid-March 1943 Tresckow arranged for his cousin Fabian von Schlabrendorff to smuggle a briefcase containing a bomb on board Hitler's personal aircraft. The plan was for it to detonate above the vast expanses of Russia as the Führer was flying back from visiting the Eastern Front. However, the device failed to explode after the trigger mechanism froze solid in the aircraft's hold.

The Bendlerblock now became the new epicentre of the plot to assassinate Hitler. The resistance network, which had steadily grown ever wider, now extended as far as the military commander of Occupied France, Carl-Heinrich von Stülpnagel, and his staff officers in Paris, as well as the high commands of a number of army groups and divisions. Nor did it stop there. In this time of moral resurgence, the conservative conspirators also reached out to Christian Democrats, Social Democrats, and the trade unions. It was the tragedy of the non-military resistance that it had been unable, in the totalitarian society of the Third Reich, to develop any viable infrastructure of opposition.

For far too long, the homogenised 'Führer state', with its social achievements, its foreign policy successes, and its all-pervasive propaganda machine, had forged an emotional bond between the masses and Hitler. When his enduring star began to wane, it was supplanted by growing domestic political pressure, which threatened to stifle even the most covert activities of opponents of the regime. The Gestapo had long since ceased to have any inhibitions about extending its campaign of terror past the portals of churches and monasteries. As a result, resistance from the churches, and from the ranks of not only Christian and Social Democrats but also communists, had to confine itself to symbolic individual actions like painting slogans and distributing leaflets. Notably, the 'White Rose' student resistance movement led by Sophie and Hans Scholl engaged in these forms of protest.

Meanwhile the Kreisau Circle founded by Count Helmuth James von Moltke, a member of the Armed Forces High Command administrative council, was a resistance group that brought together people of different political persuasions. These included, among others, the former Social Democrat MP Julius Leber, the Jesuit priest Alfred Delp, the educationalist Adolf Reichwein, and the lawyer Count Peter Yorck von Wartenburg. The latter was a descendant of the Prussian field marshal who in 1812 had signed the Convention of Tauroggen armistice between Prussia and Russia, against the express orders of his king, and in so doing had spared Prussia from being caught up in the debacle of Napoleon's defeat outside Moscow. The common denominator of the Kreisau Circle was that they were all patriots who were determined to salvage anything from 'their' Germany that could still be saved.

For a long time, these men had pinned their hopes on a rift developing in the unnatural alliance of countries opposing Hitler. In August 1943 the diplomat Ulrich von Hassell wrote:

all it would take is some sleight of hand to bring home to either the Russians or the British and Americans that it would be in their best interest for Germany to remain intact. In this game of Nine Men's Morris, I'd prefer to go with the West, but if need be I'm prepared to countenance an agreement with Russia.[17]

The problem for the resistance, the overwhelming majority of whom favoured an arrangement with the Western allies, was the 'unconditional surrender' formula that the anti-Hitler coalition had settled on at Casablanca.

The formulation put the efforts of the German resistance at the worst conceivable disadvantage. Even so, Hitler's adversaries left no stone unturned in trying to make contact with the Western allies to win them round to their way of thinking. In Stockholm in 1942, even before the Casablanca Conference, Dietrich Bonhoeffer, the leading theologian of the anti-regime Confessing Church, attempted to establish contacts in Britain using the Anglican Bishop of Chichester, George Bell, as a middleman. The following year, the German counterintelligence officer Bernd Gisevius opened a line of communication with the American secret service, the OSS, in Switzerland and held meetings with its head of operations there, Allen Dulles.

The worse Germany's military predicament became – in the autumn of 1943, Italy dropped out of the Axis, and German forces on the Apennine Peninsula were forced to retreat steadily north in the face of the advancing Allies following the landings at Anzio – the more hopeless the prospects for the resistance of entering into any sort of dialogue with the British or Americans. For why would they negotiate with an enemy whose collapse was only a matter of time? Nonetheless, in March 1944 the diplomat Adam von Trott zu Solz travelled to Stockholm for the third time to make contact, via his Swedish intermediary from the *Svenska*

*Dagbladet* newspaper, with a junior minister in Churchill's cabinet, Walter Monckton.

The key question for von Trott in arranging this meeting, according to the Swedish middleman, was whether Britain would continue its air raids against Germany even after Hitler had been successfully overthrown. The German diplomat was referring here to the intensive 'area bombing' campaign being conducted by the Royal Air Force's Strategic Bomber Command under its head air marshal Arthur Harris, which was reducing city after city to smoking ruins. It had begun with the bombing of Lübeck in April 1942. There then followed the first 'Thousand Bomber Raid' on the city of Cologne on the night of 30–1 May 1942. The campaign continued with large-scale attacks on Dortmund, Düsseldorf, Wuppertal, Remscheid, Essen, Nuremberg, and Berlin, which was targeted on numerous occasions. At the end of July and beginning of August 1943, it was the turn of Hamburg. In the devastating firestorm caused by the bombing 37,000 people lost their lives. And in many other cities and towns across Germany, women, children, and old people were asphyxiated, burned to death, or blown to pieces by the aerial bombardment.

Von Trott told Monckton that if Bomber Command continued its onslaught even after the demise of Hitler, the German people 'would conclude that Britain was fighting not against Hitler but against Germany as a whole, with the aim of destroying it completely'.[18] This remark went to the heart of the matter: namely, that the Western allies were less concerned about getting rid of the National Socialist regime and Hitler and more about eradicating Germany as a power factor in Europe. This objective had made Roosevelt first and foremost, and for a long time now Churchill too, blind to the fact that their ally Stalin wasn't so very different from Hitler and that he would stop at nothing to try and extend his sphere of power deep into the heart of the old continent. Their clashes with the Georgian-born dictator over where the borders of a future Poland were to be drawn should have alerted them to this possibility.

One can only speculate what an impetus the German resistance would have gained if the formula about 'unconditional surrender' had not existed, and if the Western allies had given Hitler's internal opposition some cause for hope. Everything would have been infinitely easier, for in such a case even doubters would have rallied to the cause. One scarcely dares to imagine what would have happened if Hitler had been eliminated and a peace concluded with the West. Stalin's room for manoeuvre in Eastern and Central Europe would have been decisively constricted. Such an outcome could even have acted as a springboard for bringing the war in the East to an end too. The lives of countless millions of people might have been spared, people who could have helped with the post-war reconstruction.

The men and women of the resistance had a clear idea of what a post-war Germany should look like. Prior to the 20 July assassination attempt, Stauffenberg had, along with Beck (who was to be made head of state), Goerdeler, and Leber, drafted a series of public appeals. He was also instrumental in drawing up a government statement, whose signatories, clearly under the influence of the Kreisau Circle, affirmed their support for a democratic welfare state and free elections. Stauffenberg, who had become the prime mover of the resistance movement, had thereby demonstrated his willingness to compromise. In 1944, together with his brother Berthold and his friend Rudolf Fahrner, he articulated his actual conception of a future German state in a pathos-laden oath full of sentimentality and reverence for conservative German values that was not meant for public consumption. In their so-called 'Guidelines for Germany's Rebirth' they reaffirmed the 'mission' of the German people and its obligation 'to lead the peoples of the West towards a better life'.[19]

The plotters dared to entertain a dream while knowing all along that it was fated to be just a dream. For a long time, their hopeless situation rendered them incapable of taking decisive action. Another major contributory factor in this was that, since Casablanca, any plan to get rid of Hitler was tainted with the disgrace of high treason. Shouldering such a heavy responsibility required an inner strength that few people could muster. However, with their 'rebellion of conscience' they wanted to send a clear signal to the outside world that another Germany existed, committed to Western norms and civilised values, in spite of all state-sponsored barbarism and Hitler.

After Stauffenberg had been promoted to chief of staff of the *Ersatzheer* in June 1944, thereby gaining direct access to Hitler, he decided to act himself. Quite how challenging a task this would be for him – a war invalid with severe disabilities, having lost one eye, an arm, and two fingers on his remaining hand – is indicated not least by the fact that even he found himself assailed by doubts despite being the most resolute member of the group. Following the success of the Allies' Normandy landings at the beginning of June 1944, he even checked with Tresckow whether their plan to overthrow Hitler had any further purpose in view of the Allied invasion and the impending end of the war. The general gave the following reply:

> The attempt on Hitler's life must succeed at all costs. But even if it fails, there should still be an attempted coup. For it is no longer about practical considerations, but about the German resistance movement having dared to put their lives on the line in front of the world and history by making a decisive move. Set against this, everything else is irrelevant.[20]

On 20 July 1944, the bomb that Stauffenberg had placed beneath a map table in the briefing room at Hitler's 'Wolf's Lair' operational headquarters in East Prussia exploded. As if by some miracle, the Führer survived this assassination attempt as well. Operation Valkyrie, which had been instigated at the Bendler-block and which the conspirators hoped would bring them to power, thus came to nothing. This endeavour marked the failure of the final attempt on Hitler's life – the thirteenth, since a Swabian cabinet maker by the name of Georg Elser had placed an explosive charge on a time fuse at the annual gathering in the Bürgerbräukeller in Munich on 9 November 1939; contrary to his normal practice, Hitler left the meeting early on that occasion.

The madness thus continued. Churchill took a disparaging view of the would-be assassins, while Hitler proceeded to settle scores with what he called a 'very small clique of ambitious, unscrupulous, and at the same time criminal and foolish officers'.[21] In all, nineteen generals, twenty-six colonels plus numerous ministry officials – a total of around a hundred individuals – were either executed or forced to take their own lives. They included Claus von Stauffenberg, who together with his fellow officers Friedrich Olbricht, Albrecht Mertz von Quirnheim, and Werner von Haeften, was shot dead by a firing squad in the courtyard of the Bendlerblock on the very same day, 20 July. Plotters like Witzleben, Stülpnagel, and Moltke were tortured to death in Plötzensee prison after being condemned by the People's Court. They were strangled in pairs by means of a single wire garotte; as each of them struggled, he choked the other to death. Hitler had these barbaric executions filmed, so that he could enjoy watching them later. Tresckow was one of those who chose suicide, blowing himself to pieces with a hand grenade in Białystok. Erwin Rommel, the darling of the German public, was also forced to commit suicide. Although he had never entertained the possibility of getting rid of his 'Führer', the field marshal was still implicated in the resistance movement and the plot. After the war Rommel's widow, concerned that the 'field marshal's honour should be preserved', was insistent that his unswerving loyalty should be emphasised, along with his steadfast refusal, as a military man, to go down the path of resistance.[22]

The conspirator Count Yorck von Wartenburg wrote in his final letter before his execution: 'Perhaps there will one day come a time when people will view the stance we took very differently, and when we will be adjudged patriots warning of catastrophe rather than as scoundrels.'[23] In the event, it would take a long time for his hope to be fulfilled, since the bulk of Germans, for all their war-weariness, continued to regard the activities of the resistance as incompatible with a soldierly conception of honour and duty. For them, it remained an act of treason. While the war was still ongoing, a security service report found that the general populace believed 'that the traitors had for a long time been sabotaging the Führer's aims and orders', and that this was what accounted for the difficult situation at the front.[24]

Popular repudiation of the assassination plot was further stoked by propaganda stories claiming that the conspirators had been in contact with the enemy – the same forces that continued to wage their relentless bombing campaign against the German civilian population. By November 1944, forty-five of the sixty larger conurbations in Germany had been devastated on the orders of Arthur Harris. Now the remaining fifteen, including Nuremberg, Munich, Leipzig, and Magdeburg, were in line for the same treatment. Berlin, meanwhile, remained the target of repeated air raids and had been reduced to a wasteland of rubble. Churchill and Stalin were united in their conviction that the sustained and systematic bombing of the German population would shatter morale and thereby shorten the war, but it actually achieved the opposite. Germans on the home front closed ranks. Hitler's much-trumpeted 'national community' had long since become an emergency mutual assistance association.

Perseverance, soldiering on regardless, was the order of the day – although, as shown by people's attitudes to the 20 July conspirators, this was oddly at variance with a strong desire for the war to end. Germans simply saw no alternative to staying the course. Besides, they did not even dare to contemplate one in circumstances where anyone who engaged in defeatist talk – in effect, who simply told the truth – was liable to be sentenced to death for 'subverting the war effort'. Anyone assisting Jews who had gone 'underground' also faced the executioner's axe.

Even the most minor of offences, such as listening to 'enemy radio stations', was punishable by a term in prison or a spell in a concentration camp. Thousands of people thus fell victim to the rough justice meted out by the president of the People's Court, a fanatical Nazi called Roland Freisler. In the 'total war' proclaimed by Goebbels after Stalingrad, which only really came into operation after 20 July 1944, extreme circumspection was called for.

On the subject of the extermination of the Jews, which was common knowledge, this circumspection required people to have seen and heard nothing. Of course, people discussed the topic but only within their closest family circle. If even an acquaintance dropped by, the topic of conversation was immediately changed. People closed their eyes to what was happening – in many cases quite literally – right outside their front doors. The fate of millions of the regime's slave labourers who were held in concentration camps such as Buchenwald, Bergen-Belsen, Flossenbürg, or Dachau, to name just a few, must have been witnessed by countless Germans. People's chief concern was to convey the impression of being a perfectly normal and good 'national comrade'.

The Nazi Party and Hitler, formerly such a luminary, had since become a matter of indifference to Germans. The latter had become something of a shadowy figure, avoiding any public appearances and for the most part delegating to Goebbels the task of speaking to the German people. The propaganda minister now increasingly came to the fore as a demonic rabble-rouser. His propaganda skilfully played upon the horrors that would supposedly await the German population in the event of defeat. When Henry Morgenthau, the US treasury secretary, produced a plan to turn Germany, the 'world's troublemaker', back into an agrarian state,[25] this was a complete gift for Goebbels. In September the *Völkischer Beobachter* ran headlines proclaiming 'Roosevelt and Churchill Adopt Jewry's Murderous Plan'[26] or 'Even Worse Than Clemenceau – Forty Million Germans Too Many'.[27] National Socialist propaganda quite deliberately invoked parallels with Versailles and exposed the alleged genocidal urge of international Jewry to eradicate the German people. There could only be one answer to all this, the propagandists suggested, and that was to fight on to the last breath.

From September 1944, this existential struggle appeared to have entered a new dimension with the deployment of Germany's so-called wonder weapons, much vaunted by the propaganda machine. Indeed, as the world's first ballistic missile, the V2 represented a major technological innovation. As with the Luftwaffe's first jet fighters (the twin-engined Messerschmitt Me 262), the British and Americans – let alone the Soviets – had nothing technically comparable with which to combat it. Many Germans may well have been inclined to believe the propaganda slogans, which claimed that the V2 was a war-winning weapon. In truth these rockets, which Hitler launched against London from early September 1944 onwards in the deluded hope of still getting Britain to see reason and switch sides at the eleventh hour, achieved very little. For each V2's payload was only a ton of high explosive, and its accuracy left much to be desired. By contrast, an antiquated-looking Lancaster bomber could carry at least five times that weight of bombs, while bomb-aiming accuracy improved towards the end of the war. Yet the German population learned nothing of this, being treated instead in the weekly newsreels to stirring images of the rockets lifting off.

As things turned out, the final false hopes linked to the 'wonder weapons' quickly dissipated, since they could do nothing to prevent the steady advance of the Allied armies towards Germany. Germans' main concerns were focused on the Eastern Front. As early as April 1944, the domestic security services registered people's fears on this score. One report on the public mood concluded: 'If the Russians keep on the way they're going, they really will reach Germany. They're already in Romania, the General Government, and threatening the borders of Hungary and Slovakia.'[28] Anxious Germans knew all too well about the trail of millions of deaths and devastation that the Wehrmacht and the SS had left behind them on their advance through the Soviet Union. No one doubted for an instant that the 'Ivans', as the Russians were colloquially called, would exact bloody revenge in return when they reached the territory of the Reich. Propaganda only heightened these fears, having for many years portrayed Stalin's soldiers as 'Jewish-Bolshevik hordes' who would set about 'massacring people in droves'.[29] Hitler referred to them as 'beasts from the Asiatic steppe'.[30]

After the Normandy landings, many Germans hoped that their country would be occupied by the Western powers. However, American units only reached German territory in the region around Aachen in September 1944, dashing the hopes of those living in the east of the Reich that they would liberated by British and US troops. The invasion of East Prussia by the Red Army in November of that year fulfilled people's gloomiest expectations as scenes of horror unfolded in villages that were briefly retaken by the Wehrmacht. In Nemmersdorf, for example, which Goebbels was quick to hold up as conclusive proof of the true 'grotesque face of Bolshevism', the inhabitants had been massacred, an atrocity that was graphically documented by the

*Wochenschau* newsreel. Unlike the SS and the Wehrmacht, who had shown a degree of discipline in selecting and liquidating their victims in the Soviet Union according to service regulations, an unruly Soviet soldiery now rampaged through German territory, raping, killing, and pillaging as it went – the result of a coldly calculated order on Stalin's part, designed to drive out the German population from the region east of the rivers Oder and Neisse. The latter was the line at which a post-Hitler Germany would stop, as agreed by Stalin with Roosevelt and Churchill at the Yalta Conference.

In view of how the military situation was unfolding on the Eastern Front, Germans must have been alarmed when, in December 1944, Hitler chose to launch a major counterattack – his final one – against the Americans in the west. The Ardennes offensive, which soon ground to a halt, was his attempt to consolidate the German position in the west before turning his attention to the final showdown with 'Jewish Bolshevism'.

As 1945 dawned, Hitler's apocalyptic fantasies envisaged this struggle being played out on German soil. As he had written in *Mein Kampf*: 'Germany will either be a world power or annihilated.'[31] Hitler's notorious 'Nero Order' of March 1945, which instructed retreating army units to destroy all remaining infrastructure as they pulled back, was also intended to scorch the earth of his own country. He believed that the German people had not shown themselves to be worthy of his leadership.

However, this was of little concern to ordinary Germans now, as the Eastern and Western fronts pressed in on their country, turning it into a battleground. For them, Hitler was now nothing but the individual whose continued existence was prolonging the war. They found themselves in an agonising predicament, desensitised by the constant presence of death – in the shape of fallen soldiers, civilians who had been killed, or executed deserters whose bodies were left hanging from trees to deter others.

The downtrodden population just wanted to survive. Yet that was particularly difficult for those in the east, where the depredations of the Red Army continued during the forcible expulsion of ethnic Germans, resulting in the deaths of two million people. At the same time, the equally pointless bombing campaign went on unabated. With the aim of killing even more civilians, from the beginning of 1945 the British and Americans deliberately targeted cities that were packed with refugees. Between 14,000 and 20,000 people were killed in a raid on Swinemünde, while most notoriously in Dresden, the capital of Saxony, between 22,000 and 40,000 perished, according to the most recent studies.[32] At the time, the Royal Air Force boasted that over 135,000 died in the Dresden raid,[33] which was carried out jointly with the USAAF. It has been estimated that some 600,000 civilians lost their lives as a result of the area bombing of German cities by the British and Americans during the Second World War, although the actual figure may well have been even higher.

Just one point of potential relief interrupted Germany's death throes, when President Franklin D. Roosevelt died suddenly and unexpectedly on 12 April 1945. Would the unbalanced anti-Hitler coalition now fall apart, in the same way as the death of Tsarina Elizabeth of Russia in 1762, during the Seven Years' War, fractured the Austro-Russian alliance and saved Emperor Frederick II's Prussia from disaster at the very last moment? Hitler grasped desperately at the idea that the 'miracle of the House of Brandenburg' might now be repeated. The question on everyone's lips on the street was whether, if the anti-Hitler coalition disintegrated, the Western powers would join forces with Germany to fight against Stalin's Soviet Union. Speculation was once more rife. There was even talk of a joint British and German army. Meanwhile, the time simply seemed to pass Hitler by. Only teenagers and children, who were put in uniform and thrown into the fight against the Soviets armed with just a rifle or an anti-tank grenade, still believed in him. No one in Germany was therefore especially moved when, on the evening of 1 May 1945, state radio broadcast the lie that 'our Führer Adolf Hitler ... has fallen, fighting against Bolshevism to his dying breath in his command post at the Reich Chancellery'.[34]

Thereafter, fighting only continued against the Red Army, bringing the battle for control of the Reich's capital to a victorious conclusion. By 1 May 1945, the Red Flag was flying over the battle-scarred Reichstag building. Over the preceding months, the last-ditch combined efforts of the Wehrmacht, the SS, and the home defence volunteers known as the 'Volkssturm' had tried to defend every metre of German territory from the massively superior Soviet forces. Their dogged resistance enabled millions of civilians to flee from the advance of the Red Army and head west. Eventually, when all the overland routes were cut off, the German navy undertook round-the-clock operations to evacuate refugees from any ports that remained in German hands and ferry them to safety across the Baltic Sea. This unprecedented rescue mission continued even beyond the unconditional surrender of German forces that took place on 8–9 May 1945. For the first time during the Second World War, in these final months the Wehrmacht was fighting on behalf of ordinary German citizens rather than in pursuit of the criminal aims of the man whose body his last remaining acolytes had burned and buried in a shallow grave in the garden of the Reich Chancellery.

In the West, Hitler's death essentially brought the fighting to an end. Even over the preceding days, the Western allies' advance into the heart of Germany had – quite contrary to their worst fears – met with very little resistance. Guerrilla warfare conducted by so-called 'Werewolf' Nazi terror cells and the fanatical defence of an 'Alpine redoubt' turned out to be largely fantasies of Goebbels' propaganda. Overwhelmingly, people were happy that it was all over at last. Portraits of the Führer were taken down and the insignia of National Socialist power consigned to the bin. In an instant, Hitler became history, not least because the Germans never really understood him.

Now the Germans were no longer prisoners of the Nazi dictatorship and the unrelenting pressures of the war, from which there had been no escape. Yet they had not been truly liberated. They were now prisoners of the new circumstances. They placed their hopes and trust above all in the British and Americans, on the assumption that the Western allies, having put an end to National Socialism, would not tolerate the barbarism of the Russians and the imposition of the Soviet system throughout Central Europe. Even when the West proceeded to do exactly that, the great majority of Germans who now fell within Stalin's sphere of influence came to terms with the new realities of life, just as they always had.

# Bibliography

Achmann, Klaus and Buhl, Hartmut, *20. Juli 1944* (Berlin and elsewhere, 1994).

*Akten zur Deutschen Auswärtigen Politik 1918–1945*, Serie D, 1937–1945 (Baden-Baden, 1950).

Albrecht, Dieter, 'Der Vatikan und das Dritte Reich' in The history working group of the Rottenburg-Stuttgart Diocese, eds, *Kirche im Nationalsozialismus* (Sigmaringen, 1984).

Allard, Sven, *Hitler und Stalin* (Berne and Munich 1974).

Aly, Götz et al., eds, *Die Verfolgung und Ermordung der europäischen Juden durch das nationalsozialistische Deutschland 1933–1945*. 14 vols. Edited on behalf of the Federal German Archive, the Institute of Contemporary History and the Faculty of Recent and Contemporary History at Alberts-Ludwigs-University (Freiburg im Breisgau and Munich, 2008–17).

Bayerlein, Bernhard H., *Tagebücher 1933–1943*, edited by Georgi Dimitroff (Berlin, 2000).

Bayerlein, Bernhard H., 'Stalin und die Kommunistische Partei Deutschlands in der Weimarerer Republik' in *Der Rote Gott. Stalin und die Deutschen* (Berlin, 2018).

Benz, Wolfgang, *Der Holocaust* (Munich, 2008).

Benz, Wolfgang, *Antisemitismus und Antisemitismusforschung*, Version 1.0 in Dokupedia-Zeitgeschichte, 11. 2. 2010, http://docupedia.de/zg/benz_antisemitismus_v1_de_2010.

Benz, Wolfgang, *Der Holocaust* (Munich 2008).

Bernier, François, 'Nouvelle division de la terre par les

differentes espèces ou race d'hommes qui habitent', *Journal des scavans*, vol. 6 (1684), pp. 133–40.

Besier, Gerhard, *Die Kirchen und das Dritte Reich. Spaltungen und Abwehrkämpfe 1934–1937* (Berlin and Munich, 2001).

Besymenski, Lew, *Stalin und Hitler. Das Pokerspiel der Diktatoren* (Berlin, 2002).

Birkelund, John P., *Gustav Stresemann. Patriot und Staatsmann* (Hamburg and Vienna, 2002).

Boberach, Heinz, ed., *Meldungen aus dem Reich. Die geheimen Lageberichte des Sicherheitsdienstes der SS 1938–1945*, 16 vols. (Herrsching, 1984).

Boehlich, Walter, ed., *Der Berliner Antisemitismusstreit* (Frankfurt a. M., 1965).

Brakel, Alexander, *Der Holocaust. Judenverfolgung und Völkermord* (Berlin, 2008).

Broszat, Martin, 'Plädoyer für eine Historisierung des Nationalsozialismus', *Merkur* 39 (1985).

Brumlik, Micha, *Antisemitismus. 100 Seiten* (Stuttgart, 2020).

Brumlik, Micha, 'Das Gesetz ist erhaben', *Die Welt* (7 February 2004).

Bullock, Alan, *Hitler. A Study in Tyranny* (London, 1952).

Burckhardt, Carl J., *Meine Danziger Mission 1937–1939* (Munich, 1960).

Chamberlain, Houston Stewart, *Die Grundlagen des neunzehnten Jahrhunderts* (Munich, 1899).

Churchill, Winston S., *The Second World War*, 6 vols. (Boston, 1948–53).

Churchill, Winston S., *Great War Speeches: A unique collection of the finest and most stirring speeches by one of the greatest Leaders of our time* (London, 1957).

Clark, Christopher, *The Sleepwalkers: How Europe Went to War in 1914* (London, 2012).

Claß, Heinrich (published under the pseudonym Daniel

Frymann), ed., *Wenn ich Kaiser wär … Politische Wahrheiten und Notwendigkeiten* (Leipzig, 1912).

Conze, Eckart, Frei, Norbert, Hayes, Peter, and Zimmermann, Moshe, *Das Amt und die Vergangenheit. Deutsche Diplomaten im Dritten Reich und in der Bundesrepublik* (Munich, 2010).

Courtois, Stéphane, ed., *The Black Book of Communism: Crimes, Terror, Repression*, translated by Jonathan Murphy and Mark Kramer (Cambridge MA and London, 1999).

Cüppers, Martin, *Wegbereiter der Shoah. Die Waffen-SS, der Kommandostab des Reichsführers-SS und die Judenvernichtung 1939–1945* (Darmstadt, 2005).

Darwin, Charles, *On the Origin of Species by Means of Natural Selection, or the Preservation of Favoured Races in the Struggle for Life* (London, 1859).

*Das Dritte Reich und der Zweite Weltkrieg*, The Military History Research Department, eds, 10 vols. (Stuttgart, 1979–2008).

*Die Wehrmachtsberichte 1939–1945*, 3 vols. (Cologne, 1989).

Diedrich, Torsten, *Paulus. Das Trauma von Stalingrad. Eine Biographie* (Paderborn and elsewhere, 2008).

Dimitrov, Georgi, *The Working Class Against Fascism. Report Delivered at the Seventh World Congress of the Communist International on 2 August 1935*, www.marxists.org/reference/archive/dimitrov/works/1935/08_02.htm.

Dohm von, Christian Wilhelm, 'Über die bürgerliche Verbesserung der Juden'in Wolf Christoph Seifert, ed., *Ausgewählte Schriften*, vol. 1 (Göttingen, 2015).

Domarus, Max, ed., *Hitler. Reden und Proklamationen 1932–1945*, 2 vols. (Wiesbaden, 1973) (English edition: *Hitler: Speeches and Proclamations 1932–1945. The Chronicle of a Dictatorship*, 4 vols, translated by Mary Fran Gilbert and Chris Wilcox (Wauconda IL, 1990–2004).

Eberle, Henrik and Uhl, Mathias, eds, *Das Buch Hitler. Geheimdossier des NKWD für Josef W. Stalin. Zusammengestellt aufgrund der Verhörprotokolle des Persönlichen Adjutanten Hitlers, Otto Günsche, und des Kammerdieners Heinz Linge* (Moscow, 1948–9 and Bergisch Gladbach, 2005).

Eberle, Henrik, *Hitlers Weltkriege. Wie der Gefreite zum Feldherrn wurde* (Hamburg, 2014).

Eckart, Dietrich, *Der Bolschewismus von Moses bis Lenin. Zwiegespräch zwischen Adolf Hitler und mir* (Munich, 1924) (English edition: *Bolshevism from Moses to Lenin: A Dialogue Between Adolf Hitler and Me*, translated by William L. Pierce (Hillsboro WV, 1999).

Eich, Martin, 'Als Deutschland den Frieden verlor', *Frankfurter Allgemeine Zeitung* (11 Mar. 2018).

Eichholtz, Dietrich, *Geschichte der deutschen Kriegswirtschaft* (Munich, 2013).

Eliasberg, David, 'Russischer und Münchner Bolschewismus', *Die Ausbreitung des Bolschewismus, Süddeutsche Monatshefte* (Apr. 1919).

Fest, Joachim C., *Hitler. Eine Biographie* (Berlin and Munich, 2002).

Fetscher, Iring, 'Deutscher Geist und Judenhass. Judenliebe, Judenhass' (21 Jan. 2001) tagesspiegel.de.

Fischer, Fritz, *Griff nach der Weltmacht. Die Kriegszielpolitik des kaiserlichen Deutschland 1914/18* (Düsseldorf, 1961) (English edition: *Germany's Aims in the First World War*, translated by Hajo Holborn and James Joll (New York, 1968).

Fischer, Jens Malte, 'Richard Wagners Das Judentum in der Musik. Entstehung – Kontext – Wirkung' in Dieter Borchmeyer, Ami Maayani, and Susanne Vill, eds, *Richard Wagner und die Juden* (Stuttgart and Weimar, 2000).

Fishman, Talya, *Becoming the People of the Talmud. Oral Torah as Written Tradition in Medieval Jewish Cultures* (Philadelphia, 2011).

Ford, Henry, *The International Jew: The World's Foremost Problem* (Dearborn, 1920).

Furet, François and Nolte, Ernst, *Feindliche Nähe. Kommunismus und Faschismus im 20. Jahrhundert. Ein Briefwechsel* (Munich, 1998).

Furet, François, *The Passing of an Illusion. The Idea of Communism in the Twentieth Century* (Chicago, 1999).

Gasser, Markus, *Die Postmoderne* (Stuttgart, 1997).

Gellermann, Günther W., *Geheime Wege zum Frieden mit England ... Ausgewählte Initiativen zur Beendigung des Krieges 1940/1942* (Bonn, 1995).

Gellinek, Christian, *Philipp Scheidemann. Eine biographische Skizze* (Cologne, Weimar, and Vienna, 1994).

Gobineau, Arthur de, *Essai sur l'inégalité des races humaines* (Paris, 1853–5).

Goebbels, Joseph, *Die Tagebücher von Joseph Goebbels*. Compiled on behalf of the Institute of Contemporary History and with the support of the National Archives Service of Russia. Elke Fröhlich et al., eds, 36 vols. (Munich and elsewhere, 1987–2008) (English editions: *The Goebbels Diaries 1939–1941*, edited and translated by Fred Taylor (London, 1982); *The Goebbels Diaries 1942–1943*, edited and translated by Louis P. Lochner (New York, 1948).

Goldhagen, Daniel Jonah, *Hitler's Willing Executioners. Ordinary Germans and the Holocaust* (New York, 1996).

Goozé, Marianne E., 'Wilhelm von Humboldt und die Judenemanzipation. Leistungen und Widersprüche', *A Journal of Germanic Studies*, XLVIII/3 (Sept. 2012).

Górny, Majiej, 'Die Experten', *Frankfurter Allgemeine Zeitung* (20 Jan. 2020).

Gorodetsky, Gabriel, ed., *Die Maiski-Tagebücher. Ein Diplomat im Kampf gegen Hitler 1932–1943* (Munich, 2016).

Groener, Wilhelm, Notes by the First Quartermaster on the events of 18–20 June 1919 in Weimar, Military Archive of the Federal German Republic, Schleicher bequest, N 42/12.

Haberl, Othmar Nicola, 'Kommunistische Internationale' in *Pipers Wörterbuch zur Politik*, vol. 4, Sozialistische Systeme (Munich and Zurich, 1981).

Haensel, Carl, *Das Gericht vertagt sich. Aus dem Tagebuch eines Nürnberger Verteidigers* (Hamburg, 1950).

Haffner, Sebastian, *Die verratene Revolution* (Berne, 1969).

Haffner, Sebastian, *Anmerkungen zu Hitler* (Munich, 1978) (English edition: *The Meaning of Hitler*, translated by Ewald Osers (Cambridge MA, 1979).

Haffner, Sebastian *1918/19. Eine deutsche Revolution* (Hamburg, 1981).

Halder, Franz, *Kriegstagebuch. Tägliche Aufzeichnungen des Chefs des Generalstabes des Heeres 1939 – 1942*, ed., Arbeitskreis für Wehrforschung, vol. I–III (Stuttgart, 1962–64).

Hamann, Brigitte, *Hitlers Wien. Lehrjahre eines Diktators* (Munich and Zürich, 1996) (English edition: *Hitler's Vienna: A Dictator's Apprenticeship*, translated by Thomas Thornton (Oxford and New York, 1999).

Hartmann, Christian, *Halder. Generalstabschef Hitlers 1938–1942* (Paderborn and elsewhere, 1991).

Hassell, Ulrich von, *Die Hassel-Tagebücher 1938–1944. Aufzeichnungen vom Anderen Deutschland*, ed., Friedrich Hiller von Gaertringen (Berlin, 1988).

Heiber, Helmut, ed., *Goebbels-Reden, 1933–1945*, 2 vols. (Munich, 1972).

Heidemann, Gerd, Recherchen und Interview in Santiago de

Chile Gesprächspartner General a. D. Karl Wolff (ehem. SS-Oberstgruppenführer) (25 June–2 July 1979).

Heiden, Konrad, *Adolf Hitler. Das Zeitalter der Verantwortungslosigkeit. Ein Mann gegen Europa. Die Biographie* (Berlin and elsewhere, 2016) (English edition: *Hitler: A Biography* (London, 1938).

Held, Ludger, 'Wenn die Olympiade vorbei ist, schlagen wir die Juden zu Brei', zeit.de, (1 Aug. 2016).

Heresch, Elisabeth, *Geheimakte Parvus. Die gekaufte Revolution* (Munich, 2000).

Herzl, Theodor, *Der Judenstaat. Versuch einer modernen Lösung der Judenfrage* (Leipzig and Vienna 1896) (English edition: *The Jewish State*, translated by Sylvie D'Avigdor, new ed., with an introduction by Alan Dershovitz (New York, 2019) www.gutenberg.org/files/25282/25282-h/25282-h.htm.

Heusinger, Adolf, *Befehl im Widerstreit* (Tübingen and Stuttgart, 1950).

Heydecker, Joe J., *Der große Krieg 1914–1918* (Frankfurt and Berlin, 1988).

Hildebrandt, Klaus *Deutsche Außenpolitik 1939–1945* (Stuttgart and elsewhere, 1980).

Hill, Leonidas E., ed., *Die Weizsäcker-Papiere 1933–1950* (Berlin and Frankfurt, 1974).

Hillgruber, Andreas, *Staatsmänner und Diplomaten bei Hitler*, 2 vols. (Frankfurt a. M., 1967 and 1970).

Hillgruber, Andreas, *Deutsche Großmacht und Weltpolitik im 19. und 20. Jahrhundert* (Düsseldorf, 1977).

Hillgruber, Andreas/Hümmelchen, Gerhard, *Chronik des Zweiten Weltkrieges. Kalendarium militärischer und politischer Ereignisse, 1939–45* (Düsseldorf, 1978).

Hillgruber, Andreas, *Hitlers Strategie. Politik und Kriegführung 1940–1941* (Koblenz, 1982).

Hitler, *Monologe* (16 and 17 Jan. 1942).

Hitler, *Reden, Schriften, Anordnungen, Februar 1925 bis Januar 1933*, 5 vols. (13 subvolumes), edited by Institute of Contemporary History (Munich and elsewhere, 1992–98).

Hitler, *Mein Kampf. Eine kritische Edition*, 2 vols., ed., Christian Hartmann, Thomas Vordermayer, Othmar Plöckinger, and Roman Töppel, on behalf of the Institute of Contemporary History (Munich and Berlin, 2016).

*Hitlers politisches Testament. Die Bormann Diktate vom Februar und April 1945*. With an essay by Hugh R. Trevor-Roper (n.p., n.d.).

'Hitlers Zweites Buch. Außenpolitische Standortbestimmung nach der Reichstagswahl Juni–Juli 1928' in *Hitler. Reden. Schriften. Anordnungen*, vol. II (Munich and elsewhere, 1995).

Hoeres, Peter, *Versailler Vertrag. Ein Frieden, der kein Frieden war*. Bundeszentrale für politische Bildung. Aus Politik und Zeitgeschichte, *Pariser Friedensordnung* (Jahrgang 15/2019) bpb.de.

Hofer, Walter, ed., *Der Nationalsozialismus. Dokumente 1933–1945* (Frankfurt a. M,. 1957).

Hoffmann, Peter, *Claus Schenk Graf von Stauffenberg und seine Brüder* (Stuttgart, 2004).

Höhne, Hein, *Die Zeit der Illusionen* (Düsseldorf and elsewhere, 1991).

Hossbach, Friedrich, *Zwischen Wehrmacht und Hitler 1934–1938* (Göttingen, 1965).

Hubatsch, Walther, ed., *Hitlers Weisungen für die Kriegführung 1939–1945* (Koblenz, 1983).

Hürter, Johannes, ed., *Notizen aus dem Vernichtungskrieg. Die Ostfront 1941/42 in den Aufzeichnungen des Generals Heinrici* (Darmstadt, 2016).

Hürter, Johannes, *Hitlers Heerführer. Die deutschen*

*Oberbefehlshaber im Krieg gegen die Sowjetunion 1941/42, Quellen und Darstellungen zur Zeitgeschichte*, edited by Institute of Contemporary History (Munich, 2006).

Hurwicz, E., 'Die Weltexpansion des Bolschewismus. Versuch einer Prognose' in *Die Ausbreitung des Bolschewismus, Süddeutsche Monatshefte* (Leipzig and Munich, April 1919).

International Military Tribunal Nuremberg, ed., IMT, *Trial of the principal war criminals before the International Military Tribunal, Nuremberg 14 November 1945–1 October 1946*, 24 vols. (Nuremberg, 1949), reprinted (Munich and Zurich, 1984).

Jäckel, Eberhard and Kuhn, Axel, eds, *Hitler. Sämtliche Aufzeichnungen 1905–1925* (Stuttgart, 1980).

Jacobsen, Hans-Adolf, *Der Weg zur Teilung der Welt. Politik und Strategievon 1939 bis 1945* (Koblenz and Bonn, 1979).

Jasch, Hans-Christian, *Staatssekretär Wilhelm Stuckart und die Judenpolitik. Der Mythos von der sauberen Verwaltung* (Berlin, 2012).

Jensen, Uffa, 'Die Juden sind unser Unglück', zeit.de, (27 Dec. 2013).

Joachimsthaler, Anton, *Hitlers Weg begann in München 1913–1923*, with a foreword by Ian Kershaw (Munich, 2000).

Jochmann, Werner, ed., *Adolf Hitler. Monologe im Führerhauptquartier 1941–1944. Die Aufzeichnungen Heinrich Heims* (Hamburg, 1980).

Jung, Rudolf, *Der nationale Sozialismus. Seine Grundlage, sein Werden, seine Ziele* (Aussig, 1919).

Kant, Immanuel, *Werke*. Akademie-Textausgabe, vol. 9, *Logik, Physische Geographie, Pädagogik* (Berlin and elsewhere, 1987).

Keil, Lars-Broder and Kellerhoff, Sven Felix, *Lob der Revolution. Die Geburt der deutschen Demokratie* (Darmstadt, 2018).

Keil, Lars-Broder and Kellerhoff, Sven Felix, *Deutsche Legenden. Vom 'Dolchstoß' und anderen Mythen der Geschichte* (Berlin, 2002).

Kellerhoff, Sven Felix, *'Mein Kampf'. Die Karriere eines deutschen Buches* (Stuttgart, 2015).

Kellerhoff, Sven Felix, *Die NSDAP. Eine Partei und ihre Mitglieder* (Stuttgart, 2017).

Kennan, George F., *The Decline of Bismarck's European Order. Franco-Russian Relations 1875–1890* (Princeton NJ, 1979).

Kershaw, Ian, *The 'Hitler Myth': Image and Reality in the Third Reich* (Oxford, 1987).

Kershaw, Ian, *Hitler*, vol. 1. *1889–1936: Hubris*, vol. 2. *1936–1945: Nemesis* (London, 1998 and 2000).

Kershaw, Ian, *The End. Hitler's Germany 1944–45* (London, 2011).

Kessler, Harry Graf, *Das Tagebuch. Neunter Band 1926–1937*, edited by Sabine Gruber and Ulrich Ott (Stuttgart, 2010).

Keil, Lars-Broder and Kellerhoff, Sven Felix, *Deutsche Legenden. Vom 'Dolchstoß' und anderen Mythen der Geschichte* (Berlin, 2002).

Keynes, John Maynard, *The Economic Consequences of the Peace* (London, 1920).

Kilb, Andreas 'Putin als Historiker', *Frankfurter Allgemeine Zeitung* (20 June 2020).

Kipling, Rudyard, 'The White Man's Burden' (n.p. 1899).

Klemperer, Victor, *Man möchte immer weinen und lachen in einem. Revolutions-Tagebuch* (Berlin, 2015).

Knopp, Guido, *Holocaust* (Munich, 2000).

Koenen, Gerd, *Die Farbe Rot. Ursprünge und Geschichte des Kommunismus* (Munich, 2017).

Kogon, Eugen, *Der SS-Staat. Das System der deutschen Konzentrationslager* (Munich, 1946). (English edition: *The*

*Theory and Practice of Hell*, translated by Heinz Norden (New York, 1950).

Kolb, Eberhard, *Der Frieden von Versailles* (Munich, 2011).

Kotze, Hildegard von, ed., 'Heeresadjutant bei Hitler. Aufzcichnungen des Major Engel 1939–1945', *Schriftenreihe der Vierteljahrshefte für Zeitgeschichte*, 29 (Stuttgart, 1974).

Kulka, Otto Dov, 'Die Nürnberger Rassegesetze und die deutsche Bevölkerung im Lichte geheimer NS-Lage- und Stimmungsberichte', *Vierteljahrshefte für Zeitgeschichte*, 32 (1984) www.ifz.muenchen.de/heftarchiv.html.

Lagarde, Paul de, 'Juden und Indogermanen' (1887), quoted in Alexander Bein, *Der moderne Antisemitismus und seine Bedeutung für die Judenfrage*, in: *Vierteljahrshefte für Zeitgeschichte*, Jg. 6, (1958), Heft 4, p. 359, www.ifz. muenchen.de/heftarchiv.html.

Large, David Clay, *Where Ghosts Walked: Munich's Road to the Third Reich* (New York, 1997).

Lenhard, Philipp, *Volk oder Religion? Die Entstehung moderner jüdischer Ethnizität in Frankreich und Deutschland 1782–1848*, www.igk-religioesekulturen.uni. muenchen.de/mitglieder/ehemalige_kollegiat/lenhard/ dissproj_lenhard/index.html.

Lenin, Vladimir Ilyich, *Ausgewählte Werke*, vol. I (East Berlin, 1961).

Lessing, Gotthold Ephraim, *Nathan der Weise* ('Nathan the wise') (n.p., 1779).

Lloyd George, David, *Some Considerations for the Peace Conference before they finally draft their terms* (1919). Transcript from the National Archives, Kew, Extracts from a document setting out British Prime Minister David Lloyd George's views on a treaty with Germany, 25 March 1919 (Catalogue ref: CAB 1/28).

Lloyd George, David, *Daily Mail* (17 Sept. 1936).

Longerich, Peter, ed., *Die Ermordung der europäischen Juden. Eine umfassende Dokumentation des Holocaust 1941–1945* (Munich, 1989).

Longerich, Peter, *Heinrich Himmler, Biographie* (Munich, 2008) (English edition: *Heinrich Himmler: A Life*, translated by Jeremy Noakes and Lesley Sharpe (Oxford, 2011).

Loßberg, Bernhard von, *Im Wehrmachtführungsstab* (Hamburg, 1949).

Lukacs, John, *The Duel. The Eighty-Day Struggle Between Churchill and Hitler* (New York, 1991).

Lukacs, John, *The Hitler of History* (New York, 1997).

Luther, Martin, *Von den Juden und ihren Lügen*('On the Jews and their lies'), new edition, edited and with a commentary by Matthias Morgenstern (Berlin, 2016).

Luxemburg, Rosa, 'Zur Russischen Revolution (1918)', in Rosa Luxemburg, *Gesammelte Werke*, vol. 4 (East Berlin, 1974) (English edition: *The Russian Revolution*, translated by Bertram Wolfe (New York, 1940). www.marxists.org/archive/luxemburg/1918/russian-revolution.

Mann, Thomas, *Tagebücher*, edited by Peter de Mendelsohn (Frankfurt a. M., 1959).

Marx, Karl, *Zur Judenfrage* ('On the Jewish question') www.marxists.org/archive/marx/works/1844/jewish-question.

Marx, Karl and Engels, Friedrich, *Werke*, edited by the Institute for Marxism-Leninism of the Central Committee of the Socialist Unity Party (East Berlin, 1955–81).

Maser, Werner, *Hitlers Briefe und Notizen. Sein Weltbild in handschriftlichen Dokumenten* (Graz and Stuttgart, 2002).

Mayer, Michael, 'NSDAP und Antisemitismus 1919–1933', *Münchner Wirtschaftswissenschaftliche Beiträge* (July 2002).

Meining, Stefan, 'Ein neuer Ansturm der Antisemiten: 1919–1923' in Douglas Bokovoy and Stefan Meining, eds, *Versagte*

*Heimat. Jüdisches Leben in Münchens Isarstadt 1914–1945*
(Munich, 1994).

*Meldungen aus dem Reich,* 17, 10 Aug. 1944.

Menzel, Thomas, *Die Ermordung von Rosa Luxemburg und Karl Liebknecht,* www.bundesarchiv.de.

Merz, Kai-Uwe, *Das Schreckbild. Deutschland und der Bolschewismus 1917–1921* (Frankfurt and Berlin, 1995).

Montefiore, Simon Sebag, *Stalin: The Court of the Red Tsar* (London, 2003).

Müller, Rolf-Dieter, *Der Feind steht im Osten. Hitlers geheime Pläne für einen Krieg gegen die Sowjetunion im Jahr 1939* (Berlin, 2011) (English edition: *Enemey in the East: Hitler's Secret Plans to Invade the Soviet Union,* translated by Alexander Starritt (London, 2015).

N'Diaye, Tidiane, *Le génocide voilé. Étude de la traite négrière arabo-musulmane* (Paris, 2008).

Neitzel, Sönke, *Abgehört. Deutsche Generäle in britischer Kriegsgefangenschaft 1942–1945* (Berlin, 2007).

Nevins, Michael, *Bloody Bacchanalia. The Pogroms of Proskurov and Felshtin,* p. 5 in www.felshtin.org/resources/bloodybaccanalia.pdf.

Nitti, Francesco, *Peaceless Europe* (London and New York, 1922).

Nolte, Ernst, *Der Faschismus in seiner Epoche* (Munich, 1963).

Nolte, Ernst, *Frankfurter Allgemeine Zeitung* (6 June 1986).

Nolte, Ernst, *Die Weimarer Republik. Demokratie zwischen Lenin und Hitler* (Munich, 2006).

Noske, Gustav, *Von Kiel bis Kapp. Zur Geschichte der deutschen Revolution* (Berlin, 1920).

O'Brien, Phillips, *How the War Was Won. Air-Sea Power and Allied Victory in World War II* (Cambridge, 2015).

Overy, Richard, *The Bombing War: Europe 1939–1945* (London, 2013).

Petersen, Jens, 'Mussolini. Wirklichkeit und Mythos eines Diktators' in Karl Heinz Bohrer, ed., *Mythos und Moderne* (Frankfurt a. M., 1983).

Picker, Henry, *Hitlers Tischgespräche im Führerhauptquartier 1941–1942* (Frankfurt and Berlin, 1989).

Pipes, Richard, 'Jews and the Russian Revolution', *Polin*, 9 (1999).

Pius XI, Pope, Encyclical 'Mit brennender Sorge' ('With burning concern') on the Church and the German Reich, 14 March 1937 (full text) www.vatican.va/content/pius-xi/en/encyclicals/documents/hf_p-xi_enc_14031937_mit-brennender-sorge.html.

Platthaus, Andreas, *Der Krieg nach dem Krieg. Deutschland zwischen Revolution und Versailles* (Berlin, 2018).

Popper, Karl, *The Open Society and Its Enemies*, with a new foreword by George Soros (Princeton, 2020)

Pufelska, Agnieszka, 'Vernunft jenseits der Vernunft. Zur Judenfeindschaft in der Zeit der Aufklärung' in Hans-Joachim Hahn and Olaf Kistenmacher, eds, *Beschreibungsversuche der Judenfeindschaft. Zur Geschichte der Antisemitismusforschung vor 1944*. Europäisch-jüdische Studien (Berlin and elsewhere, 2015).

Puschner, Marco, *Antisemitismus im Kontext der Politischen Romantik* (Berlin and elsewhere, 2008).

Pyta, Wolfram, *Hitler. Der Künstler als Politiker und Feldherr. Eine Herrschaftsanalyse* (Munich, 2015).

Quinkert, Babette, *Deutsche Besatzung in der Sowjetunion 1941–1944. Vernichtungskrieg, Reaktionen, Erinnerung* (Paderborn, 2014).

Rauschning, Hermann, *Die Revolution des Nihilismus*, (Zürich and New York, 1938).

Rauschning, Hermann, *Gespräche mit Hitler* (Vienna, 1973).

Reuth, Ralf Georg, *Entscheidung im Mittelmeer. Die südliche*

*Peripherie Europas in der deutschen Strategie des Zweiten Weltkrieges 1940–1942* (Koblenz, 1985).

Reuth, Ralf Georg, ed., *Joseph Goebbels. Tagebücher 1924–1945*, 5 vols. (Munich and Zurich 1992).

Reuth, Ralf Georg, *Goebbels. Eine Biographie* (Munich, 1990) (English edition: *Goebbels*, translated by Krishna Winston (London, 1993).

Reuth, Ralf Georg, *Hitler. Eine politische Biographie* (Munich and Zurich, 2003).

Reuth, Ralf Georg, 'Vielleicht wird man uns einmal als Patrioten sehen', *Welt am Sonntag* (18 July 2004).

Reuth, Ralf Georg, *Erstickt, verkohlt, zerstückelt*, *Welt am Sonntag* (6 Feb. 2005).

Reuth, Ralf Georg, *Hitlers Judenhass. Klischee und Wirklichkeit* (Munich and Zürich, 2009).

Reuth, Ralf Georg, *Rommel. Das Ende einer Legende* (Munich and Zurich ,2004) (English edition: *Rommel: The End of a Legend*, translated by Debra Marmor and Herbert Danner (London, 2009).

Reuth, Ralf Georg, *Kurze Geschichte des Zweiten Weltkriegs* (Berlin, 2018).

Ribbentrop, Joachim von, *Zwischen London und Moska* (Leoni am Starnberger See, 1953) (English edition: *The Ribbentrop Memoirs*, with an introduction by Alan Bullock, translated by Oliver Watson (London, 1954).

Rindl, Peter, *Der internationale Kommunismus* (Munich, 1961).

Rogalla von Bieberstein, Johannes, *Jüdischer Bolschewismus. Mythos und Realität* (Dresden, 2002).

Röhl, John C. G., *Wilhelm II. Der Aufbau der persönlichen Monarchie 1888–1900* (Munich, 2001).

Römer, Felix, *Der Kommissarbefehl. Wehrmacht und*

*NS-Verbrechen an der Ostfront 1941/42* (Paderborn, Munich, Vienna, and Zürich, 2008).

Rosenberg, Arthur, *Entstehung und Geschichte der Weimarer Republik*, edited and with an introduction by Kurt Kersten (Frankfurt a. M., 1983).

Rotte, Ralph, *Die Außen- und Friedenspolitik des Heiligen Stuhls. Eine Einführung* (Wiesbaden, 2014).

Rürup, Reinhard, ed., *Der Krieg gegen die Sowjetunion 1941–1945. Eine Dokumentation* (Berlin, 1991).

Salewski, Michael, *Die deutsche Seekriegsleitung*, 2 vols, (Frankfurt a. M., 1970 and 1973).

Sammons, Jeffrey L., ed., *Die Protokolle der Weisen von Zion. Die Grundlage des modernen Antisemitismus – eine Fälschung. Text und Kommentar* (Göttingen, 1998).

Scheel, Wilhelm, *Deutschlands Kolonien in achtzig farbenphotographischen Abbildungen* (Berlin, 1914).

Schmidt, Paul, *Statist auf diplomatischer Bühne 1923–1945* (Bonn, 1950).

Schmidt, Rainer F., *Rudolf Heß. 'Botengang eines Toren'? Der Flug nach Großbritannien vom 10. Mai 1941* (Munich, 2000).

Schmitt, Carl, 'Der Führer schützt das Recht. Zur Reichstagsrede Adolf Hitlers vom 13. Juli 1934', *Deutsche Juristenzeitung* 15 (1934).

Schramm, Percy Ernst, ed., *Kriegstagebuch des Oberkommandos der Wehrmacht (Wehrmachtführungsstab)*, vols. I – IV (Munich, 1982)

Schwabe, Klaus, ed., *Quellen zum Friedensschluss von Versailles* (Darmstadt, 1997).

Seidler, Fritz W., *Deutscher Volkssturm. Das letzte Aufgebot 1944/45* (Munich and Berlin, 1989).

Seraphim, Hans Günther, *Die deutsch-russischen Beziehungen 1939–1941* (Hamburg, 1949).

Sloterdijk, Peter *Zorn und Zeit. Politisch-psychologischer Vergleich* (Frankfurt a. M., 2006).

Solzhenitsyn, Alexander, *Zweihundert Jahre zusammen. Die Juden in der Sowjetunion* (Munich, 2003).

Sommer, Theo, 'Deutschland und Japan zwischen den Mächten 1935–1940' in Hans Rothfels et al., eds, *Tübinger Studien zur Geschichte und Politik*, 15 (Tübingen, 1962).

Speer, Albert, *Erinnerungen* (Frankfurt, Berlin and Vienna, 1969) (English edition: *Inside the Third Reich: Memoirs,* translated by Richard and Clara Winston (London, 1970).

Spencer, Herbert, *Social Statics* (London, 1851).

Spengler, Oswald, *Der Untergang des Abendlandes. Umrisse einer Morphologie der Weltgeschichte* (Munich, 1920) (English edition: *The Decline of the West: Perspectives of World History,* translated by Charles Francis Atkinson (New York, 1926 and 1928).

Spengler, Oswald, *Jahre der Entscheidung* (Munich, 1933).

Spengler, Oswald, *Preußentum und Sozialismus* (Munich, 1919) (English edition: *Prussianism and Socialism,* translated by Charles Francis Atkinson (New York, 1922).

Stalin, Josef W., *On the Great Patriotic War of the Soviet Union* (Moscow, 1944).

Stargardt, Nicholas, *The German War: A Nation Under Arms, 1939–1945* (London, 2015).

*Statutes of the Pan-German League 1897*, Bundesarchiv, R 8048/4, fol. 2–5.

Stead, William T., *The Last Will and Testament of Cecil Rhodes* (London, 1902).

Striefler, Christian, *Kampf um die Macht. Kommunisten und Nationalsozialisten am Ende der Weimarer Republik* (Frankfurt and Berlin, 1993).

Thamer, Hans Ulrich, *Verführung und Gewalt. Deutschland 1933–1945* (Berlin, 1986).

Töppel, Roman, *Kursk 1943. Die größte Schlacht des Zweiten Weltkriegs* (Paderborn, 2017). (English edition: *Kursk 1943: The Greatest Battle of the Second World War*, translated by Katharina Straub (Warwick, 2018).

Überschär, Gerd R., *Der deutsche Angriff auf die Sowjetunion 1941* (Darmstadt, 1998).

Uhl, Mathias, et al., eds, *Verhört. Die Befragungen deutscher Generale und Offiziere durch die sowjetischen Geheimdienste 1945–1952* (Berlin, 2015).

Ullrich, Volker, *Adolf Hitler*, vol. 1. *Die Jahre des Aufstiegs*, vol. 2 *Die Jahre des Untergangs* (Frankfurt a. M., 2013 and 2018) (English edition: *Hitler*, vol. 1. *Ascent 1889–1939*, vol. 2. *Downfall 1939–1945*, translated by Jefferson Chase (London, 2016 and 2020).

*Ursachen und Folgen. Vom deutschen Zusammenbruch 1918 und 1945 bis zur Staatlichen Neuordnung Deutschlands in der Gegenwart*, vol. X, edited by by Herbert Michaelis and Ernst Schraepler (Berlin n.d.).

*Versailles 1919. Aus der Sicht von Zeitzeugen*. With contributions by Sebastian Haffner, Lloyd George, Ernst Jünger et al. (Munich, 2002).

Warlimont, Walter, *Im Hauptquartier der deutschen Wehrmacht 1939 bis 1945. Grundlagen, Formen, Gestalten* (Frankfurt, 1962) (English edition: *Inside Hitler's Headquarters 1939–45*, translated by R. H. Barry (London, 1964).

Weber, Thomas, *Hitlers erster Krieg. Der Gefreite Hitler im Weltkrieg. Mythos und Wahrheit* (Berlin, 2001) (English edition: *Hitler's First War: Adolf Hitler, the Men of the List Regiment, and the First World Wa*, (Oxford, 2010).

Weber, Thomas, *Wie Adolf Hitler zum Nazi wurde. Vom unpolitischen Soldaten zum Autor von »Mein Kampf«*

(Berlin, 2016) (English edition: *Becoming Hitler: The Making of a Nazi* (New York, 2017).

Wegner, Bernd, 'Hitlers Besuch in Finnland. Das geheime Tonbandprotokoll seiner Unterredung mit Mannerheim am 4. Juni 1942' *Vierteljahrshefte für Zeitgeschichte* (1993).

Wehler, Hans-Ulrich, *Deutsche Gesellschaftsgeschichte*, vol. 4, *Vom Beginn des Ersten Weltkrieges bis zur Gründung der beiden deutschen Staaten 1914–1949* (Munich, 2003).

Weinberg, Gerhard L., *Eine Welt in Waffen. Die globale Geschichte des Zweiten Weltkrieges* (Stuttgart, 1995).

Wenzel, Otto, *1923. Die gescheiterte Deutsche Oktoberrevolution* (Münster, 2003).

Westemeier, Jens, *Himmlers Krieger. Joachim Peiper und die Waffen-SS in Krieg und Nachkriegszeit* (Paderborn, 2012) (English edition: *Joachim Peiper: A Biography of Himmler's SS Commander*, translated by Christine Wisowaty (Atglen PA, 2007).

Wiedemann, Friedrich, *Der Mann, der Feldherr werden wollte. Erlebnisse und Erfahrungen des Vorgesetzten Hitlers im I. Weltkrieg und seines späteren persönlichen Adjutanten* (Velbert and Kettwig, 1964).

Winkler, Heinrich August, *Geschichte des Westens. Die Zeit der Weltkriege 1914–1945* (Munich, 2011) (English edition: *The Age of Catastrophe: A History of the West 1914–1945*, translated by Stewart Spencer (New Haven CT, 2015).

Witte, Peter, Wildt, Michael, and Vogt, Martina, *Der Dienstkalender Heinrich Himmlers 1941/42.* (Hamburg, 1999).

Wörner, Hansjörg, 'Rassenwahn – Entrechtung – Mord' in Elmar Krautkrämer and Paul-Ludwig Weinacht, eds, *Zeitgeschehen. Erlebte Geschichte – Lebendige Politik* (Freiburg i. Br., 1981).

Zieblatt, David in Andreas Christoph Schmidt, *Musste Weimar scheitern?* RBB-Documentary, ARD (first broadcast 4 Feb. 2019).

Zoller, Albert, *Hitler privat. Erlebnisbericht einer Geheimsekretärin* (Düsseldorf, 1949).

# Notes

## Introduction

1   Sloterdijk, Peter, *Zorn und Zeit. Politisch-psychologischer Vergleich* (Frankfurt a. M., 2006), p. 72.

2   Fest, Joachim C., *Hitler. Eine Biographie* (Berlin and Munich, 2002) (cited hereafter as Fest, *Hitler*).

3   An overview of different interpretative approaches to Hitler can be found in Lukacs, John, *The Hitler of History* (New York, 1997).

4   Kershaw, Ian, *Hitler*, vol. 1. *1889–1936: Hubris*, vol. 2. *1936–1945 Nemesis* (London, 1998 and 2000) (cited hereafter as Kershaw, *Hitler*).

5   Ullrich, Volker, *Adolf Hitler*, vol. 1. *Die Jahre des Aufstiegs*, vol. 2 *Die Jahre des Untergangs* (Frankfurt a. M., 2013 and 2018) (cited hereafter as Ullrich, *Hitler*).

6   Pyta, Wolfram, *Hitler. Der Künstler als Politiker und Feldherr. Eine Herrschaftsanalyse* (Munich, 2015) (cited hereafter as Pyta, *Hitler*).

7   Furet, François, *The Passing of an Illusion. The Idea of Communism in the Twentieth Century* (Chicago, 1999).

8   Furet, François and Nolte, Ernst: *Feindliche Nähe. Kommunismus und Faschismus im 20. Jahrhundert. Ein Briefwechsel* (Munich, 1998) (cited hereafter as Furet/Nolte *Briefwechsel* ), p. 91.

9   Ibid.

10  Popper, Karl, *The Open Society and Its Enemies*, with a new foreword by George Soros (Princeton, 2020).

11  Fest, *Hitler*, p. VIII.

12  As, for example, the then head of the Institute of Contemporary History in Munich. See: Broszat, Martin, 'Plädoyer für eine Historisierung des Nationalsozialismus', *Merkur* 39 (1985), p. 273 ff.

13  The 'historians' dispute' was triggered by an essay by Ernst Nolte that appeared in the *Frankfurter Allgemeine Zeitung* on 6 June 1986.

14  Kilb, Andreas, 'Putin als Historiker', *Frankfurter Allgemeine Zeitung,* 30 June 2020.

15  Hillgruber, Andreas, *Hitlers Strategie. Politik und Kriegführung 1940–1941* (Koblenz, 1982) (cited hereafter as Hillgruber, *Strategie*); see also Hillgruber, *Deutsche Großmacht und Weltpolitik im 19. und 20. Jahrhundert* (Düsseldorf, 1977) (cited hereafter as Hillgruber, *Weltpolitik*).

## 1: Anti-Semitism in Europe

1   The full quotation runs: '*I contend that we are the first race in the world, and that the more of the world we inhabit the better it is for the human race.*' Quoted in: Stead, William T., *The Last Will and Testament of Cecil Rhodes* (London, 1902), p. 58.

2   N'Diaye, Tidiane, *Le génocide voilé. Étude de la traite négrière arabo-musulmane* (Paris, 2008), p. 13.

3   Scheel, Wilhelm, *Deutschlands Kolonien in achtzig farbenphotographischen Abbildungen* (Berlin, 1914), p. 9 f.

4   Kipling's poem 'The White Man's Burden' (1899) begins: '*Take up the White Man's burden – / Send forth the best to breed – / Go bind your sons to exile / To serve your captives' need.*'

5   Herzl, Theodor, *Der Judenstaat. Versuch einer modernen Lösung der Judenfrage* (Leipzig and Vienna, 1896), quoted

here from the Manesse Edition (Zürich, 1988) (cited hereafter as Herzl, *Judenstaat*), p. 13.

6   Fishman, Talya, *Becoming the People of the Talmud. Oral Torah as Written Tradition in Medieval Jewish Cultures* (Philadelphia, 2011).

7   Luther, Martin, *Von den Juden und ihren Lügen*. New edition, edited and with a commentary by Matthias Morgenstern, and with a preface by Heinrich Bedford-Strohm, Chair of the Council of the Evangelical Church in Germany (Berlin, 2016).

8   Bernier, François, *Nouvelle division de la terre par les differentes espèces ou race d'hommes qui habitent*, in: *Journal des Scavans*, vol. 6 (1684), pp. 133–40.

9   Kant, Immanuel, *Werke*. Akademie-Textausgabe, vol. 9, *Logik, Physische Geographie, Pädagogik* (Berlin and elsewhere, 1987), p. 316.

10  Pufelska, Agnieszka, Vernunft jenseits der Vernunft. Zur Judenfeindschaft in der Zeit der Aufklärung, in: Hans-Joachim Hahn and Olaf Kistenmacher, eds., *Beschreibungsversuche der Judenfeindschaft. Zur Geschichte der Antisemitismusforschung vor 1944*. Europäisch-jüdische Studien. Beiträge (Berlin and elsewhere, 2015), p. 27 ff.

11  Brumlik, Micha, *Das Gesetz ist erhaben Die Welt* (7 Feb. 2004).

12  Dohm, Christian Wilhelm, *Über die bürgerliche Verbesserung der Juden*, edited by Wolf Christoph Seifert, in Dohm, *Ausgewählte Schriften*, vol. 1 (Göttingen, 2015).

13  Goozé Marianne E., 'Wilhelm von Humboldt und die Judenemanzipation. Leistungen und Widersprüche', *A Journal of Germanic Studies*, XLVIII/3 ( Sept. 2012), p. 317 ff., here p. 320.

14  From the abstract of the dissertation by Philipp Lenhard,

*Volk oder Religion? Die Entstehung moderner jüdischer Ethnizität in Frankreich und Deutschland 1782–1848*, www.igk-religioesekulturen.uni.muenchen.de/mitglieder/ehemalige_kollegiat/lenhard/dissproj_lenhard/index.html.

15 Fetscher, Iring, *Deutscher Geist und Judenhass. Judenliebe, Judenhass*, tagesspiegel.de (21 Jan. 2001).

16 Puschner, Marco, *Antisemitismus im Kontext der Politischen Romantik* (Berlin and elsewhere 2008), p. 190.

17 Marx, Karl, *Zur Judenfrage* ('On the Jewish question') www.marxists.org/archive/marx/works/1844/jewish-question.

18 Letter of Karl Marx to Friedrich Engels, 30 July 1862, in Karl Marx and Friedrich Engels, *Werke*, vol. 30, edited by the Institute for Marxism-Leninism of the Central Committee of the Socialist Unity Party (East Berlin, 1955–81), pp. 257–9.

19 Ibid., vol. 6, p. 172.

20 Ibid., p. 168.

21 George Watson interviewed in the 2008 documentary film *The Soviet Story* by the Latvian direction Edvīns Šnore. (Incidentally, Watson translates the term 'Völkerabfälle' that Engels uses in his *Neue Rheinische Zeitung* article as 'racial trash').

22 Gobineau, Arthur de, *Essai sur l'inégalitédes races humaines* (Paris, 1853–55).

23 Fest, *Hitler*, p. 301.

24 Darwin, Charles, *On the Origin of Species by Means of Natural Selection, or the Preservation of Favoured Races in the Struggle for Life* (London, 1859).

25 Spencer, Herbert, *Social Statics* (London, 1851).

26 Benz, Wolfgang, *Antisemitismus und Antisemitismus-forschung*, version 1.0 in Dokupedia-Zeitgeschichte, 11. 2.

2010, http://docupedia.de/zg/benz_antisemitismus_v1_
de_2010 (cited hereafter as Benz, *Antisemitismus*).

27  Quoted in Fischer, Jens Malte, 'Richard Wagners Das
Judentum in der Musik. Entstehung – Kontext – Wirkung',
in Dieter Borchmeyer, Maayani, Ami, and Vill, Susanne,
eds., *Richard Wagner und die Juden* (Stuttgart and Weimar,
2000), p. 35 ff., here p. 44 f.

28  Brumlik, Micha *Antisemitismus. 100 Seiten* (Stuttgart,
2020) (cited hereafter as Brumlik, *Antisemitismus*), p. 64.

29  Ibid.

30  Ibid.

31  Rauschning, Hermann, *Gespräche mit Hitler* (Vienna,
1973), p. 216.

32  Chamberlain, Houston Stewart *Die Grundlagen des
neunzehnten Jahrhunderts* (Munich, 1899).

33  Ibid., p. 259.

34  Liebenfels promulgated his views in the magazine *Ostara*,
which he founded in 1905 and of which he became the sole
author and editor in 1908. This publication ran for a total
of eighty-nine editions (Rodaun and Mödling 1905–17).

35  Benz, *Antisemitismus*.

36  Koenen, Gerd, *Die Farbe Rot. Ursprünge und Geschichte
des Kommunismus* (Munich, 2017), p. 845.

37  Sammons, Jeffrey L., ed., *Die Protokolle der Weisen von
Zion. Die Grundlage des modernen Antisemitismus – eine
Fälschung. Text und Kommentar* (Göttingen, 1998) (cited
hereafter as Sammons, *Protokolle*).

38  Herzl, *Judenstaat*, p. 33.

39  Hitler, *Mein Kampf. Eine kritische Edition*, 2 vols., edited
by Christian Hartmann, Thomas Vordermayer, Othmar
Plöckinger, and Roman Töppel, on behalf of the Institute
of Contemporary History (Munich and Berlin, 2016) (cited
hereafter as *Mein Kampf*), vol. I, p. 799 ff.

40  On the provenance and dissemination of the *Protocols*, see Sammons, *Protokolle*, p. 8 f.

41  Benz, *Antisemitismus.*

42  Fest, *Hitler*, p. 65.

43  Hamann, Brigitte, *Hitlers Wien. Lehrjahre eines Diktators* (Munich and Zürich, 1996).

44  Brumlik, *Antisemitismus*, p. 53.

45  Boehlich, Walter, ed., *Der Berliner Antisemitismusstreit* (Frankfurt a. M., 1965) (cited hereafter as Boehlich, *Antisemitismusstreit*), p. 8.

46  Jensen, Uffa, 'Die Juden sind unser Unglück', zeit.de, 27 Dec, 2013).

47  Brumlik, *Antisemitismus*, p. 51.

48  Ibid.

49  Lagarde, Paul de, 'Juden und Indogermanen, 1887', quoted in Alexander Bein, ed., *Der moderne Antisemitismus und seine Bedeutung für die Judenfrage*, in: *Vierteljahrshefte für Zeitgeschichte*, Jg. 6, (1958), issue 4, p. 359, www.ifz. muenchen.de/heftarchiv.html.

50  Brumlik, *Antisemitismus*, p. 57.

51  Mommsen, Theodor, *Auch ein Wort über unser Judentum*, Quoted in Boehlich, *Antisemitismusstreit*, p. 222.

52  *Statutes of the Pan-German League 1897*, Bundesarchiv, R 8048/4, fol. 2–5.

53  Röhl, John C. G., *Wilhelm II.: Der Aufbau der persönlichen Monarchie 1888–1900* (Munich, 2001), p. 1055.

54  Ibid.

55  Claß, Heinrich (published under the pseudonym Daniel Frymann), ed., *Wenn ich Kaiser wär ... Politische Wahrheiten und Notwendigkeiten* (Leipzig, 1912).

56  Clark, Christopher, *The Sleepwalkers: How Europe Went to War in 1914* (London, 2012).

57  Reuth, Ralf Georg, *Hitlers Judenhass. Klischee und*

*Wirklichkeit* (Munich and Zürich, 2009) (cited hereafter as Reuth, *Judenhass*), p. 33 f.

58  Ibid., p. 34.

59  Weber, Thomas, *Hitlers erster Krieg. Der Gefreite Hitler im Weltkrieg. Mythos und Wahrheit* (Berlin, 2001).

60  Wiedemann, Friedrich, *Der Mann, der Feldherr werden wollte. Erlebnisse und Erfahrungen des Vorgesetzten Hitlers im I. Weltkrieg und seines späteren persönlichen Adjutanten* (Velbert and Kettwig, 1964), p. 33. See also Reuth, *Judenhass*, p. 37 ff.

61  Weber, Thomas, *Wie Adolf Hitler zum Nazi wurde. Vom unpolitischen Soldaten zum Autor von »Mein Kampf«* (Berlin, 2016) (cited hereafter as Weber, *Nazi*).

## 2: The Civil War after the Great War

1   Koenen, Gerd, *Die Farbe Rot. Ursprünge und Geschichte des Kommunismus* (Munich, 2017), p. 856.

2   Quoted in Heresch, Elisabeth, *Geheimakte Parvus. Die gekaufte Revolution* (Munich, 2000), p. 362.

3   Keil, Lars-Broder and Kellerhoff, Sven Felix: *Lob der Revolution. Die Geburt der deutschen Demokratie* (Darmstadt, 2018) (cited hereafter as Keil and Kellerhoff, *Revolution*).

4   Ibid., p. 25.

5   Ibid., p. 28.

6   Eich, Martin 'Als Deutschland den Frieden verlor', *Frankfurter Allgemeine Zeitung* (3 Nov. 2018).

7   Quoted in the *Vossische Zeitung* (9 Nov. 1918).

8   *Vossische Zeitung* (10 Nov. 1918).

9   Heydecker, Joe J., *Der große Krieg 1914–1918* (Frankfurt and Berlin, 1988), p. 383.

10  In *Mein Kampf* (p. 487) Hitler refers to a mass demonstration. Since no such event took place in the days

immediately after Hitler's discharge from the Pasewalk
Hospital, this can only refer to the obsequies for the
victims of the revolution held on 20 November, which many
thousands of people attended. See Weber, *Nazi*, p. 11 ff.

11  *Vorwärt* (11 Dec. 1918).
12  *Rote Fahne* (7 Dec. 1918).
13  Ibid., 14 (Dec. 1918).
14  Luxemburg, Rosa, *Zur Russischen Revolution (1918)*, in
    Rosa Luxemburg, *Gesammelte Werke*, vol. 4 (East Berlin,
    1974), p. 365.
15  Keil and Kellerhoff, *Revolution*, p. 93 f.
16  Noske, Gustav, *Von Kiel bis Kapp. Zur Geschichte der
    deutschen Revolution* (Berlin, 1920) (cited hereafter as
    Noske, *Kiel*), p. 68.
17  Reuth, Ralf Georg, *Hitler. Eine politische Biographie*
    (Munich and Zürich, 2003) (cited hereafter as Reuth,
    *Hitler*), p. 74.
18  Quoted in Merz, Kai-Uwe *Das Schreckbild. Deutschland
    und der Bolschewismus 1917–1921* (Frankfurt and Berlin,
    1995) (cited hereafter as Merz, *Schreckbild*), p. 180.
19  Menzel, Thomas, *Die Ermordung von Rosa Luxemburg
    und Karl Liebknecht*, www.bundesarchiv.de.
20  *Vorwärts* (17 Jan. 1919).
21  Haffner, Sebastian, *Anmerkungen zu Hitler* (Munich,
    1978), p. 69 f.
22  Haffner, Sebastian, *1918/19. Eine deutsche Revolution*
    (Hamburg, 1981), p. 208. Haffner's book was originally
    published in Berne in 1969, under the title *Die verratene
    Revolution*.
23  Rosenberg, Arthur, *Entstehung und Geschichte der
    Weimarer Republik*, edited and with an introduction by
    Kurt Kersten (Frankfurt a. M., 1983) (cited hereafter as
    Rosenberg, *Weimarer Republik*).

24 Hurwicz, E., 'Die Weltexpansion des Bolschewismus. Versuch einer Prognose' (cited hereafter as Hurwicz, *Weltexpansion*) in *Die Ausbreitung des Bolschewismus, Süddeutsche Monatshefte* (Leipzig and Munich, April 1919), p. 9.

25 Ullrich, *Hitler*.

26 David Zieblatt in Andreas Christoph Schmidt, *Musste Weimar scheitern?*, RBB-Documentary, ARD first broadcast 4 Feb. 2019, (cited hereafter as Schmidt, *Weimar*).

27 Rosenberg, *Weimarer Republik*, p. 24.

28 Reuth, *Hitlers Judenhass*, p. 82, photograph on p. 88.

29 Spengler, Oswald, *Preußentum und Sozialismus* (Munich, 1919), p. 9.

30 Joachimsthaler, Anton, *Hitlers Weg begann in München 1913–1923* (Munich, 2000) (cited hereafter as Joachimsthaler, *München*), p. 238.

31 Ibid., p. 202.

32 *Münchner Post* (24 and 25. Mar. 1923).

33 Ibid.

34 Heiden, Konrad, Adolf Hitler. *Das Zeitalter der Verantwortungslosigkeit. Ein Mann gegen Europa. Die Biographie* (Berlin and elsewhere 2016) (cited hereafter as Heiden, *Hitler*), p. 127.

35 Joachimsthaler, *München*, p. 187 f.

36 Kershaw, *Hitler*, vol. 1, p. 162.

37 Jochmann, Werner, ed., *Adolf Hitler. Monologe im Führerhauptquartier 1941–1944. Die Aufzeichnungen Heinrich Heims* (Hamburg, 1980) (cited hereafter as Hitler, *Monologe*), 1 Feb. 1942, p. 248.

38 Klemperer, Victor, *Man möchte immer weinen und lachen in einem. Revolutions-Tagebuch* (Berlin, 2015), 17 April 1919, p. 117.

39 Eliasberg, David, *Russischer und Münchner Bolschewismus,* in *Die Ausbreitung des Bolschewismus, Süddeutsche Monatshefte* (April 1919), p. 69.

40 Rindl, Peter, *Der internationale Kommunismus* (Munich, 1961), p. 19.

41 Quoted in Ernst Nolte, *Die Weimarer Republik. Demokratie zwischen Lenin und Hitler* (Munich, 2006), p. 57.

42 The relevant document is held in the main Bavarian State Archives in Munich (Gruko 4, Nr. 478, Bund 67, Akt 4 ). See: Reuth, *Judenhass*, p. 93 f.

43 Almost all Hitler biographies from Fest to Kershaw identify Hitler's hatred of the Jews as having originated during his early years in Vienna, a chronology which tallies with the impression he himself was keen to convey in *Mein Kampf*.

44 Noske, *Kiel*, p. 136.

45 Gellinek, Christian *Philipp Scheidemann. Eine biographische Skizze* (Cologne,Weimar, andVienna, 1994) (cited hereafter as Gellinek, *Scheidemann*), p. 60.

46 Quoted in Schmidt, *Weimar*.

### 3: The Dictated Peace of Versailles

1 Hoeres, Peter, *Versailler Vertrag. Ein Frieden, der kein Frieden war*. Bundeszentrale für politische Bildung. Aus Politik und Zeitgeschichte, *Pariser Friedensordnung,* Jahrgang 15/2019, bpb.de (cited hereafter as *Friedensordnung*); the text of the peace treaty is reprinted in: *Versailles 1919. Aus der Sicht von Zeitzeugen*. With contributions by Sebastian Haffner, Lloyd George, Ernst Jünger et al. (Munich, 2002) (cited hereafter as *Versailles 1919*), p. 112 ff.

2 Kennan, George F. ,*The Decline of Bismarck's European*

*Order. Franco-Russian Relations 1875–1890* (Princeton, 1979), p. 3.

3 Quoted in Conze, Eckart, *Verhasster Vertrag. »Versailles« als Propagandawaffe gegen die Weimarer Republik*, in *Friedensordnung*.

4 Spengler, Oswald, *The Decline of the West*, translated by Charles Francis Atkinson, abridged edition (New York and Oxford, 1991).

5 Solzhenitsyn, Alexander, *Zweihundert Jahre zusammen. Die Juden in der Sowjetunion* (Munich, 2003), p. 135.

6 See for example the illustration on the title page of the magazine *Welt-Echo* from 7 Mar. 1919.

7 Quoted in Merz, *Schreckbild*, p. 182 f.

8 Keynes, John Maynard, *The Economic Consequences of the Peace* (London, 1920 (cited hereafter as Keynes, *Consequences*), p. 56.

9 Górny, Majiej, 'Die Experten', *Frankfurter Allgemeine Zeitung* (20 Jan. 2020). See also Platthaus, Andreas, 18 and 19. *Der Krieg nach dem Krieg. Deutschland zwischen Revolution und Versailles* (Berlin, 2018), p. 350 ff.

10 Schwabe, Klaus, ed., *Quellen zum Friedensschluss von Versailles* (Darmstadt, 1997), p. 156.

11 *Versailles 1919*, p. 222.

12 Keynes, *Consequences*, p. 225.

13 Smuts, Jan C., Letter to Woodrow Wilson 30 May 1919, in *Versailles 1919*, p. 397.

14 Nitti, Francesco, *Peaceless Europe* (London and New York, 1922), p. 150.

15 Quoted in Gellinek, *Scheidemann*, p. 61.

16 Groener, Wilhelm, Notes by the First Quartermaster on the events of 18–20 June 1919 in Weimar, Military Archive of the Federal German Republic, Schleicher bequest, N 42/12.

17 Lenin, Vladimir Ilyich, *Ausgewählte Werke*, vol. I (East Berlin, 1961), p. 713.

18 Lenin, 'Entlarvt ist der Friede von Versailles' in *Versailles 1919*, p. 380.

19 Quoted in Keil, Lars-Broder and Kellerhoff, Sven Felix, *Deutsche Legenden. Vom »Dolchstoß« und anderen Mythen der Geschichte* (Berlin, 2002), p. 33.

20 Reuth, *Judenhass*, p. 106.

21 The guiding principles of the NSDAP can be found in www.dokumentarchiv.de/wr/1920/nsdap-programm.html.

22 Hitler, *Reden, Schriften, Anordnungen, Februar 1925 bis Januar 1933*, 5 vols. (13 sub-volumes), edited by the Institute of Contemporary History (Munich and elsewhere, 1992–98) (cited hereafter as *Hitler, Reden, Schriften, Anordnungen*), vol. I.1, Dok. 6, 27. Feb. 1925, p. 24.

23 See Reuth, *Hitler*, p. 118.

24 *Rote Fahn*, (19 Oct. 1920).

25 Ibid., (18 Mar. 1921).

26 Wenzel, Otto 1923. *Die gescheiterte Deutsche Oktoberrevolution* (Münster, 2003) (cited hereafter as Wenzel, *Oktoberrevolution*), p. 150.

27 Birkelund, John P., *Gustav Stresemann. Patriot und Staatsmann* (Hamburg and Vienna, 2002), p. 325.

28 Wenzel, *Oktoberrevolution*, p. 201 f.

29 *Rote Fahne* (24. Sept. 1923). See also Besymenski, Lew, *Stalin und Hitler. Das Pokerspiel der Diktatoren* (Berlin, 2002), p. 35.

## 4: Hitler's National Socialism

1 Furet and Nolte, *Briefwechsel*, p. 50 f.

2 Reuth, *Judenhass*, p. 5.

3 Herzl, *Judenstaat*, p. 2.

4   *Illustrated Sunday Herald* (8 Feb. 1920). See also Reuth, *Judenhass*, p. 61.

5   Solzhenitsyn, *Juden*, p. 136 f.

6   Pipes, Richard , 'Jews and the Russian revolution', in *Polin*, 9 (1999), p. 55.

7   Rogalla von Bieberstein, Johannes, *Jüdischer Bolschewismus. Mythos und Realität* (Dresden, 2002) (cited hereafter as Rogalla, *Mythos*).

8   Quoted in Weber, *Nazi*, p. 135.

9   Quoted in Reuth, *Judenhass*, p. 148.

10  Ibid.

11  Nevins, Michael *Bloody Bacchanalia. The Pogroms of Proskurov and Felshtin*, p. 5, www.felshtin.org/resources/bloodybaccanalia.pdf.

12  *The Jewish Chronicle* (30 May 1919); Reuth, *Judenhass*, p. 150.

13  Reuth, *Hitler*, p. 50.

14  Mann, Thomas, *Tagebücher*, edited by Peter de Mendelsohn (Frankfurt a. M.,) 1959, 1 May 1919, p. 218 f.

15  Quoted in Reuth, *Judenhass*, p. 136.

16  Quoted in Joachimsthaler, *München*, p. 237.

17  Ibid., p. 243.

18  Weber, *Nazi*, p. 154.

19  *Auf gut deutsch* (14 Feb. 1919).

20  Weber, *Nazi*, p. 160 ff.

21  Reuth, *Judenhass*, p. 126.

22  Ibid., p. 127.

23  Ibid., p. 142.

24  Meining, Stefan, 'Ein neuer Ansturm der Antisemiten: 1919–1923' in Douglas Bokovoy and Stefan Meining, eds, *Versagte Heimat. Jüdisches Leben in Münchens Isarstadt 1914–1945* (Munich, 1994), p. 61.

25 Large, David Clay, *Where Ghosts Walked: Munich's Road to the Third Reich* (New York, 1997).

26 Quoted in Weber, *Nazi*, p. 183.

27 Reuth, *Judenhass*, p. 165 f.

28 Ibid., p. 166.

29 Ibid., p. 158 ff.

30 Jung, Rudolf, *Der nationale Sozialismus. Seine Grundlage, sein Werden, seine Ziele* Aussig 1919.

31 www.documentarchiv.de/wr/1920/nsdap-programm.html.

32 Maser, Werner, *Hitlers Briefe und Notizen. Sein Weltbild in handschriftlichen Dokumenten* (Graz and Stuttgart, 2002), p. 224 ff.

33 Ibid., p. 225.

34 *Auf gut deutsch* (10 Jan. 1919).

35 Ibid. (21 Feb. 1919).

36 Hitler, *Monologe*, (16 and 17 Jan. 1942), p. 208.

37 Heiden, *Hitler*, p. 119.

38 Reuth, *Judenhass*, p. 144.

39 Ibid., p. 142.

40 Ibid.

41 Ibid., p. 144.

42 www.documentarchiv.de/wr/1920/nsdap-programm.html.

43 *Mein Kampf*, vol. II, p. 1161.

44 Reuth, *Judenhass*, p. 197.

45 Quoted in Reuth, *Judenhass*, p. 194.

46 Ford, Henry, *The International Jew: The World's Foremost Problem* (Dearborn MI, 1920).

47 Ibid., p. 23 (Chapter II: 'Germany's Reaction Against the Jew').

48 Reuth, *Judenhass*, p. 222.

49 Jäckel, Eberhard and Kuhn, Axel, eds, *Hitler. Sämtliche Aufzeichnungen 1905–1925* (Stuttgart, 1980) (cited

hereafter as Jäckel/Kuhn, *Aufzeichnungen*), Dok. 578, (October 1923), p. 1024.

50  *Mein Kampf*, vol. I, p. 213.

51  Ibid., p. 223.

52  Ibid., vol. II, p. 1739.

53  Kershaw, *Hitler*, vol. I, p. 26.

54  *Mein Kampf*, vol. I, p. 733.

55  Ibid.

56  Ibid., p. 837.

57  Ibid.

58  Ibid., p. 853.

59  Ibid., vol. II, p. 1657.

60  Ibid., p. 1675.

61  Ibid., p. 1619.

62  Ibid.

63  Ibid., p. 1615.

64  Ibid., vol. I, p. 231.

65  Jäckel and Kuhn, *Aufzeichnungen*, Dok. 91, (6 Apr. 1920), p. 119 f.

66  Ibid., Dok. 129, (7 Aug. 1920), p. 119 f.

67  Eckart, Dietrich, *Der Bolschewismus von Moses bis Lenin. Zwiegespräch zwischen Adolf Hitler und mir* (Munich, 1924).

68  Quoted in Nolte, Ernst, *Der Faschismus in seiner Epoche* (Munich, 1963), p. 407.

69  Hitler, *Zweites Buch. Außenpolitische Standortbestimmung nach der Reichstagswahl Juni–Juli 1928* (cited hereafter as Hitler, *Zweites Buch*), in Hitler, *Reden, Schriften, Anordnungen*, p. 186.

## 5: Hitler's Rise to Power

1   Hitler, *Reden, Schriften, Anordnungen*, vol. I, Dok. 6, (27 Feb. 1925), p. 20.

2   Reuth, *Hitler*, p. 198.

3   Reuth, Ralf Georg, *Goebbels. Eine Biographie* (Munich and Zürich, 2021) (cited hereafter as Reuth, *Goebbels*), p. 102.

4   Reuth, *Hitler*, p. 200.

5   Feder, letter to Hitler, 9 Sept. 1927, from the author's own archive.

6   *Die Tagebücher von Joseph Goebbels*. Compiled on behalf of the Institute of Contemporary History and with the support of the Russian State Archive Service, edited by Elke Fröhlich et al., 36 vols. (Munich and elsewhere, 1987– 2008) (cited hereafter as Goebbels, *Tagebücher*), Part I, vol. 1/II, (15 Feb. 1926), p. 55.

7   *Mein Kampf*, vol. 2, p. 1581.

8   Quoted in Schmidt, *Weimar*.

9   Hitler, *Reden, Schriften, Anordnungen*, vol. II, 2, Dok. 237, (29 Feb. 1928), p. 699.

10  Rauschning, Hermann, *Die Revolution des Nihilismus* (Zürich and New York, 1938), p. 23.

11  Bayerlein, Bernhard H., 'Stalin und die Kommunistische Partei Deutschlands in der Weimarerer Republik' in *Der Rote Gott. Stalin und die Deutschen* (Berlin, 2018), p. 15.

12  Reuth, *Hitler*, p. 219.

13  *Rote Fahne* (29 Aug. 1929).

14  Hitler, *Reden, Schriften, Anordnungen*, vol. III, 3, Dok. 20, (24 Feb. 1930), p. 101.

15  Mayer, Michael, 'NSDAP und Antisemitismus 1919–1933' (cited hereafter as Mayer, *Antisemitismus*), in *Münchner Wirtschaftswissenschaftliche Beiträge* (July 2002), p. 15.

16  Quoted in Gasser, Markus, *Die Postmoderne* (Stuttgart, 1997), p. 232.

17  Striefler, Christian, *Kampf um die Macht. Kommunisten und Nationalsozialisten am Ende der Weimarer Republik* (Frankfurt and Berlin, 1993), p. 312.

18  Ibid., p. 216.
19  Goebbels, *Tagebücher*, Part 1, 1924–1941, vols. 1–4 (Munich and elsewhere, 1987) (cited hereafter as Goebbels, *Kaiserhof*), vol. 2 (23 Apr. 1932), p. 160. The first four-volume edition of Joseph Goebbels' diaries released by the Institute of Contemporary History (IfZ) in 1987 drew upon the published texts that had appeared under the title *Vom Kaiserhof zur Reichskanzlei* (Eher-Verlag, Munich) in 1934.
20  Reuth, *Hitler*, p. 263 f.
21  Quoted in Fest, *Hitler*, p. 469.
22  Kessler, Harry Graf, *Das Tagebuch. Neunter Band 1926–1937*, edited by by Sabine Gruber and Ulrich Ott (Stuttgart, 2010), (27 June 1932), p. 452, and (12 July 1932), p. 461 f.
23  *Frankfurter Zeitung* (1 Jan. 1933).
24  Quoted in Thamer, Hans Ulrich, *Verführung und Gewalt. Deutschland 1933–1945* (Berlin, 1986), p. 232.

## 6: Chancellor and Führer

1  Goldhagen, Daniel Jonah, *Hitler's Willing Executioners. Ordinary Germans and the Holocaust* (New York, 1996) (cited hereafter as Goldhagen, *Executioners*).
2  Ullrich, *Hitler*, vol. I, 419 f.
3  Domarus, Ma ed., *Hitler. Reden und Proklamationen 1932–1945*, 2 vols. (Wiesbaden, 1973) (cited hereafter as Domarus, *Hitler*), vol. 1, (1 Feb. 1933), p. 192 f.
4  Reuth, *Hitler*, p. 309.
5  Ibid., p. 308.
6  Goebbels, *Tagebücher*, Part I, vol. 2.III, (1 Feb, 1933), p. 121.
7  Domarus, *Hitler*, vol. I.1 (21 Mar. 1933), p. 226 ff.
8  Spengler, Oswald *Jahre der Entscheidung* (Munich, 1933), p. VIII.

9   Besier, Gerhard, *Die Kirchen und das Dritte Reich. Spaltungen und Abwehrkämpfe 1934–1937* (Berlin and Munich, 2001), p. 12.

10  Reuth, *Hitler*, p. 321.

11  *Verhandlungen des Reichstags*, VIII. Wahlperiode, vol. 457, p. 36 ff.

12  Records of the discussion with Egon Krenz are in the author's archives.

13  Höhne, Hein, *Die Zeit der Illusionen* (Düsseldorf and elsewhere, 1991), p. 87.

14  Quoted in *Ursachen und Folgen. Vom deutschen Zusammenbruch 1918 und 1945 bis zur Staatlichen Neuordnung Deutschlands in der Gegenwart*, edited by Herbert Michaelis and Ernst Schraepler (Berlin n.d.) vol. X, p. 166.

15  The text of the speech delivered by Joseph Goebbels on 1 July 1934 was reprinted in the Berlin Nazi newspaper *Der Angriff* on 2 July 1934. See also Reuth, *Goebbels*, p. 341.

16  Kershaw, Ian, *The 'Hitler Myth': Image and Reality in the Third Reich* (Oxford, 1987) (cited hereafter as Kershaw, *Hitler Myth*), p. 80 f.

17  Schmitt, Carl, 'Der Führer schützt das Recht. Zur Reichstagsrede Adolf Hitlers vom 13. Juli 1934', *Deutsche Juristenzeitung* 15 (1934), p. 945 ff.

18  *Frankfurter Allgemeine Zeitung* (3 July 1934).

19  The swearing by the Reichswehr of an oath of allegiance to Adolf Hitler on the day of Hindenburg's death (2 August 1934), *Deutsche Geschichte in Dokumenten in Bildern*, https://ghdi.ghi-dc.org/print_document.cfm ?document_id= 1982.

20  Reuth, *Goebbels*, p. 72.

21  Rudolf Hess, in a speech delivered to the Nuremberg

National Socialist Party Congress on 10 September 1934; see the *Völkischer Beobachter* (12 Sept. 1934).

22  Reuth, *Hitler*, p. 358.

23  *Völkischer Beobachter* (11 Sept. 1935).

24  Hofer, Walter, ed., *Der Nationalsozialismus. Dokumente 1933–1945* (Frankfurt a. M., 1957), Dok. 160, p. 285.

25  Reuth, *Hitler*, p. 366.

26  Ibid.

27  Kulka, Otto Dov, 'Die Nürnberger Rassegesetze und die deutsche Bevölkerung im Lichte geheimer NS-Lage- und Stimmungsberichte' in *Vierteljahrshefte für Zeitgeschichte*, Jg. 32 (1984), Heft 4, p. 602 f., www.ifz.muenchen.de/heftarchiv.html. See also Longerich, Peter, »*Davon haben wir nichts gewusst*« (Munich, 2006), p. 85 ff.

28  Domarus, *Hitler*, vol. I.2, (14 Mar. 1936), p. 606.

29  Reuth, *Goebbels*, p. 366.

30  Reuth, *Hitler*, p. 373.

31  Held, Ludger, *Wenn die Olympiade vorbei ist, schlagen wir die Juden zu Brei*, zeit.de (1 Aug. 2016).

32  David Lloyd George in the *Daily Mail* (17 Sept. 1936).

33  Transcript of the meeting held in the Reich Chancellery on 5 November 1937 from 16.15 to 20.30 (Hossbach-Protokoll) (10 Nov. 1937) in 1000dokumente.de.

34  *Völkischer Beobachter* (21 Sept. 1938).

35  Reuth, Ralf Georg, *Kurze Geschichte des Zweiten Weltkriegs* (Berlin, 2018) (cited hereafter as Reuth, *Zweiter Weltkrieg*), p. 69.

36  Goebbels, *Tagebücher*, Part I, vol. 6, (1 Oct. 1938), p. 122.

37  Pope Pius XI, Encyclical 'Mit brennender Sorge' ('With burning concern') on the Church and the German Reich, 14 March 1937 (full text): www.vatican.va/content/pius-xi/en/encyclicals/documents/hf_p-xi_enc_14031937_mit-brennender-sorge.html.

38   Domarus, *Hitler*, vol. II.1, (30 Jan. 1939), p. 1058.

39   See Kershaw, *Hitler*, p. 28.

40   Petersen, Jens, 'Mussolini. Wirklichkeit und Mythos eines Diktators', in Karl Heinz Bohrer, ed., *Mythos und Moderne* (Frankfurt a. M., 1983), p. 246.

## 7: The Hitler–Stalin Pact

1    Kilb, Andreas, 'Putin als Historiker', *Frankfurter Allgemeine Zeitun,* (20 June 2020).

2    Lloyd George, David, *Some Considerations for the Peace Conference before they finally draft their terms* (1919). Transcript from the National Archives, Kew, Extracts from a document setting out British Prime Minister David Lloyd George's views on a treaty with Germany, 25 March 1919 (Catalogue ref: CAB 1/28). www.nationalarchives.gov.uk/education/greatwar/transcript/g5cs1s2t.htm.

3    Domarus, *Hitler*, vol. II.1, (21 Aug. 1939), p. 1233.

4    Hitler, *Zweites Buch*, p. 185.

5    Quoted in the 2008 documentary film *The Soviet Story* by Edvīns Šnore.

6    Reuth, *Zweiter Weltkrieg*, p. 172.

7    Hitler, *Zweites Buch*, p. 134.

8    Dimitrov, Georgi, *The Working Class Against Fascism. Report Delivered at the Seventh World Congress of the Communist International on 2 August, 1935.* www.marxists.org/reference/archive/dimitrov/works/1935/08_02.htm.

9    Allard, Sven, *Hitler und Stalin* (Berne and Munich, 1974), p. 64 f.

10   Ribbentrop, Joachim von *Zwischen London und Moskau* (Leoni am Starnberger See, 1953), p. 88 f.

11   Quoted in Sommer, Theo, 'Deutschland und Japan zwischen den Mächten 1935–1940'in*Tübinger Studien zur*

*Geschichte und Politik,* 15, edited by Hans Rothfels et al. (Tübingen, 1962), p. 34.

12 *Reichsgesetzblatt* (1937), Teil II, 4.

13 *Dokumentation. Das Geheime Abkommen zum Antikominternpakt* in *Vierteljahrshefte für Zeitgeschichte,* Jg. 2 (1954), Heft 2, www.ifz.muenchen.de/heftarchiv.html.

14 Quoted in the documentary film *The Soviet Story* by Edvīns Šnore.

15 Goebbels, *Tagebücher,* Part I, vol. 3.II, (25 Jan. 1937), p. 343.

16 Hitler, *Zweites Buch,* p. 113.

17 Goebbels, *Tagebücher,* Part I, vol. 3.II, 26 Jan. 1937, p. 345.

18 Ibid., Part I, vol. 5, (22 Dec. 1937), p. 65.

19 Ibid.

20 From a speech given by Hitler in Würzburg on 27 June 1937. Quoted in Bullock, Alan, *Hitler. A Study in Tyranny* (London, 1952), p. 384.

21 Hubatsch, Walthe, ed., *Hitlers Weisungen für die Kriegführung 1939–1945* (Koblenz, 1983) (cited hereafter as Hubatsch, *Weisungen*), p. 17.

22 Domarus, *Hitler,* vol. II.1, (28 Apr. 1938), p. 1148 ff.

23 Quoted inSeraphim, Hans Günther*Die deutsch-russischen Beziehungen 1939–1941* (Hamburg, 1949), p. 49.

24 Domarus, *Hitler,* vol. II.1 (6 June 1939), p. 1210.

25 Burckhardt, Carl J., *Meine Danziger Mission 1937–1939* (Munich, 1960) p. 348.

26 Quoted in Kershaw, *Hitler,* vol. 2, p. 292.

27 Reuth, *Zweiter Weltkrieg,* p. 82.

28 *Akten zur Deutschen Auswärtigen Politik,* Serie D, 1937–1945, Baden-Baden1950 ff. (cited hereafter as ADAP) 271, (25 Aug. 1939), p. 239.

29 ADAP, vol. VII, 192 and 193, both (22 Aug. 1939), p. 167 ff.

30 Ibid., 265, p. 235.

31  Hill, Leonidas E., ed., *Die Weizsäcker-Papiere 1933–1950*
    (Berlin and Frankfurt, 1974), p. 162.

## 8: Hitler's Other War

1   *Trial of the principal war criminals before the
    International Military Tribunal*, Nuremberg 1948 (cited
    hereafter as IMT), IMT, vol. X, p. 583.

2   Schmidt, Paul, *Statist auf diplomatischer Bühne 1923–1945*
    (Bonn, 1950), p. 363.

3   Bayerlein, Bernhard H., edited by *Georgi Dimitroff.
    Tagebücher 1933–1943* (Berlin, 2000), (7 Sept. 1939), p. 273.

4   Reuth, *Hitler*, p. 464.

5   Salewski, Michael, *Die deutsche Seekriegsleitung*, 2
    vols. (Frankfurt a. M., 1970 and 1973) (cited hereafter as
    Salewski, *Seekriegsleitung*), vol. 1, p. 116.

6   Hartmann, Christian, *Halder. Generalstabschef Hitlers
    1938–1942* (Paderborn and elsewhere, 1991) (cited hereafter
    as Hartmann, *Halder*), p. 197.

7   Warlimont, Walter, *Im Hauptquartier der deutschen
    Wehrmacht 39–45 Grundlagen, Formen, Gestalten*
    (Munich, 1978) (cited hereafter as Warlimont,
    *Hauptquartier*), p. 112.

8   Ibid., p. 114, note 9.

9   Lukacs, John, *The Duel. The Eighty-Day Struggle Between
    Churchill and Hitler* (New York, 1991), p. 127.

10  Zoller, Albert, *Hitler privat. Erlebnisbericht einer
    Geheimsekretärin* (Düsseldorf, 1949), p. 85.

11  Churchill, Winston S., *The Second World War*, 6 vols.
    (Boston, 1948–53) (cited hereafter as Churchill, *Second
    World War*), vol. 2 *Their Finest Hour*.

12  Quoted in Gellermann, Günther W., *Geheime Wege zum
    Frieden mit England ... Ausgewählte Initiativen zur
    Beendigung des Krieges 1940/1942* (Bonn, 1995), p. 32.

13  Domarus, *Hitler*, vol. II.1, (19 July 1940), p. 1558.

14  Hitler, *Zweites Buch*, p. 32.

15  Halder, Franz,*Kriegstagebuch. Tägliche Aufzeichnungen des Chefs des Generalstabes des Heeres 1939 – 1942*, edited by the Arbeitskreis für Wehrforschung, vol. I–III (Stuttgart, 1962–64) (cited hereafter as Halder, *Kriegstagebuch*), vol. II (31 July 1940), p. 49.

16  Hildebrandt, Klaus, *Deutsche Außenpolitik 1939–1945* (Stuttgart and elsewhere, 1980), p. 62.

17  Reuth, *Zweiter Weltkrieg*, p. 132.

18  Hubatsch, *Weisungen*, p. 84.

19  Kotze, Hildegard von. ed., 'Heeresadjutant bei Hitler. Aufzeichnungen des Major Engel 1939–1945' in *Schriftenreihe der Vierteljahrshefte für Zeitgeschichte*, 29 (Stuttgart, 1974), (18 Dec. 1940), p. 92.

20  Halder, *Kriegstagebuch*, vol. II, (28 Jan. 1941), p. 261.

21  Wegner, Bernd, 'Hitlers Besuch in Finnland. Das geheime Tonbandprotokoll seiner Unterredung mit Mannerheim am 4. Juni 1942', in *Vierteljahrshefte für Zeitgeschichte* (1993), p. 135.

22  ADAP, vol. XI.2, (10 Nov. 1940), p. 538.

23  Boberach, Heinz, ed., *Meldungen aus dem Reich. Die geheimen Lageberichte des Sicherheitsdienstes der SS 1938–1945*, 16 vols., Herrsching 1984 (cited hereafter as *Meldungen aus dem Reich*), here vol. 7, 191 (5 June 1941, p. 2366).

24  Hillgruber, Andreas, *Staatsmänner und Diplomaten bei Hitler*, 2 vols., Frankfurt a. M. 1967 and 1970, here vol. I, (11 May 1941), p. 541.

25  Hitler – Speech to the Reichstag on 4. 5. 1941 after the Balkans campaign (1 h 10 m), archive.org.

26  Schmidt, Rainer F., *Rudolf Heß. »Botengang eines Toren«*

*? Der Flug nach Großbritannien vom 10. Mai 1941* (Munich, 2000).

27  Helmut Kohl in an interview with Ralf Georg Reuth on 19 February 2004. The former German chancellor, with whom the present author had many discussions about recent history and current affairs, justified his sensational claim by pointing out that Margaret Thatcher was an almost fanatical admirer of Winston Churchill. Her alleged motive for having Rudolf Hess silenced was to prevent him from possibly tarnishing Churchill's reputation by talking to the press, in the event that the Soviets unilaterally instigated and effected his release from Spandau Gaol.

28  See: Reuth, *Hitler*, p. 517.

29  Gorodetsky, Gabriel, ed., *Die Maiski-Tagebücher. Ein Diplomat im Kampf gegen Hitler 1932–1943* (Munich, 2016) (18 June 1941), p. 534.

30  Ibid., p. 540.

31  Domarus, *Hitler*, vol. II.2 (22 June 1941), p. 1731.

32  Hubatsch, *Weisungen*, p. 85.

33  *Meldungen aus dem Reich*, vol. 7, 193 (12 June 1941), p. 2394.

34  Quoted in Rürup, Reinhard, ed., *Der Krieg gegen die Sowjetunion 1941–1945. Eine Dokumentation* (cited hereafter as Rürup, *Krieg*) (Berlin, 1991), p. 85.

35  Halder, *Kriegstagebuch*, vol. III (3 July 1941), p. 38.

36  Reinhardt, Klaus, *Die Wende vor Moskau. Das Scheitern der Strategie Hitlers im Winter 1941/42* (Stuttgart, 1972), p. 36.

37  Goebbels, *Tagebücher*, Part II, vol. 1 (19 Aug. 1941), p. 262.

38  Hillgruber, *Strategie*, p. 548 f.

39  Goebbels, *Tagebücher*, Part II, vol. 1 (24 July 1941), p. 116

40  Jacobsen, Hans-Adolf, *Der Weg zur Teilung der Welt. Politik und Strategie von 1939 bis 1945* (Koblenz and Bonn,

1979) (cited hereafter as Jacobsen, *Teilung der Welt*) (14 Aug. 1941), p. 157.

41 Ibid. (22 June 1941), p. 155.

42 Rürup, *Krieg*, p. 122.

43 Hitler, *Monologe* (21 Oct. 1941), p. 99.

44 Ibid. (26 and 27 Oct. 1941), p. 110.

45 Halder, *Kriegstagebuch*, Part III, (19 Nov. 1941), p. 295.

46 Hillgruber, Andreas and Hümmelchen, Gerhard, *Chronik des Zweiten Weltkrieges. Kalendarium militärischer und politischer Ereignisse, 1939–45* (Düsseldorf, 1978), (1 Dec. 1941).

## 9: The Genocide of the Jews

1 The term 'global struggle' (*Weltkampf*) appears, for example, in: Hitler, *Zweites Buch*, p. 184.

2 *Mein Kampf*, vol. II, p. 1657.

3 Goebbels, *Tagebücher*, Part I (30 Nov. 1937), p. 429.

4 Reuth, *Judenhass*, p. 289.

5 Wörner, Hansjörg, 'Rassenwahn – Entrechtung – Mord' in Elmar Krautkrämer and Paul-Ludwig Weinacht, eds, *Zeitgeschehen. Erlebte Geschichte – Lebendige Politik*, ed. (Freiburg i. Br., 1981), p. 29.

6 *Völkischer Beobachter* (13 Sept. 1938).

7 Ibid. (8 Nov. 1938).

8 IMT, vol. XXVIII, 1816-PS, p. 539.

9 Jasch, Hans-Christian, *Staatssekretär Wilhelm Stuckart und die Judenpolitik: Der Mythos von der sauberen Verwaltung* (Berlin, 2012), p. 294.

10 Goebbels, *Tagebücher*, Part I, vol. 8 (17 Aug. 1940), p. 276.

11 Reuth, *Judenhass*, p. 304.

12 Cüppers, Martin, *Wegbereiter der Shoah. Die Waffen-SS, der Kommandostab des Reichsführers-SS und die Judenvernichtung 1939–1945* (Darmstadt, 2005), p. 183.

13  From the interrogation of a sergeant of a police unit that
    was detailed to cordon off the site of the shootings at
    Babi Yar (19 Nov. 1965), quoted in Longerich, Peter, ed.,
    *Die Ermordung der europäischen Juden. Eine umfassende
    Dokumentation des Holocaust 1941–1945* (Munich, 1989)
    (cited hereafter as Longerich, *Ermordung*), p. 123 f.

14  From a written directive by Heinrich Himmler to Arthur
    Greiser, the *Gauleiter* of the German-occupied territory of
    Wartheland, announcing the impending arrival in Łodz of
    trains carrying Jews from the Reich (18 Sept. 1941), ibid.,
    p. 157.

15  Quoted in Knopp, Guido, *Holocaust* (Munich, 2000) (cited
    hereafter as Knopp, *Holocaust*), p. 178.

16  From the police interrogation of Adolf Eichmann on
    Hitler's 'extermination order' (1960) in Longerich,
    *Ermordung*, p. 81.

17  Reuth, *Judenhass*, p. 179.

18  Domarus, *Hitler*, vol. II.2, (30 Jan. 1942), p. 1828 f.

19  *Der Dienstkalender Heinrich Himmlers 1941/42.* Edited
    and with a commentary and introduction by Peter Witte et
    al. on behalf of the Centre for Research in Contemporary
    History (Hamburg, 1999) (cited hereafter as Himmler,
    *Dienstkalender*) (17 Nov. 1941), p. 265.

20  Ibid., p. 262, note 46.

21  Goebbels, *Tagebücher*, Part II, vol. 2 (13 Dec.. 1941),
    p. 498.

22  Transcription of the 'Wannsee Conference' ( 20 Jan. 1942 )
    in Longerich, *Ermordung*, p. 83 ff.

23  Ibid., p. 87.

24  Interrogation of Adolf Eichmann on the 'Wannsee
    Conference' during the course of his trial in Jerusalem (24
    July 1961) in Longerich, *Ermordung*, p. 93.

25  Goebbels, *Tagebücher*, Part II, vol. 3 (27 Mar. 1942), p. 561.

26 Schnell, Felix, *Gewalt und Gruppenmilitanz in der Ukraine 1905–1933* (Hamburg, 2012).

27 Telegram sent by Reinhard Heydrich to the heads of the mobile death squads, regarding 'independent clean-up operations' in the Soviet Union (29 June 1941) in Longerich, *Ermordung*, p. 118 f.

28 Kellerhoff, Sven Felix, 'So antisemitisch war Polen vor dem Holocaust', *Die Welt* (9 Mar. 2018).

29 Snyder, Timothy, *Bloodlands. Europe Between Hitler and Stalin* (New York, 2010).

30 Order sent by Himmler to Friedrich-Wilhelm Krüger, the Supreme Head of the SS and Police in the General Government, regarding the 'resettlement' of the entire Jewish population (19 July 1942) in Longerich, *Ermordung*, p. 201.

31 Haensel, Carl, *Das Gericht vertagt sich. Aus dem Tagebuch eines Nürnberger Verteidigers* (Hamburg, 1950), p. 61.

32 Himmler, *Dienstkalender*, p. 456, note 24.

33 Chronicle of Rudolf Höss, the commandant of Auschwitz regarding the 'final solution' of the Jewish Question in the Auschwitz concentration camp (1947) in Longerich, *Ermordung*, p. 79.

34 Chronicle of Rudolf Höss, the commandant of Auschwitz, on the exterminations using poison gas in Auschwitz (1941), ibid., p. 379 f.

35 Heidemann, Gerd, *Recherchen und Interview in Santiago de Chile, 25.6.–3. 7. 1979, Gesprächspartner General a. D. Karl Wolff (ehem. SS- Oberstgruppenführer), »Partisanen«- Erschießungen in Minsk, Aug. 41*, p. 43 ff.

36 Order issued by Himmler to Krüger regarding the destruction of the Warsaw Ghetto (16 Feb. 1943) in Longerich, *Ermordung*, p. 222.

37 Quoted in Albrecht, Dieter 'Der Vatikan und das Dritte

Reich' in *Kirche im Nationalsozialismus*, edited by the history working group of the Rottenburg-Stuttgart Diocese (Sigmaringen, 1984), p. 42.

38 news.bbc.co.uk/onthisday/hi/dates/stories/.../17/.../3547151.stm

39 Hillgruber, *Staatsmänner*, vol. II (5 Aug. 1944), p. 494.

40 Reuth, *Zweiter Weltkrieg*, p. 278.

41 Longerich, Peter, *Der ungeschriebene Befehl. Hitler und der Weg zur »Endlösung«* (Munich and Zürich, 2001), p. 189 f.

42 From Himmler's speech in Posen (4 Oct. 1943) www.nationalsozialismus.de/dokumente.

43 Adolf Hitler. *Politisches Testament 1945*, in NS-Archiv. Dokumente zum Nationalsozialismus, ns.archiv.de.

## 10: Defeat

1 See for example the introductory remarks on Hitler in Kershaw, *Hitler*, p. 15 ff.

2 *Meldungen aus dem Reich* (8 Dec. 1941), p. 3069 f.

3 Ibid. (15 Dec. 1945), p. 3089.

4 Eichholtz, Dietrich, *Geschichte der deutschen Kriegswirtschaft* (Munich, 2013), p. 484.

5 Heusinger, Adolf, *Befehl im Widerstreit* (Tübingen and Stuttgart, 1950), p. 201.

6 Reuth, Ralf Georg, *Rommel. Das Ende einer Legende* (Munich, 2004). (cited hereafter as Reuth, *Rommel*), p. 73 f.

7 *Die Wehrmachtsberichte 1939–1945*, 3 vols. (Cologne, 1989), vol. 2, (3 Feb. 1943), p. 435 f.

8 Heiber, Helmut, ed., *Goebbels-Reden*, vol. 2 : 1939–1945 (Munich, 1972), p. 158 ff.

9 *Meldungen aus dem Reich* (22 Feb. 1943), p. 4831.

10 Quoted in Kershaw, *Hitler-Mythos*, p. 170.

11 Achmann, Klaus and Buhl, Hartmut, *20. Juli 1944* (Berlin and elsewhere, 1994), p. 145.

12  Reuth, Ralf Georg, 'Vielleicht wird man uns einmal als Patrioten sehen' (cited hereafter as Reuth, *Patrioten*) *Welt am Sonntag* (18 July 2004).

13  Knopp, *Holocaust*, p. 32

14  Reuth, *Hitler*, p. 609.

15  Ibid.

16  Reuth, *Patrioten*.

17  Ibid.

18  Hoffmann, Peter, *Claus Schenk Graf von Stauffenberg und seine Brüder* (Stuttgart, 2004) (cited hereafter as Hoffmann, *Stauffenberg*), p. 396.

19  Ibid., p. 388.

20  Domarus, *Hitler*, vol. II.2 (20 July 1944), p. 2118.

21  Quoted in Reuth, *Rommel*, p. 260 f.

22  Reuth, *Patrioten*.

23  *Meldungen aus dem Reich*, vol. 17, (10 Aug. 1944), p. 6700.

24  Reuth, *Zweiter Weltkrieg*, p. 300 ff.

25  *Völkischer Beobachter* (26 Sept. 1944).

26  Ibid. (16 Sept. 1944).

27  *Meldungen aus dem Reich*, vol. 16, (14 Apr. 1944), p. 6489.

28  *Das Reich* (25 Feb. 1945).

29  Quoted in Irving, David, *Hitlers Krieg. »Götterdämmerung« 1942–1945* (Herrsching, 1988) p. 361.

30  *Mein Kampf*, vol. II, p. 1657.

31  The figures given in historical accounts for the number of German civilians killed by Allied bombing vary widely. There are grounds for conjecturing that these discrepancies may derive from the differing political standpoints of particular writers.

32  Reuth, Ralf Georg, 'Erstickt, verkohlt, zerstückelt', i*Welt am Sonntag* (6 Feb. 2005).

33  Reuth, *Zweiter* Weltkrieg, p. 344.

# Acknowledgements

I would like to express my gratitude – first and foremost for my long-running collaboration with Piper Verlag, which has now spanned some three and a half decades. My thanks are due especially to the managing director, Felicitas von Lovenberg, but also to Anne Stadler, head of non-fiction at Piper, and chief press officer Eva Brenndörfer, who has been involved since the inception of this project. Charlyne Bieniek showed great skill in managing the editing and production of this book. Not only did she bring a high degree of professionalism to bear in her role but also exercised an admirable sensitivity and objectivity of judgement throughout. I am greatly indebted to her for this.

# Index